The Lore of the
NEW
TESTAMENT

The Lore of the
NEW
TESTAMENT

By JOSEPH GAER

GROSSET & DUNLAP
PUBLISHERS   NEW YORK

To
FAY

Contents

The Lore of the
NEW
TESTAMENT

Jesus in Folk Imagination

I

Nearly two thousand years ago, according to legend, a certain fisherman named John and his elder brother James were in their father's boat one day nearing Bethsaida after a long fishing trip on the harp-shaped Sea of Galilee. As they neared the shore they heard someone calling to them.

James turned to his brother and said: "What can that child on the shore want?"

John looked up toward the nearing shore and asked in surprise: "What child?"

"The one beckoning to us," said James.

"Because of our long watches at sea, Brother, your eyes deceive you," said John. "For that is no child on the shore, but a man, fair and comely, and of a cheerful countenance."

James looked again. "I can see no man," he said. "Come, let us bring our boat in and see what the child wants."

When they brought their ship to shore Jesus came to help them secure it. And John saw him as a tall man with a thick flowing beard; but to James he now appeared as a youth whose beard had just begun to grow.

When their boat was secure, Jesus said to the two brothers: "Come, follow me!"

And the brothers followed Jesus along the shore, still perplexed that he had appeared so differently to each of them.

In this story we have the key to the nature of the lore of the New Testament. And it is underscored in another legend that when Jesus arose to preach before a multitude, John would look up at him from time to time: and sometimes he saw Jesus as a small man and uncomely; and sometimes he saw him so tall that he reached to heaven, his eyes sparkling, and beautiful to behold. And everyone in that multitude saw Jesus differently. As they saw him, so was he to them.

The library shelves are filled with huge tomes by learned men who have devoted their years in search of Jesus "the historic man." They have gathered facts by the bushel, as they would gather them for the biography of a great military leader or the distinguished ruler of a principality. The times in which Jesus lived and the books that presumably influenced him have all been studied and analyzed. Many of these chroniclers have grieved because the chroniclers of Jesus' day failed to tell us much, if anything, about him; and what was said about him by his contemporaries, later historians sadly rejected as interpolations of sectarians. And each man writing of Jesus constructed a skeleton theory of his own upon which to mold a neatly conceived image.

Yet anyone wishing to know the true Jesus of Nazareth need only look for him in the lore. For Jesus belongs to no denomination or sect. He belongs to the people. Those who read the lore attentively will come to know Jesus as the people know him and see him and adore him.

Nowhere more than in the lore does Jesus appear with the lowly, as the healer of the afflicted, as the man of sorrows, as the wise teacher who distinguishes between the letter and the spirit of the Law, and as the crucified, that truth and justice might not perish. And nowhere more than in the lore does Jesus emerge as the hope of the world, that love and not hatred may rule the hearts of men.

From the day of his birth, according to the lore, all the lowly of the earth, all the afflicted, all the heavy-laden and sorrowful, all the seekers after truth, all those willing to suffer martyrdom for their faith, all those seeking salvation sought Jesus out. And each one, according to the lore, saw him differently, just as John and James saw him differently, each according to his spiritual need.

For the lore of the New Testament is not a collection of legends, beliefs, superstitions, myths, parables, proverbs and discourses that were created and assembled at a given time in the past and then, as of a given day, sealed with a canonical period. This lore, like the

*lore of every other great and living religion, is a constant spring.
Some legends, like those in the Protevangelium of James, may date
back to the third century or even the second; whereas other parts
of it, like the legends in the Aquarian Gospel, were printed less than
half a century ago. A number of acanonical works now accounted
as of a very early date did not come to light until recent times,
and some, like a few of the Sayings of Jesus in the Oxyrhynchus
papyri, were not discovered until early in this century. Even material known for many centuries has gone through so many translations and revisions that it is often difficult to determine how far a
given legend, as we now have it, may be from the original. The
merit of the lore, therefore, cannot be gauged by age alone. As an
early sage pointed out long ago, "There may be a new flask full of
old wine, and an old flask that has not even new wine in it." The
test of this lore does not lie in its antiquity but rather in how nearly
it reflects a clearer image of Jesus.*

II

*The events in the life of Jesus and the precepts of his teachings
are the themes and the inspiration of the vast lore of the New
Testament.*

*Those fond of counting words might discover that four times as
many words, or four times four times as many words, are devoted
in this lore to people other than Jesus. The lore formally begins
with Joachim and Anna, the parents of Mary; though actually it
wanders back, all the way back, to the days of Adam and Eve and
their good son Seth. Mary's miraculous birth and exceptional childhood occupy a prominent place and her role remains constant in
the lore. The legends about Joseph the Carpenter are many, from
the day he appears in the temple with his rod, one of the Ten Wonders of the World, to the day he dies at the age one year greater
than that of Joseph the Patriarch. Zacharias and Elizabeth and their
son John appear in brief but unforgettable roles. And, after the
Passion, they are followed by a procession of apostles and disciples,
admirers and accusers, the steadfast and the wavering. As in the
Canon, the attention in the lore turns entirely from the Gospel story
to the Acts of the Apostles and their missionary activities. There
exist so many books about the adventures, miraculous deeds and*

martyrdom of the apostles and the disciples and the saints of the apostolic period that one is apt to think that this lore, by sheer volume, is devoted to them.

Yet, in essence, whatever the topic, the central theme is Jesus; and whatever the occurrence, the object of the occurrence is Jesus. Whether the legends are about the marvelous events in the lives of Joachim and Anna long before Jesus was born, or in the life of Thecla of Iconium who had never seen Jesus in the flesh; whether they are about Zebel, the doubting midwife at the time of Jesus' birth, or about Nicanora in the city of the Serpent, so many years later — they are all and always in fact about Jesus.

This lore might be likened to an epic drama about a far-famed king with a great household and many ambassadors. The stage is always full of people; the ambassadors come and go upon the stage, each relating new incidents, impending dangers, violent conflicts, approaching disasters and great triumphs. The king may not appear upon the stage at all. But all that happens, happens because of him; and without him none would have any meaning.

Even that area in the life of Jesus which the theologians refer to as "the hidden years" has been speculated upon and explored in the lore. The so-called unknown life of Jesus (from his early boyhood to the time he appeared to be baptized by John) is accounted for and becomes familiar in the lore. And the legends of "the hidden years," expounded in a number of strange gospels, appeared in lands as remote as Kashmir, Palestine and Tibet, and as near to us as the United States; among the Tamils in India, and the very proximate mystics of California of our own day.

In every legend of this vast and, at times, extravagant lore, Jesus is the essence, and the canonical Gospels of the New Testament are the source of inspiration. For the image of Jesus reflected in the folk imagination could not have existed without the Gospels of the New Testament and the recorded utterances of Jesus in them.

To appreciate the lore of the New Testament one must not only know the Gospels and how they came to be in the form we have them today, but also the kinship of the New Testament, as a whole, to the Old Testament, as a whole.

III

At first glance, the Old and the New Testaments appear disparate. In literary form, the Old Testament consists of chronicles, genealogies, laws, directives, precepts, commandments, histories of migrations, wars and conquests, personal histories, the rise and fall of kingdoms, collections of prayers, dramatic poems, miraculous contests, legends of great adventures, stirring wedding songs, collections of gnomic poetry, expressions of great despair and of doubt, idyllic stories, riddles, lamentations, prophetic warnings, and a large collection of lyric hymns that probe the human heart in its multitude of joys and sorrows. The literary form of the New Testament is simple and may be divided into three parts: the Gospels, the Acts and the Epistles. In their basic objectives, too, the Old and the New Testaments seem disparate. The Old Testament, as a whole, stresses the Law as a light to guide man along his dark journey so that he may know how to live and find favor in the eyes of his Creator. It is a way of life. The World to Come is barely hinted at and rarely underscored. The Old Testament is preoccupied with the search for justice and the differentiation between right and wrong in a world which will last forever. The New Testament seems preoccupied with the problem of personal salvation and preparation for the World to Come. The end of the world is at hand, it seems to say; the last judgment and the inauguration of the Kingdom of God on Earth might take place any moment, and the Judge stands at the door. This is the central theme. In this eschatological concept, faith replaces knowledge and love replaces justice. And, most important of all, the Old Testament is the long history of a very old nation; whereas the New Testament centers about the teachings of Jesus of Nazareth.

These and other differences may be pointed out. On the strength of them a bill of divorcement might be prepared for the Testaments.

But on closer examination it becomes apparent that, in the Canon and in the lore, the Old and the New Testaments belong together, parts of the same whole. The New Testament and its lore are as inconceivable without the Old Testament and its lore as branches without a trunk, or a tree without roots. For the two collections of books, and most of the lore that grew up about them, are the prod-

ucts of the same creative process in the experience of the same people.

Throughout the New Testament the Old is quoted for corroboration. According to one biblical scholar, Dr. John Paterson, the Old Testament is quoted 287 times in the New Testament; 116 of these quotations are from the Psalms, that fortress of faith built by the Jews over many troubled centuries to which they always turned in all their troubled times. "Those of you who are afflicted, pray," James counseled the followers of Jesus, "those of you who are gay, sing the psalms." The followers of Jesus sang the psalms in gladness and in sorrow. The Psalter, like the rest of the Law and the Prophets, remained a source of strength and a rock for those who early accepted the teachings of Jesus. The apostles often quoted the Old Testament to prove their points; though they quoted freely, from memory, "in the fullness of the spirit of revelation," and often adapted the text to their particular arguments. But the new teachings were still a direct extension, and in the tradition of the old.

In the New Testament lore the affinity with the Old Testament is even more evident. The major events, of course, take place on the same soil. And even in literary form the kinship is clear: the names are proximate; the numbers used symbolically are similar; and the precepts taught by example are familiar. At every turn one encounters the Patriarchs, the Prophets, the Jewish kings, judges and priests so familiar in the Old Testament lore — though they now appear in apocalyptic robes.

As literature the Bible is clearly one book, or rather, one collection of books. And in ethical content and form, the sayings, parables and discourses of Jesus as found in the Gospels belong with the sayings, parables and discourses of the Prophets, the Proverbs, the Psalms and the other books of the Hagiographa.

The reason one senses a break between the Old and the New Testaments is due to the great gap that yawns between them in time — the gap of nearly four centuries which separate Malachi from Matthew. During these eventful and bitter years in the lives of the Jewish people a number of now-apocryphal works were created which constitute the bridge between the Old and the New Testaments and which establish the continuity from Genesis to Revelation. Without this bridge, and without knowledge of the

stirring events which took place during these years, the New Testa-
ment and its lore naturally seem alien to what preceded them in the
Bible and the earlier lore. (The parallel might be made to one
reading English poetry in continuity from Beowulf *to* Auden *and*
halfway through the book suddenly encountering a gap of many
missing pages. The reader might conclude, though erroneously,
that the earlier and latter parts, because of their great differences,
do not belong together, and are separate works.)

Anyone wishing to gain insight into the lore of the New Testa-
ment with its asceticism and martyrdoms, its astounding miracles,
and its portrayal of the life of Jesus and his mission, should have a
general notion of the events that transpired between the days of
Malachi and the birth of Jesus.

IV

For several centuries preceding the times of the New Testa-
ment, a large number of Jews dwelt in Babylonia, in Egypt and in
other parts of the Persian and Greek world. Some migrated to those
countries of their own free will to seek their fortune or because they
were attracted by the dazzling star of the now post-Alexandrian
Greek civilization; and others were the children of people taken into
captivity who had not returned to their homeland when return was
permitted them under King Cyrus. A time arrived when there were
almost as many Jews abroad as at home. They kept in touch with
their brothers in Judea and the majority were not lost through as-
similation. But in Babylonia, and more particularly in Egypt, the
Jews were profoundly influenced by the civilization around them.
They spoke Greek; they began to dress like the Greeks; they
adopted many Greek customs; they read the Scriptures in Aramaic
and Greek; and they accepted a number of scriptural works which
were rejected by their brothers in Judea. They even added to the
Scriptures works of their own, written in Greek, which showed
clearly the influence of Greek philosophy and ethics and which
interpreted the Law and the Prophets in more universal terms.

The bond between the Jewish communities abroad and in Judea
was never broken. And whenever a Jew was in trouble in his home-
land, he would escape to Egypt for refuge among his brethren
and remain there permanently or until the particular danger that

threatened him and his family was over. The bond was never broken; but the bond was strained. For while the extra-Judean Jews continued to liberalize their concepts of the Law in terms of the spirit, the leaders of the Jews in Judea turned increasingly to a stricter and narrower observance of the Law and a more fundamentalist interpretation of the letter of the Law. In time, particularly during periods of great stress, the Orthodoxy extolled the ritual above the meaning; watched jealously for any deviation from the precept and the rule; and punished severely every infraction. And they accused the people of their sins against the Lord, or their failure to observe the Law to the last of the Six Hundred and Thirteen Commandments, as the cause for their sufferings under oppression.

Judging from the written record of restrictions it is evident that the strain to loosen the bonds, especially by those who had ties with brethren in other lands, must have been very great.

The struggle between the "purists" who taught the Mosaic Law as eternal and inflexible, and thought of Judaism as a religion exclusively for the Jews as a chosen people, and those who strained to transform Judaism into a universal religion, resulted in many sects and in many strange new works of a mystic and apocalyptic nature. The theological schism was sharpened by the deteriorating economic and political situation in Judea.

During the century preceding the ministry of Jesus, not a year passed without war, preparation for war, or the fear of war. These were accompanied by outbreaks among the poor who organized in secret societies and openly rebelled against the oppressive hand of the priests and the landowners. In the midst of all these troubles Judea was struck by an earthquake that killed thousands of people and destroyed a great part of their cattle. This was followed closely by a severe drought of disastrous proportions.

Many of the strong in body died in the wars and many of the weak in body perished of hunger and disease.

The Jews interpreted their misfortunes as signs of the imminent arrival of the Messiah. Immanuel the Deliverer was on everybody's lips. A number of apocalyptic works appeared that were read avidly, and each work gave "signs of the coming of the Messiah." Before the Messiah arrived, the people were told, the trees and the herbs of forest and field would be covered with a dew of blood. Great buildings would crumble into dust. Tempests would level the mountains of the earth into plains. And the people read Tobit and other works for descriptions of the world after the arrival of the Messiah, whom they eagerly awaited.

Among the Jewish sects one, called the Righteous, prepared for the coming of the Messiah. The members of this sect ate no meat; they drank no wine; they owned neither slaves nor gold; they shared in common all they possessed; and they refused to bear arms because they believed it was just as evil to kill an enemy as to kill a friend.

With each new disaster the ranks of this sect increased, and among these the people of Judea began to seek the Messiah.

Into this environment Jesus was born.

And the lore of the New Testament is the folk chronicle of what Jesus meant to his people, first, and what he came to mean to the people of the world. In the lore, as in the Gospels, Jesus emerges steeped in the Jewish ritual and liturgy of his day, and all his expressions are founded upon Judaic concepts and Hebraic ethics. That is the soil upon which Jesus grew; and for some time the Nazarene community was a Judaic manifestation, no more divergent than Reform Judaism is from Orthodox Judaism today. The wedge between Jesus and the Jews was not driven in until Paul of Tarsus impressed his apostolic concepts on the new creed, and Luke had written his Gospel for the Greeks rather than for the Hebrews; followed by the many apostolic works, each adding a stroke to the wedge.

V

In assembling the material for this book from the vast body of the lore, the constant problem was one of selection. This applied particularly to the stories about the apostles. These exist in many versions, and often a story is attributed to one apostle in one source, and to another apostle in a different source. In this book, as the Notes on Sources indicate, several different legends are often combined into one story. Yet even this device did not assure the inclusion of more than a very small portion of the legends available.

In chronology this book follows the New Testament, a procedure

*that imposed additional limitations. For although the legends were
selected on the basis of their merit, the sequence in time had to be
considered.*

*The reader will find many anachronisms in the lore: Joseph the
Carpenter is called a priest, though in the same lore he is described
as a Levite (a group excluded from the priesthood); virgins are
described as dwelling in the temple of Jerusalem, counter to all
historical fact; a Roman King of Jerusalem orders a throne to be
built for him in that city, though no Roman was ever king in Jerusalem; a river flows along the outskirts of Nazareth, where no river
ever existed. And so on. But in legend all things are possible. The
lore is not bound by history, or geography, or mathematics, or any
other science, exact or otherwise, excepting the moral science. For
all the lore is dedicated to teaching a moral.*

*And the moral of the New Testament lore might be summed up
in the legend about the good man who died and whose soul
knocked upon the gates of heaven.*

The voice of God from within asked: "Who is there?"

"It is I," said the soul of the good man, and gave his name.

"Heaven will not hold both you and me," came the reply.

*The soul of the good man went away sorrowfully, perplexed by
the reply he had received. But after a while he returned and
knocked again upon the gates of heaven.*

"Who is there?" came the question.

"It is you," the good soul answered.

And the gates of heaven opened to him.

PART I
The Lineage

From the New Testament we gain scant knowledge about Mary's origins, her childhood, her appearance, her nature. But the lore dwells with tender redundance upon every conceivable phase of her person and character.

The Gospel According to St. Luke merely mentions that Mary was of the House of David. And The Gospel According to St. Matthew concerns itself with tracing the ancestry of Joseph the Carpenter all the way back to the Patriarch Abraham.

The lore, however, underscores Mary's lineage as a descendant of King David and of the Tribe of Judah. That written records of Mary's genealogy could not be found is accounted for by the wickedness of the acts of Herod, himself an Idumean, who felt insecure in his rule of Judea and was forever afraid that a true descendant of David might rightfully claim the throne. He therefore, according to legend, commanded that all genealogies kept in the secret chests of the temple be burnt.

CHAPTER ONE

Joachim and Anna

1. The Good Joachim Takes a Bride

In the days of Antipater the Idumean and his wicked son Herod there lived in the city of Nazareth, in Galilee, a young man, well-born and rich, named Joachim. Although he was of noble parentage and had inherited great wealth, yet was he from his childhood a fearer of God, endowed with a good heart and crowned with humility. And though he was exceedingly rich in cattle, gold and silver, he lived as one who cared for his father's flocks and herds. People called him Noble Joachim; but he called himself humbly ben Eliezer — the Son of the Man Who Depends on the Help of Cod. In Nazareth he was known best as Joachim Zadok, meaning Joachim the Righteous.

Three times each year Joachim went up to Jerusalem with his father and kindred to make the offering on the altar of God. There they marveled at the new walls of the city, rebuilt by permission of Julius Caesar; they listened in the temple court to the whispered rumors that young Herod the Idumean flattered the tyrants whose very names made the hearts of the just to tremble; and the young Levite priests consoled them with the accounts of the glorious Maccabees of the past, and the still more glorious days of the future when the Messiah would come.

Each time Joachim returned from the Holy City, he devoted himself with greater zeal to help the widow, the orphan, the stranger, and the poor; and he gave to those who had too little of what he had too much. Yet the more Joachim gave away, the more his wealth increased. For God was with him.

When Joachim reached the age of eighteen, his parents began to seek a bride for their son, worthy of his goodness and, like himself, a descendant of the tribe of Judah and of the House of David.

They found her in the adopted daughter of Mathan of Judah, in Bethlehem. As an infant she had been abandoned and exposed in the fields by her parents. But a doe had found and nourished her. And when the childless Mathan and his wife discovered the child, they saw written on her breast in letters of gold the name: ANNA.

While all Judea mourned the marriage of the wicked Herod the Idumean to the beautiful Hasmonean Princess Mariamne, Bethlehem celebrated the marriage of Joachim the Righteous, in his twentieth year, to the good Anna, who was eighteen years old on her wedding day, and known throughout Judea as much for the goodness of her heart as for the beauty of her countenance.

2. Issachar's Rebuke

Joachim and Anna began their married life in joy. But as year followed year and their home remained empty of either sons or daughters, their joy turned into sorrow.

After ten years of childless marriage, Anna pleaded with her husband to divorce her and marry another, according to the Law, that he might fulfill God's will. But Joachim so loved Anna that he replied they must continue to pray for offspring. At every feast and festival they went up to the temple in Jerusalem to make their offerings, and there they vowed each time that if a child were granted them, they would dedicate the child to the service of God.

In the twentieth year of their marriage, Joachim and Anna went up with their kin to the temple in Jerusalem to celebrate the Feast of Encenia, which is the festival of the Rededication of the Temple. When Anna entered the Court of the Women, the women drew away from her, saying:

"Touch us not, for you are barren, and your infirmity might pass to us so that we, too, might become childless and our husbands despise us."

And the men similarly withdrew from Joachim.

Later, as Joachim came up to the altar with his offerings and his gifts, Issachar the high priest pointed an accusing finger at him and asked:

"Have you brought forth seed in Israel?"

Joachim bowed his head and answered: "Indeed, I have not."

And Issachar said: "Your sin must be great for the curse of barrenness is upon you. It is written: 'There shall nothing cast their young, nor be barren, in your land.'"

And Joachim said: "I know it is so written."

And Issachar said: "If a man and his wife remain barren for ten years, it is the duty of the faithful to divorce his barren wife and marry again so as to fulfill God's law. Yet twice that many years have passed and still you cleave to your wife. Therefore depart from this altar and from among this congregation who have fulfilled God's law!"

Joachim covered his face with his cloak and left the temple in distress. He prayed: "O God of our fathers! You have heard and seen the shame heaped upon me and my unhappy wife. Though I know not what our sins are, yet must they be altogether greater than the sins of all the assembled before the altar who have been blessed with offspring."

And he said to Anna his wife: "This day I have been shamed before the altar and all the assembly before God in Jerusalem. I cannot return to Nazareth to be branded by my own kin with the reproach they have heard from the lips of the high priest. Therefore I leave my house in your hands; and I shall go to the desert and pray."

Joachim went into the desert and made a vow: "I will give neither sleep to my eyes, nor slumber to my eyelids, until the Lord shall make my disgrace pass away from me; nor shall I put food in my mouth nor water to my lips, until the Lord has answered my supplication."

And thus he remained for forty days and forty nights, fasting and praying.

Anna, his wife, returned alone to Nazareth in great sorrow and lamented: "It is meet that I should weep, for among the daughters of Israel there is none like unto me; and in all the house of Jacob there is not another woman as heavy laden as I am. For the blessing of God has not been with me; and now my husband has forsaken me and fled from me and I know not whether I shall ever see him again."

3. Visions in the Night

One night in the desert Joachim dreamt a dream and saw a vision. He dreamt that he stood beside the waters of a spring, and a white dove came to rest upon his head. Then it rose again and circled about him.

The same night, and at the same time, Anna, asleep in her home, dreamt a dream and saw a vision. She dreamt that she was walking toward a laurel tree which grew beside a flowing spring, and a white dove flew out from the tree and came to rest upon her hands. But when they awoke, neither Joachim in the desert nor Anna in her home knew what their dreams and visions meant. Many weeks passed; and no sign was given them.

4. Joachim and the Angel

After the good Joachim had been in the desert for five months, an angel came to him and said:

"Arise, Joachim, for your reproach has been heard and your shame has been seen. But Issachar's reproach is not your reproach. When God closes the womb, it is not as a punishment, but only to open it later more marvelously. The first Mother of Israel, Sarah, was barren until the ninetieth year of her life, and then she gave birth to Isaac to whom the benediction of all people was promised. And the Mother Rebekah was barren for twenty years before she gave birth to Esau and Jacob, called Israel. And the Mother Rachel was childless for many years, until God gave her Joseph who saved the world from starvation.

"And who was stronger than Samson or holier than Samuel? Yet their mothers were barren for many years before they gave birth to their sons. Thus you may believe by example that the child that will be given you will be more marvelous. For you shall have a daughter, and you shall call her Mary; and from her infancy she shall be dedicated to the Lord. And this shall be your sign:

"Return to Jerusalem and go to the gate of the temple called the Beautiful. There, thirty days from today, in the sixth hour of the day, you will find your wife waiting for you, and she will rejoice in your return."

Then Joachim said: "If I have found favor in your eyes, come and sit with me awhile in my tent, and partake of my food, and bless me, your servant, as Father Abraham was blessed and Father Jacob was blessed by the angels that visited them."

And the angel replied: "Do not ask me to enter your tent, for my food is invisible and my drink cannot be seen by men."

Joachim then took a lamb without blemish and sacrificed it to the Lord, and the angel and the odor of the sacrifice went up together straight to heaven.

5. Tidings Under the Laurel Tree

On the day that Joachim was visited by the angel, Anna was in her chamber, lamenting: "O Lord, God of Israel, how you have smitten me! First I was deprived of children, and now I am also deprived of my husband; and I do not know whether he is alive or whether he is dead. And I sorrow with two sorrows: my childlessness and my widowhood."

Anna's maidservant, Judith, came into the chamber to remind her mistress that the Feast of Tabernacles was drawing near and that it was not meet to mourn on the day dedicated to God.

Anna took off her garments of mourning, anointed her head, and put on festive clothes to greet the holiday. Then she went into her garden and sat down under a laurel tree.

In the branches of the tree before her she could see a sparrow's nest in which there were young birds, and their mother was hovering over them and giving them food. The tears rose to Anna's eyes, and she said:

"Alas! To what am I likened? I am not even as this sparrow in the tree; for the sparrow has her young and see how happy she is in feeding them. O Lord! Why have you made me a reproach and a mockery in the eyes of my people? If my sin be great, in your mercy cast it away like a pebble into the sea, and hearken to my prayer!"

Suddenly she heard a voice beside her, saying: "Fear not, Anna, for I am an angel of the Lord and I bring you tidings of your husband Joachim, for whose safety you are anxious." The angel repeated to Anna what he had told to Joachim, and he gave her the sign of the meeting at the temple gate, called the Beautiful. Then the angel vanished.

When the servants in the house saw Anna on her return from the garden, they asked: "What news have you? For you went out sorrowing and now you come in rejoicing!"

"I rejoice," said Anna, "because God has given me a message of glad tidings by the hand of his angel."

And after the Feast of Tabernacles was over, Anna put on her wedding dress, and departed for Jerusalem to meet her husband.

6. *Reunion at the Gate*

Anna passed through the Golden Gate of Jerusalem and walked quickly ahead of her maidens through the market place filled with the smell of herbs and oils and spices. She passed through the stalls of fine linens and glittering ornaments, looking neither to the right nor to the left, and hastened her step until she reached the temple and the gate called the Beautiful.

There Anna waited, for the hour was still early. And to calm her impatience, she recited the psalm she had been taught in childhood: "The earth is the Lord's, and the fullness thereof; the world, and they that dwell in it. For he has founded it upon the seas, and established it upon the floods."

When she wearied from waiting, Anna lifted her eyes and, behold, her husband was coming. She ran to him joyously and threw her arms about him and hung upon his neck.

"I was a widow, and behold, my husband is alive; I was childless, and behold, I am about to conceive."

And together they went to the temple.

7. *The Great Celebration*

Anna's time was fulfilled in her home in Nazareth.
"What have I brought forth?" she asked.

"A girl," answered the midwife.

And Anna said: "I thank you, O Lord, God of our forefathers, who today magnified my soul and put away my reproach from among my people."

The women in the neighborhood came to the house with gifts for Anna and the men brought gifts for Joachim. And Anna's sister, Hismeria, came from the hill country with her daughters Elizabeth and Eliud; and Elizabeth's husband, the priest Zacharias, came with them. And all their other relatives from out of town assembled in Joachim's house for the celebration.

After the days of purification were over, Anna and her husband brought the child to the synagogue to be named. And they called her Mary, as the angel had commanded. Then Anna took her daughter in her arms, and before all those assembled she sang a song to the Lord:

"You are the Lord, who will exalt the humble, and humble the haughty;

"You are the Lord, who looked down from heaven on the houses of the poor, and made them rich;

"You, archangels of the Lord, come and rejoice with me, for my knees have carried the fruit of a child;

"You, cherubim with four faces and six wings and a thousand eyes full of light, come and rejoice with me and teach me to sing to my child;

"You, stewards of joy, you harpers and praisers of God, come and rejoice with me by reason of my joy today."

And all those assembled responded: "Amen!"

The celebration of the birth of Mary continued in her father's house for seven days. And everyone in Nazareth rejoiced over what God had done for Joachim and Anna of the Tribe of Judah.

CHAPTER TWO

Mary in the Temple

1. *The Late Weaning*

When Mary was one year old her mother put her down upon the ground to see if she was able to walk. The child stood up firmly and walked without faltering to her mother's apron. Anna lifted the child in her arms and kissed her and said to her husband Joachim:

"Let us build a chamber for Mary our daughter to abide in until we take her up to the temple in Jerusalem, as we vowed. And let us make her chamber as a shrine and a sanctuary, where her feet shall not touch the bare ground."

Joachim built a beautiful chamber and furnished it as a shrine and covered the ground with costly silks from Persia and precious purple cloth from Tyre and Sidon. And there Mary dwelt for two years.

On Mary's third birthday Joachim gave a great feast, as was customary, to celebrate the weaning of the child. To this feast were invited many priests and scribes and the elders of the city, as well as relatives and neighbors.

When the guests were at the feasting tables, Anna brought her daughter for the blessing. And the priests said:

"The Lord, God of our fathers, bless this maiden, and grant her a noble, and exalted, and glorious name, for ever and ever, throughout all generations; and may she be found worthy that from her shall spring the Messiah, son of David, for whom the nation waits."

And all the guests responded: "Amen!"

After the feast Joachim said to his wife: "The time has come for us to take our daughter to the temple of the Lord, as we vowed before she was born."

But Anna pleaded: "Let us wait a while longer, for the child is still frail."

Some time later, when Joachim again spoke of their vow and his fear that the Lord might be angered by their delay, Anna again pleaded: "Let us wait just a little longer, that the child may not suffer so with longing when she is left in the temple."

Until one day Joachim said to Anna with firmness: "Come, call the maidens to accompany us to Jerusalem, and let each virgin take a lamp as on the eve when the bridegroom is met; and when we reach the temple grounds, let them go before us with the lighted lamps, so that our child will watch them and not turn back. And her heart will be distracted."

2. Anna's Three Marys

In the year that Mary was left in the temple, Joachim died in the prime of his age and in the vigor of his youth. And Anna mourned with two mournings: one for her widowhood; and another because her daughter, her beloved daughter, was not at home to console her.

At the end of her days of mourning, an angel of the Lord came to Anna and commanded her to marry again and not to tarry in her widowhood. And she married Cleophas, a brother of Joseph the Carpenter, a native of Bethlehem and of the House of David.

Within a year Anna gave birth to a daughter. But her joy was canceled by her new sorrow, for Cleophas died before the birth of his child. And Anna named the second child also Mary.

Mary, daughter of Cleophas, was not yet weaned, when an angel appeared to Anna and commanded her to marry again. And she married Shalom, to whom she bare a daughter. And this daughter, too, was named Mary.

And so it came to pass that the good Anna, who had been visited by an angel three times and had lived by the command of God, lived many years to be consoled in her offspring.

3. Mary's Guardian

After the death of Mary's father, Joachim, the priests in the temple, twenty-five in number, disputed as to who should become her guardian. Each of them wanted to take care of her, and each advanced a claim of his own. Finally they decided to settle the matter by lots.

They went down to the shores of the Jordan and each threw into the flowing waters a reed with an inscription from the Holy Law. Twenty-four of the reeds sank; only the reed belonging to the priest Zacharias floated upon the water and did not sink.

All the other priests congratulated Zacharias, saying: "You and your wife are full of days and you have no son and no daughter of your own. Now the Lord has rewarded you and you shall guard and teach Mary as if she were your own child."

And Zacharias and his wife thanked God for having given them in trust a daughter so perfect in every way.

4. Mary and the Sabbath

Mary was unlike any of the many virgins in the temple of Jerusalem. At the age of three she walked with a step so sure, spoke with such clarity and perfection, and cared for herself with such self-reliance that she astonished her elders, and they treated her as if she were thirty and not three.

As she grew, so grew her serenity and skill. She never adorned herself as a young girl, as did the other maidens in the temple, nor indulged in any outward show. She never painted her eyes, nor put saffron upon her cheeks, nor plaited her hair. She used no perfume, nor anointed her body with ointment.

During all the years that Mary was in the temple, she wore the same garments her mother had put on her when she was brought to the temple. For as she grew, so the garments grew miraculously with her. They never tore nor showed signs of wear. And they were always as fresh as on the first day she had put them on.

Mary's companions in the temple taught her how to weave, and soon there were none who could compare with her in skill.

She ate only enough to sustain her soul in her body. And she ate only the food that was brought to her from heaven by the hands of an angel.

Even her greeting was different from the greeting of her companions. Whereas they would say: "Good morning!" or "Good evening!" or "With you be peace!" Mary said: "O give thanks unto the Lord!"; and never varied the psalmic salutation.

Each day in the temple was a day of dedication for Mary. But most sacred of all was the Sabbath. She spoke very little on all other days; and not at all on the Sabbath, except when she spoke to the angel who brought her Sabbath meal.

(Her companions saw her in the attitude of speaking, yet could not see to whom she spoke; they saw her in the attitude of listening, yet could not see to whom she listened. And they all knew that she was visited by angels.)

On the Sabbath Mary repeated all she had learned about the holy day. She recited the Fourth Commandment; she communed with the Angel of the Sabbath who sits on a special Throne of Glory; she welcomed the Sabbath as a bride; and she offered up a special prayer when the Sabbath departed.

(And Saturday remains Mary's day. Those who pray to her on the Sabbath, it is believed, will have their prayers answered.)

There are a number of legends on the affinity of Mary and the Sabbath. One tells of a statue of Mary in a church called Lucerne, in the city of Constantinople. All week long this statue was hidden from view by a heavy curtain of gold and silver. But on Friday evening, when the first star appeared in the heavens, the curtain rose of its own accord and the beautiful statue was revealed in all its splendor to the worshipers. It remained unveiled until vespers on the Sabbath day; and then the curtain fell miraculously and shielded Mary's statue from view until the following Sabbath.

5. What Was Mary Like?

What was Mary like as she grew up in the temple of Jerusalem?

Mary was of medium stature, we are told, and her body was graceful and well proportioned. She was delicate in appearance and her skin the color of ripening wheat. Her face was oval but not pointed; her hair was golden and not plaited; her eyes were large, bluish in color, and sparkling; her eyebrows were arched and darker in color than the hair of her head; her nose was rather long; and her lips were fresh and full of loveliness in speech. Her hands were long and her fingers tapered. And her appearance was always so beautiful and glorious that scarcely anyone could look into the brightness of her face.

This was the vessel; lovelier still was the content.

None was more learned than Mary in the Law and the Prophets; none was more humble; none more melodious in singing; none more steadfast in the work of the temple. Daily she advanced in the perfection of knowledge and skill. She spoke little, and only that which was necessary; and then with becoming modesty, without embarrassment, and without pride. She was never seen angry, or ever heard to speak ill of anyone. And she was always careful in her speech, lest she offend one of her companions.

And all who knew her, adored her.

CHAPTER THREE

Joseph's Rod

1. *Abiathar and the High Priest*

There lived a priest named Abiathar who saw Mary in the temple when she reached her golden age; and he went to the high priest with many gifts, and said:

"Mary, the daughter of Joachim and Anna, has now reached the age of consent, and I would like nothing better than that she should become my son's wife."

The high priest replied: "Zacharias is her guardian. He is the one to be asked. But since Mary is an orphan, she must be consulted first."

But when they told Mary of Abiathar's wish, she forbade them to speak about it, saying: "It cannot be that I should ever take a husband."

The priests were astonished to hear such words. And they admonished her: "Surely you know that God is worshiped in children and adored in posterity!"

And Mary replied: "I have resolved in my heart to remain a virgin, like Abel the Righteous and Elijah the Prophet, and so to live all the days of my life."

They quoted the Law and they quoted the Prophets, but their words failed to move Mary, for she was convinced that virginity was sufficiently dear to God.

Since all the good men knew her to be worthy of admiration, they left her in peace, and Abiathar's request was denied.

2. *The Complaint of the Pharisees*

On the occasion of Mary's fourteenth birthday, the Pharisees, who guarded the Law jealously, demanded of the high priest to declare that no virgin who lived in the house of God could remain there after reaching the age of maturity; and that all the virgins who had reached that age must return to their homes to be married.

All the maidens obeyed the decree of the high priest, except Mary, who said that her parents had dedicated her to the temple and the service of God even before she was born, and that she could not violate their vow without offending the Most High.

The high priest, being in great perplexity, said to the Pharisees: "Let us go and consult Zacharias and hear what he advises us to do."

Zacharias listened to them and he said: "I am an old man and my wife is dead. And Mary, whom God has given me to guard, has become a woman. But she refuses to violate her father's vow. And it is written: 'If a man vow a vow unto the Lord, he shall not break his word.' But it is also written: 'Be fruitful and multiply, and replenish the earth.' Therefore, let us inquire of the Lord what to do concerning Mary, and whatever is his will, that shall be our answer."

3. The Advice of the Oracle

The priests assembled before the altar of God and the high priest put on the robe with the blue and scarlet and purple pomegranates embroidered on its hem and the golden bells between them; a golden bell and a pomegranate, a golden bell and a pomegranate; with seventy-two bells all around the hem (one bell for each of the twelve tribes of Israel, multiplied by the days of Creation). And while the Levites bowed their heads in prayer, the high priest entered the Holy of Holies to consult the oracle concerning Mary, and the bells of his robe tinkled so that their sound could be heard before he entered the sanctuary of the Lord.

And the priests heard a voice issuing from the oracle and the Seat of Mercy. And the voice was the voice of the angel Gabriel, who said:

"Zacharias! Zacharias! Send out your trumpeters throughout Jerusalem to call all the men of the Tribe of Judah, and those of the House of David, to gather together on the morrow at the temple. And let each man bring his rod with him. Take their rods and place them in the Holy of Holies. And to whomsoever God shall show a sign, to him shall Mary be given as a wife."

Trumpeters were sent out to all the gates of Jerusalem and to every market place, and wherever crowds gathered, letting it be known that on the morrow every man of the Tribe of Judah who had no wife must come to the temple and bring his rod with him.

The next morning three thousand men appeared in the court of the temple, waiting for the high priest. And among the crowd was Joseph of Nazareth of the Tribe of Judah, who, like the others, had come to Jerusalem for the festival that was at hand.

4. *The Old Carpenter*

The aged Joseph had been a carpenter from his youth. Yet from his youth he had been so learned that he had been ordained a priest and a preacher in the temple of God. At the age of forty he married the God-fearing Escha of Bethlehem, who bare him four sons and three daughters. The names of the sons were: Judas, Justus, Simon and James; and the names of the daughters were: Esther, Thamar and Salome. And James was the youngest of them all.

Escha died after forty-nine years of wedded bliss. And Joseph was then eighty-nine years old.

Joseph continued his work as a carpenter with his sons. And he went up to Jerusalem a year after Escha's death for the approaching Festival of the Dedication. He had just entered the Holy City when he heard the trumpeters in the streets and the heralds of the high priest in the market place, calling all the men of the Tribe of Judah and of the House of David to assemble on the morrow in the court of the temple.

Joseph, wise in the Law, understood that this was a matter of giving an orphaned daughter of Israel in marriage, which could not concern him because of his great age. But being of the Tribe of Judah and without a wife, he dared not slight the order of the high priest. And he joined the multitude of young men.

When all the men had assembled in the temple court, the high priest rose on a step so that he could be seen and heard by all, and said:

"Ever since the temple was built by Solomon, there have been virgins in its courts. And when they came of age, they returned to their homes and were given in marriage. But there is one in the temple who refuses to leave and marry. We have consulted the oracle to learn in whose keeping she should be entrusted, for she can no longer remain in the temple. And we were commanded to gather you here and place your rods in the Holy of Holies. On the morrow, when the rods are taken out of the holy place, we shall be given a sign as to whom Mary should be given in marriage."

The rods were gathered, and each of the young men spent the night in prayer for the sign, so that the beautiful Mary might be given him in marriage.

5. *One of the Ten Wonders*

The old man Joseph turned in his short and knobby rod, not knowing its wonderful history. For this rod which belonged to Joseph was one of the Ten Wonders of the World.

On the sixth day of Creation, when the twilight approached and the world with all that is in it was complete, God created the ten wonders, and the Rod of Moses was one of them.

The rod had inscribed upon it: the Exalted and Ineffable Name; the names of the patriarchs Abraham, Isaac and Jacob; the names of the Twelve Tribes of Israel; and the names of the ten plagues to be inflicted on Egypt by Moses.

Adam brought this rod out of the Garden of Eden. From Adam it descended to Enoch, the man who walked with God. Enoch gave it to the good Noah. And when Noah came out of the ark after the deluge, he gave it to his son Shem. Shem gave it to Abraham. And Abraham gave it to his grandson Jacob, who, in his old age, took it down with him to Egypt, and gave it to his favorite son, Joseph.

When Joseph died, this rod, along with all of Joseph's possessions, was placed in the royal treasury; and Jethro, Pharaoh's adviser, saw it one day and asked for it. Pharaoh could not see that it was worth much, and he gave it to Jethro. Later, when Jethro left the service of the king and returned to Midian, he took the rod with him. There he stuck it in the ground one day; but when he tried to pull it out again, he could not. All the strong men in Midian came and tried to pull it out, yet none succeeded.

One day, Moses, who had fled from Egypt to Midian, came into Jethro's garden and saw the rod with the Exalted Name engraved upon it, and he lifted it out of the ground with great ease. With this rod Moses smote the hard-hearted Pharaoh with the ten plagues, and then, for forty long years, he led the children of Israel from slavery to freedom. And during these forty years in the desert, Moses performed many miracles with the aid of the rod.

The Rod of Moses was handed down until it reached King David. And from King David it went to his descendants (who no longer knew its history and its power) until it reached Joseph the Carpenter, of Nazareth.

And Joseph did not know the rod's history, or the powers that resided in it, when he handed it in among the three thousand others to be placed in the Holy of Holies.

6. *The Dove Whiter than Snow*

Early the following morning the men of Judah assembled in the outer court of the temple. An incense offering was made and the high priest intoned the prayer.

Then the high priest entered the holy place. The assembled waited anxiously. But when the high priest reappeared with all the rods, a murmur of disappointment went through the crowd; for no sign had been given.

The high priest resolved to consult the oracle once again. He donned the sacerdotal robe with the many bells, entered the sanctuary, made a burnt offering, and bowed his head in prayer.

And as he prayed the angel Gabriel came and stood at the right of the altar on which the incense burned, and said:

"There is here a short rod which you brought in with the rest, but neglected to take out with the others. When you have returned it to the one to whom it belongs, the sign shall be given."

The high priest looked about him and he saw the short rod belonging to Joseph of Nazareth. He picked it up, went out into the court, and called out in a loud voice:

"Joseph, come and receive your rod!"

Joseph came forward with a trembling heart. He had thought that the rod had been discarded, because of his age, and he would not himself ask for its return. Now he came forward to receive it. And as his hand stretched out to take the rod, a dove, whiter than snow, its wings tipped with gold, appeared from the heavens and alighted on Joseph's head. Then the dove flew up to the pinnacle of the temple and disappeared. And as the rod passed from the high priest's hand to Joseph, its head burst into clusters of almond blossoms.

"This is our sign," said the high priest, "that God wishes you to receive the maiden Mary."

Joseph said softly: "I am an old man, and this girl is younger than some of my grandchildren. If I take her into my house as a bride I shall be a laughing stock in Israel."

"Fear the Lord our God, and not the scorn of men; for the sign came from the Lord," said the high priest sternly.

"I shall do as the Lord wills," said Joseph. "I shall take Mary and be her guardian until I can ascertain to which of my sons God wishes me to give her as wife. But meanwhile, it would be fitting that some of the virgins accompany her to my house as her companions."

The high priest appointed five virgins (one for each of the five classes of guardian angels) to accompany Mary and be with her until she was given in marriage.

7. Mary in Joseph's House

After the betrothal ceremonies, Mary was received by Joseph into his house in Nazareth. And with her came her five companions, whose names were: Rebekah "the plump one"; Sephora "the bookish"; Susanna "the joyous"; Abigea "the restful"; and Calah "the favored."

(Some say that the five virgins who came to Joseph's house with Mary were: Forgiveness, Rest, Perfection, Covenant and Holiness.)

After Mary and her companions were settled in his home, Joseph said to them: "I must leave you now, for I go to complete my work in Capernaum by the sea, and I shall be gone for many months. May the Lord protect you while I am gone."

Mary and her companions cared for Joseph's house while he was gone. And when Mary found the child James sorrowful because of the loss of his mother, she cared for him tenderly, for he was still of a tender age. And the child James loved Mary and called her "Mother." Hence she was called the mother of James, later known as James the Less.

CHAPTER FOUR

Trial by Water

1. *The Veil for the Temple*

The Levites held a council and decided that there should be a new veil made for the temple of the Lord, and they said:

"Let us call together seven maidens of the House of David skilled in the spinning of the threads, the dyeing of the wool, and the weaving of the cloth. And they shall make the new veil."

Seven virgins were selected for the honor; seven virgins like the seven strings on King David's harp. And Mary was amongst them. The maidens came to the storing place of the offerings of gold and silver, of wool and silk, of rams' skins and badgers' skins, and of ointments of many kinds. And the officers of the temple said:

"We shall choose by lot who shall spin the gold, who the fine linen and silk, and who shall work with the green, the hyacinth, the scarlet and the true purple."

They cast lots as to what each virgin should do; and the scarlet and true purple fell to the lot of Mary. The other maidens, who were older than Mary and envious that she should have drawn the scarlet and the purple, began to chide her and called her "Queen of Virgins." Whereupon the voice of an angel was heard saying:

"The words you have uttered in jest and envy, shall turn into a prophecy most true."

The virgins were troubled when they heard this, and asked Mary to forgive them. And Mary forgave them.

Then the maidens took the allotments given them by the officers of the temple, and each went to her own home.

2. *Mary and the Angel*

One day, as Mary sat alone in her chamber working on the purple for the veil of the temple, with the door of her chamber securely shut, there appeared beside her a young man of ineffable beauty. And he said: "Fear not, Mary, for I am an angel of the Lord."

Mary was accustomed to angelic voices and she was not terrified by his appearance, nor astonished at the great light of his face, nor perplexed by his greeting.

And the angel spoke again and said: "Blessed are you, Mary, above all women, and blessed is the fruit of your womb. For you, a virgin, shall conceive by his word, and shall have a son. And, as it was foretold in days of old, he shall be great and have dominion from sea to sea and from the river to the ends of the earth. He shall judge the poor of the people, he shall save the children of the needy, and he shall break the oppressor. His name shall endure as long as the sun; and all the nations of the earth shall call him blessed."

Mary had often heard such words in the temple and in the songs of the Levites; and now she wondered what could be the portent of these words as spoken by the angel. And she asked:

"How shall that come to pass? For I am a virgin even as I was born."

To this the angel replied: "Not in the manner of other women shall you conceive; but by the hearing of the ear. The Holy Spirit shall be upon you, and the power of the Most High shall envelop you. And you shall give birth to a son, and you shall call him Jeshua, meaning: Salvation Comes from God; for he shall save the Children of Israel from sin."

Mary stretched out her hands and raised her eyes to heaven, and said: "Let it be with me according to your words."

See Notes on Sources *for another version of this legend.*

3. *Joseph Returns*

Six months after the angel came to Mary, Joseph returned from Capernaum, where his house-building work was completed. And when he came into his home, he saw that Mary was big with child.

Joseph threw himself down upon the ground, trembling and weeping bitterly. From fear and sorrow, and anguish of heart, he could neither eat nor drink all day. And he prayed for death.

"O Lord! What prayer shall I make for this maiden that you have entrusted to my care? For I received her as a virgin out of your temple, and I did not watch over her. In me the history of Adam repeats itself. For just as Adam tarried in singing praise, while the serpent came and deceived his wife Eve, so also, while I was gone, a deceiver came and defiled this virgin in my house. It were better by far for me to die than to live any longer. O Lord, hear my prayer and receive my spirit!"

His spirit was not taken from him. And Joseph called Mary and said to her:

"Why have you done this thing and forgotten the Lord, our God? You, who have been brought up in the holy temple and received your food from the hands of the angels, why have you brought your soul so low?"

Mary bowed her head and wept bitterly before Joseph, and replied: "I am innocent and have known no man."

And Joseph asked again: "Have you ever heard of a crop upon the earth without the sowing of seed?"

"God, at the time of Creation," said Mary, "produced fruit without the intervention of seed."

"But whence is this offspring and who is the father of the child you bear?" asked Joseph.

"The case is the same as it was with Adam," said Mary. "God said, 'Let him be,' and he was."

Then she told him of the angel of ineffable beauty who visited her, and all that the angel had told her.

"Why do you mislead me to believe that an angel of the Lord has made you pregnant by the hearing of the ear? Is it not possible that some one pretended to be an angel and has beguiled you?"

"Call my companions," said Mary, "and let them testify whether any man has ever entered my chamber."

All of Mary's companions came and vowed that they had watched over her all the days that he was gone, and that none came nor left her chamber in all that time.

Joseph wept again in despair, saying: "With what face shall I approach the altar of God and the priests of the temple? What shall I say to them who entrusted Mary to my care? What am I to do?"

And Joseph thought to himself, "If I conceal her sin, I shall sin against the Law; but if I testify against her, and she be innocent, her blood will be upon my head."

And he thought again, "If I should flee and leave Mary behind, my name would forever be a reproach in Israel; but if Mary should flee and hide her shame, I would not reveal her secret to anyone."

He meditated in perplexity until night came upon him and he fell asleep. And he dreamt that the angel Gabriel appeared before him and said:

"Joseph, of the stem and stock of David, fear no evil, and think no evil of Mary who is of the same lineage as you are. For that which is begotten in her, and so vexes your soul, is the work of no man but of the Holy Spirit. Take her in marriage and keep her in chastity. For Mary will bring forth a son whom you shall call Jeshua, for he will save his people from their sins. Hearken to the prophecy of Isaiah, who said: 'Behold, a virgin shall conceive and she shall bear a son. And his name shall be Immanuel,' which means, God is with us. Rejoice then that this happened in your household and that the spirit of God has made his abode in Mary, your betrothed."

Joseph then wakened from his sleep and his dream, and went straightaway to Mary and her companions and told them what the angel Gabriel had said. He begged Mary to forgive the harshness of his words and the suspicion in his heart.

And after that night Mary was like a light to his eyes and to his sight.

4. Annas Accuses Joseph

The day after Joseph returned from his journey, Annas the Scribe came to learn why Joseph had not appeared at the assembly of the priests.

"I was weary from the journey," said Joseph, "and I rested and did not leave my house."

Mary entered the room as he spoke, and Annas looked with astonishment for he perceived that Mary was with child.

He hastened from Joseph's house to the high priest, to tell him that Joseph, to whose guardianship Mary had been entrusted, had committed a grievous crime in Israel.

"What has he done?" asked the high priest sternly.

And when Annas told him, the high priest said even more sternly: "Slander is accounted a cardinal sin as great as unchastity, idolatry, and bloodshed, for slander slays the speaker, the spoken of, and the spoken to. Think again, therefore, and tell us how you know that Joseph has done this thing."

"Send the officers to Joseph's house and let them inquire of the truth of my words," said Annas indignantly. "Let them see with their own eyes what I have seen with mine."

The messengers were sent; and they returned; and they confirmed the report made by Annas the Scribe.

The high priest sent for Joseph and Mary to appear before him. And to Mary he said:

"Why have you brought your soul so low and forgotten the Lord your God? You, who were brought up within sight of the Holy of Holies and heard the hymns of the Levites and danced in the temple before God, how could you have done this thing?"

Mary answered in tears: "By the God of my fathers, I swear that I am pure before him and have known no man nor committed any sin."

The high priest turned to Joseph and said: "Why have you brought your soul so low and have done this thing? You, who are honored in Israel, why have you beguiled this innocent maiden?"

Joseph vowed and swore that he had not touched Mary and was innocent concerning her.

"Since neither of you will confess your sins," said the high priest, "you shall be tried by the trial of the bitter water, and let God make manifest whether or not you speak the truth; and your punishment shall be meted out in accordance with his judgment."

5. Trial Before the Altar

On the appointed day and at the appointed hour of the trial of Joseph and Mary, a great multitude assembled in the chamber of the tribunal of the temple of the Lord. The judges took their places and the high priest sat at their head.

At a sign from the tribunal, the accused Joseph, dressed in black, and Mary, in a black garment without ornament and a cord around her breast, were brought before the judges. A hush fell as the chief of the tribunal read the accusation and asked the accused to confess their sins.

Joseph and Mary pleaded their innocence.

Then Joseph was brought before the altar, and a priest came forward with holy water he had taken from an earthen vessel. He dissolved in the water some dust from the floor of the tabernacle, and filled a cup to overflowing with this bitter water. He placed the cup in Joseph's right hand; and in his left he put incense for the offering of memorial.

The priest placed the accused under oath and burned upon the altar a handful of the memorial offering as he pronounced the curse on the bitter water. Then the high priest prayed for a sign from heaven to show whether the accused was innocent or guilty.

After a brief silent prayer, the priest told Joseph to drain the bitter cup and walk around the altar seven times.

Joseph drained the cup to the last drop and walked humbly around the altar seven times.

And the sign of guilt was not upon him.

Then the judges and the priests pronounced Joseph innocent; and the assembled people cried out: "Blessed are you, Joseph, for the charge against you has been found groundless!"

The high priest summoned Mary next and said to her severely: "Since Joseph has been absolved and found pure concerning you, reveal the truth and confess your guilt, and tell us who is the father of your child. For it is better that you confess than that God should mark your sin upon your face, and make your thigh to rot and your belly to swell, and the bitter water to curse your bowels!"

Mary replied steadfastly: "The God of our fathers knows all secrets; and he knows that I am innocent of that which you accuse me of, and that there is no pollution in me. Let me drink the bitter and cursed water and expose me to the sight of all the people, and let the Lord judge whether I lie or tell the truth!"

The priest brought Mary to the altar and caused her to uncover her head. He then mixed the water and cursed it, and he burned the tenth part of an epha of barley meal as the offering of memorial, and he said to Mary:

"If it is as you say and you have lain with no man, then shall you be free from the curse of this bitter water. But if you are guilty and have been defiled, then the Lord shall make you accursed among the Children of Israel."

He gave her the cup, and Mary drank the bitter water, and walked seven times around the altar.

And the sign of guilt was not upon her.

There was a silence in the tribunal. The people looked at each other in astonishment. For there was no sign of guilt upon Mary, yet all could see that she was with child. Some shook their heads in unbelief; and others said that she had been tried and found innocent in the eyes of the Lord, and therefore must she be holy.

The people gathered in groups, some doubting and some believing; and some saying:

"In truth, God has wrought a new thing in Israel and in our times, for a woman who has known no man is big with child."

And seeing that some still doubted her, Mary called out in a clear voice so that all assembled there could hear:

"I have been tried with the waters of bitterness before the God of our fathers, and he has judged me innocent. Will any of you do less than the Judge of Judges?"

They looked at her shining face in which there was no guilt; and many came forward and bowed to her and embraced her knees and asked her forgiveness because they had judged her. And she forgave them all.

Then Joseph took Mary and led her away from the judgment hall with exultation and joy. The priests and the people blessed both of them and followed them to the gates of the city.

And Joseph ministered to Mary as if he were her father or a faithful and adoring servant. And he feared no more those who speak with the third tongue of slander.

PART II
The Infancy

One brief chapter of less than a page in The Gospel According to St. Matthew gives the account from the birth of Jesus to his return from Egypt; and in The Gospel According to St. Luke a single chapter covers the entire period from the birth of Jesus to the time he reached maturity. Nothing more is to be found in the rest of the New Testament on the Infancy. Yet the lore abounds in a wealth of accounts of the miracles that attended the birth and the infancy of Jesus. For in folk imagination, the infancy of Jesus assumed a significance second only to the Crucifixion and the Ascension. Here were combined the adoration of Mother and Child, and the universal devotion to the young who forever represent the innocent promise of a better tomorrow.

There are many uncanonical Infancy Gospels, of which the Protevangelium of James and the Gospel of Thomas are the most ancient, and the Arabic Gospel of the Infancy of the Savior, one of the most colorful in incident and presentation. Later Infancy legends were either based on these three sources or influenced by them. The legends in this section were drawn from these Infancy Gospels.

CHAPTER FIVE

The Birth in a Cave

1. *The Census*

The wicked Herod, son of Antipater, King of Judea, knew it was forbidden to take a census in Israel; and that King David had been punished for the sin of counting the population. But Herod was an Idumean and he cared little for the Law or the Lord. He wanted to please Caesar Augustus and Rome; and he issued a decree that all the men of the country must go to the place of their birth and register themselves and the members of their families; and for each person registered they must offer a coin, so that when all the coins were counted (and placed in Herod's treasury), it would be known exactly how many people there were in Judea.

When the decree was made known, Joseph said to Mary mournfully: "We must go to Bethlehem to register; for we are both of the Tribe of Judah and the House of David. And I am troubled about taking so long a journey now that your time is near."

And Mary answered: "He who dwells in the secret place of the Most High, shall abide under the shadow of the Almighty. For God is my refuge and my fortress, in him I will trust."

Joseph sighed and said: "Another thing troubles me. How shall I register you? I cannot register you as my wife, for you are not in reality my wife. And I cannot register you as my daughter, for all the sons of Israel know that you are not my daughter."

And Mary replied calmly, again quoting the psalms she loved so well: "My soul is even as a weaned child; and let the day bring whatever it brings as the Lord wills it."

Mary then began to prepare for the long journey to Bethlehem. She baked the bread and dried the meat and filled a sack with lentils and tied together the cooking utensils.

While Mary prepared the food and gathered the swaddling clothes and other needs for the child she expected, Joseph saddled Thistle, their old and patient donkey, and packed upon its back the goat's-hair covers to sleep upon, and with which to cover themselves in the cold December nights, wherever they might have to sleep in the open.

After the preparations were completed, Joseph placed Mary upon the donkey. Then his son, Simon, led the animal, and Joseph and his son James followed behind them.

They did not cross the plains of Estradon toward the mountains of Samaria, though that was the shortest route to Bethlehem. Instead they descended toward the Jordan and followed the eastern banks of the river as far as the city of Jericho. For Joseph had decided that was the warmest route to travel at that time of the year, and it was also the least arduous route for Mary.

Many nights of this journey they slept out in the open. And once, after they had made themselves comfortable for the night, a storm arose. They looked about them in the rain and dark, and, behold, there stood a peasant's hut nearby with a fire burning bright in its hearth; and there they were welcomed and given shelter for the night.

On another night they had made their beds under a walnut tree. And when the rain fell, the branches and the leaves intertwined like a canopy and shielded Mary, Joseph and his sons. (And to this day, if one looks at the leaves of the walnut tree in the summer, one can discern them interwoven in the shape of Mary.)

After many tiring days they came within sight of Bethlehem. Joseph looked up at Mary and he saw that her face was sorrowful. He tried to comfort her, thinking she was in pain, and said: "Fear not, Mary!"

"The Lord is the strength of my life, of whom shall I be afraid?" asked Mary.

A little while later Joseph looked up and saw Mary smiling, her face shining like the sun.

And Joseph asked: "How is it that in one moment your face is full of sorrow; and in the next it is full of joy?"

And Mary said: "That is because I see two kinds of people before me: one lamenting and the other rejoicing. Just as in Mother Rebekah's womb twins struggled for good and for evil, so also our brethren who have departed from God struggle today. Whereas strangers shall be added to our faith for the time is at hand when in the seed of Abraham all nations shall be blessed."

Joseph tried to understand her words but he could not.

At sunset that day, Mary said to Joseph: "We must stop here, for my time has come."

"But this place is a desert," said Joseph in distress.

As Joseph despaired, an angel came and helped Mary down from the donkey and led her to a nearby cave near the tomb of Mother Rachel. And before Mary entered the cave into which the light of day never reached, she said to Joseph: "Go into the city and find a midwife to assist me."

Joseph left his two sons at the mouth of the cave, and he started out for Bethlehem.

2. *When the World Stood Still*

In the days of Moses and Joshua, the sun and the moon and all the heavenly constellations stood still.

In the hour of the birth of Jesus, the entire world stood still.

As Joseph hastened to Bethlehem to find a midwife, he noticed suddenly that, although he was walking as quickly as he could, he remained always on the same spot. He looked up at the sky and he saw that everything was without movement; and the birds on wing remained suspended in mid-air. Then Joseph looked about him in the fields and he saw workers resting from the day's labor and sitting at their evening meal. Yet they were not eating. The cutter of the bread was fixed in the act of cutting; the pourer of the drink remained fixed in the act of pouring; and he who conveyed food to his mouth did not convey nor put it down.

On the hillside the sheep stood fixed in the middle of their steps; the shepherd with upraised hand to urge them on, remained where he was with upraised hand; and by the river the lambs with outstretched necks, their mouths touching the water, were not drinking.

But whilst everything else stood still, the temple of Apollo in Rome, built by Romulus and used by Satan to render oracles, crumbled into dust; and all the idols on earth were in that moment thrown down to the ground.

And yet another thing did not stand still at that wondrous moment: the fountain beyond the Tiber, where now stands the Church of St. Mary, did not stop flowing, and from the fountain poured anointing oil instead of water. And the Rod of Engadi near Jerusalem, which bears the citron from which is made a balm, in that moment flowered and the fruit ripened and the liquor of balm flowed from them.

All else in the world stood still.

Joseph lifted his head heavenwards and beheld a star in the evening sky, larger and brighter than any he had ever seen before; and the star was unlike any other star for it was in the shape of a woman with an infant in her arms, and a crown of bright light rested upon the head of the infant. Joseph looked in astonishment and saw the star move across the heavens until it came over the place where Mary rested in the cave. And there the star stopped.

In that instant everything in the world that stood still began to move again.

And Joseph hastened on his way.

3. *The Doubting Zebel*

On the way to Bethlehem, Joseph met an old Hebrew woman coming from the hill country, and he asked her: "Can you tell me where I can find a midwife?"

"I am a midwife, and my name is Zelomi," said the old woman. "Are you of Israel?"

"I am," said Joseph.

"Where is the woman you speak for?"

"She is in a cave not far from here."

"Is she of Israel and your wife?"

"She is of Israel and was reared in the temple of God, and I won her by lot as my wife. Yet she is not my wife but has conceived by the Holy Spirit."

The old woman was astonished to hear such words, and asked: "Can this be truly so?"

"Come with me, Zelomi, and you will see with your own eyes that what I say is true and you shall be rewarded."

As Joseph and Zelomi approached the cave, they saw a luminous cloud hanging like a shining curtain over the entrance.

Zelomi was awed by the sight. She closed her eyes and prayed: "My soul has been magnified this day, and mine eyes have seen strange things. Surely the Lord has brought forth salvation for the Children of Israel."

When she opened her eyes the cloud was gone, and she could see a great light glowing within the cave, more splendid than the light of the sun. And within stood Mary holding an infant which was wrapped in swaddling clothes and sucking at his mother's breast.

Joseph and Zelomi stood near the entrance of the cave, and neither dared enter until Mary smiled at them and bade them enter.

"My lady, I have come here at the promise of a reward," said Zelomi. "I have long been afflicted with paralysis. Can you help me?"

"Place your hands upon my infant," said Mary.

Zelomi no sooner touched the infant than the illness that had afflicted her for so many years vanished.

"This is the greatest day of my life," said Zelomi, "and I shall remember it all the days of my life."

She left the cave and hastened home to tell all her friends and all her neighbors what had happened to her that day.

On the way she met another midwife, named Zebel.

"Where do you come from?" asked Zebel.

"I come from a miracle," answered Zelomi.

"What kind of a miracle?" asked Zebel, for she was the doubting kind.

"I have seen a virgin who conceived and gave birth. And though still a virgin, her breasts were full of milk and she fed her child when I left her."

"Seeing is believing," said Zebel with obvious doubt in her voice.

"Then come with me and see for yourself," said Zelomi.

They went to the cave, and there Zebel said to Mary: "Zelomi told me about you, and a dispute has arisen between us whether a woman can give birth and remain a virgin."

Mary allowed Zebel to examine her. But as soon as the midwife withdrew her hand it withered like a leaf thrown into the flames.

Zebel fell upon her knees, and wept and prayed: "O God of my fathers! Remember that I am of the seed of Abraham, Isaac and Jacob! All my life I have given my services to the poor who needed my help; took nothing from the widow and the orphan; and never sent the needy away from my door with empty hands. Yet now am I punished for my unbelief!"

An angel appeared in the cave and said to the kneeling midwife: "God has heard your plea and has pitied you for your past good deeds. Go, touch the child and you will be healed. And henceforth doubt no more!"

Zebel rose and touched the cloth with which the child was wrapped. Instantly her hand was cured and whole again.

And all the days of her life she never doubted again.

4. The Night of Miracles

On the night Mary's son was born in the cave outside Bethlehem, more miracles and wonders took place than in the Red Sea when the Jews crossed it on dry land under the leadership of Moses and Aaron. But most wonderful of all were the miracles that happened to the lowly birds, the insects and even the plants.

How the Nightingale Learned to Sing: In the cave where Jesus was born, deep in the recess and low on the ground, there was a little nest made of leaves and fine roots, with a cuplike hollow in the middle. And the dweller of that nest was a plain little snuff-brown bird, about half a span in length. He was a humble and shy bird, for, indeed, he had nothing to be proud of. He spent his days in the thickets, searching for insects and berries and fruit. And at night he returned to his lowly nest in the cave where it was always dark.

One night the snuff-colored bird was awakened by a light as bright as sunlight at noon. And the cave was filled with the sound of angels singing. The little bird, who had never sung before, joined in with the angels, singing after them the song they sang. And he went right on singing, and singing, and singing.

Ever since then this little bird, called *Luscinia luscinia,* has not stopped singing.

To this day, in some parts of the world, when the sun goes down and a hush falls upon the trees of the garden, one can hear (but rarely see) this little snuff-brown bird repeating the song he learned from the angels so long ago. And though he repeats it over and over again, it sounds forever new and different. And the song the nightingale, *Luscinia luscinia,* has learned to sing so prettily, is this:

"Glory to God in the highest; peace on earth, good will to men!"

How the Firefly Acquired its Light: There lived a beetle once, a small, slender, soft-bodied beetle whose black wings were marked with yellow. And his home was in a cave. One night the insect saw a sudden light fill the cave, and in the center of the light sat a woman with an infant in her arms. And surrounding them were a host of angels, singing.

The little beetle knew that such a sight had never been seen on earth, and he wanted to rush out and tell all his friends around Bethlehem of the wonderful sight he had just seen and of the wonderful song he had just heard. But it was after midnight, and dark outside, and the beetle did not know what to do.

He was still wondering how he could go out with the good tidings, when an angel took a sparkling jewel from his hair and placed it upon the tiny insect. The bright green light of the jewel lighted the insect on its way. The beetle was permitted to keep the jewel, and he has it to this day.

Some call this insect a firefly; and some call it a click beetle; and some call it snapping bug. In every country in the world it is known by a different name; but it is the same lightning bug that lived in a cave near Bethlehem.

Why the Robin Is Called Robin: It is a sin to rob a bird's nest; it is a double sin to rob a robin's nest. And, as everybody knows, to kill a robin is an act of sacrilege.

This is the reason why:

On the night that Jesus was born, a small, olive-gray warbler was fast asleep, with his head under his wing, in an olive tree outside of Bethlehem. Its nest of moss and leaves, lined with hair and feathers, was shallow and exposed; for the warbler was the last to go to sleep and the first to waken in the morning, he so loved to see the last rays of sunset and the first rays of morning.

But this night the warbler, called *rubecula*, was awakened in the middle of the night by a light brighter than sunrise. He took his head out from under his wing and shook himself. And as he marveled at the light, he heard the angels singing a song that filled the air. Then he saw a group of shepherds leave their sleeping flocks and their warm fire, and hurry to the mouth of a cave not far away.

After some time the bird noticed that the shepherds' fire was dying down. The bird flew down toward the flickering fire and, warbling the song the angels sang, he began to fan the darkening embers with his wings so that when the shepherds returned they would not be cold. As the flames flared up they were reflected on the green-olive breast, on the throat and forehead of the singing bird, and turned them into yellowish red.

And that color has remained on the warbler ever since.

The bird has been nicknamed affectionately "robin," which is short for Robert, meaning "fame bright." And to this day the robin is kept in special esteem the world over.

See Notes on Sources *for another version of this story.*

The animal stories related about the infancy of Jesus are obviously meant for children. The number of these stories is great and they vary with each country, the time of the telling, and the story-teller.

5. *The Shepherds in the Hills*

The star, the wonderful star that shone above the cave outside Bethlehem from sunset to sunrise on the night that Mary gave birth to her child, was seen by three shepherds guarding their flocks in the hills. The name of one was Zadok (meaning "the righteous"), the name of the second was Shammuah (meaning "the obeyed"), and the name of the third was Nathan (meaning "the giver"). And some say there was still a fourth, whose name was Jotham (meaning "the perfection of God").

As the shepherds looked heavenwards in astonishment at the star, larger and brighter than any they had ever seen, they heard all the stars in heaven singing in praise of the new star, with the sun and the moon in their dwelling place in the second heaven joining the celestial chorus. Then there appeared to them a host of angels, singing to God in heaven and praising him whose glory shall endure forever.

The shepherds left their fire and followed the shining star to the mouth of a cave, and the cavern had become like a radiant temple, filled with heavenly and earthly singing. They stood without the cave and listened all through the night. And to these things they testified in Bethlehem all the days of their lives.

6. *The Adoration of the Animals*

Mary and her infant remained in the cave for two days; and on the third Joseph moved them to a stable near Bethlehem where they would be more comfortable.

When the infant was placed in the stall which had been made into a crib, the ox and the ass, that were the inhabitants of the stable, came and adored the child. And they adored him for as long as he remained in the stable, fulfilling what was written about the ox knowing its owner and the ass its master.

(And ever since then, so it is believed in many parts of the world, exactly at midnight on Christmas Eve all the animals in the barns or in the fields, the plains, or the forests kneel in adoration; and the birds sing songs of praise.

The rooster spreads his wings and calls: "Christ is born!"

And the raven asks: "When?"

And the crow answers: "This night!"

And the ox asks: "Where?"

And the sheep lows: "In Bethlehem.")

And that is why in many parts of Europe the children on this day feed the animals and birds their favorite food.

CHAPTER SIX

Seth's Prophecy

1. Zoroaster's Prediction

Long ago, there lived in the region of Assyria a disciple of the Prophet Elijah, whose name was Zoroaster. He taught the Persians that in some unknown future day a child would be born who would grow up to be the savior of mankind. The birth of this child, he taught, would be heralded by the appearance of a star so bright that it would be seen even by day; and they who followed it would be guided to the child, regardless of where on the earth he would be born.

"When that star appears," Zoroaster instructed his followers, "send our high priests, the Magi, to carry gifts to the newborn babe."

"Where did you learn about this child?" Zoroaster's followers asked.

"I learned about the sign of the wonderful star in a book called the Book of Seth," said Zoroaster.

And Zoroaster went on to explain to them that Seth was the son of Adam and begotten in his father's image. The angels taught him all wisdom and knowledge of future events, including the coming of the Messiah. So pious was Seth all the days of his long life, that the people called him by the name of the Lord and his children were called "the sons of God."

Seth (meaning "the resurrection") was so named by Adam, because in him was resurrected the beauty, the wisdom and the glory which had been man's before the Fall.

Seth was the first on earth to learn to write, and he wrote down his knowledge of the future, which had been taught to him by the angels. One of his books, handed down from generation to generation, was inherited by Zoroaster. And from Seth's book, Zoroaster explained, he had learned of the sign of the coming of the Messiah.

In accord with Zoroaster's wishes, twelve Magi were selected to take their place on a high tower, and there they watched constantly for the appearance of the star that had been foretold. When one of the twelve Magi died, another was chosen to take his place, so that their number was never diminished.

Generations passed like the links of a chain going down the hold of a ship, but twelve Magi ceaselessly watched for the sign given them by the master Zoroaster.

2. *In the Temple of Juno*

In the land of the Magi there was a temple, known as the temple of Juno. There the King of Persia went to kindle the fire of Ahura-Mazda, the Power of Good, to burn the incense, and to have the Magi interpret his dreams.

One day, when the king entered the temple of Juno, the priest Propippius greeted him with these strange words:

"O King and Master, I congratulate you! For Juno has conceived!"

"Juno is dead," said the king. "How can the dead conceive?"

"She was dead," said Propippius "but she has come to life again; and now she has conceived."

"Explain it to me," said the king, still unbelieving.

"It happened in this way: Last night, as I was in the temple praying and burning incense, suddenly I saw all the images of both gods and goddesses bow down and tremble, each of them saying: 'Come, let us congratulate Juno, for she has been embraced!' And I asked what you just asked: 'How can she who is dead be embraced?' And the images answered: 'She was dead, but she has come to life again. Her name is no longer Juno, but Urania the Heavenly, who was embraced by the Mighty Sun; her name is no longer Juno, but the Heavenly Fountain who has been embraced by the Artificer; her name is no longer Juno, but it is really Myria, who bears in her womb as in the deep waters, but a single fish taken with the hook of Divinity. And when the child is born, he shall become like the Chief Artificer, who built with his great skill the roof of the third heaven where the food of the righteous is prepared,

and where the *Erelim*, the tallest angels in the heavens, reside. And
when the son of the Artificer is at hand, all the gods and goddesses
shall be given a sign.'

"And that, Master and King, was what I was told last night as I
was praying."

The king stood still, not believing what his ears had just heard,
when all the harps in the temple began to play of their own accord;
and all the gold and silver images of fowl and animals began to utter
each its different sound. The king was filled with great fear and
wanted to flee. But Propippius the priest stayed him.

"O King and Master, remain! For the full revelation is at hand!"

His lips were still moving with the words spoken, when the roof
of the temple opened, and there above them, a bright star shone
over the pillar of the Heavenly Fountain. And a voice came down
from heaven, saying:

"The hour of hours is at hand. And the Sun declares that the child
just born will be known as End and Beginning — the end of perdition and the beginning of salvation."

And all the statues in the temple of Juno fell down upon their
faces.

The King of Persia called together his sages and asked them to
interpret the signs he had seen. The sages gazed long upon the
bright star, and they interpreted:

"A root divine has sprouted in Judah from which shall arise a
kingdom on earth that shall make all other gods prostrate. And being
of a more ancient dignity, he shall make all the more recent deities
superfluous. Therefore, open the books and read what Seth, son of
Adam, predicted; and what Zoroaster our Prophet and Master commanded. And select the messengers to carry to the newborn babe
the gifts of gold, frankincense and myrrh that were offered to Adam
at his death and that were carried in Noah's ark through the flood,
and which came down into our hands. For these Zoroaster commanded us to send to the Messiah born under the sign of this star."

The King of Persia summoned Noah's three sons, Shem, Ham and
Japheth, who had been asleep in a cave waiting to be wakened
when the bright star appeared above the Heavenly Fountain. Each
of them selected a Magian, and each Magian, a prince in his own
right, selected three princes, so that there were twelve of them to

carry out the king's command. Among the princes were those skilled in the art of dealing with foreign potentates; those gifted in the knowledge of the highways; and those trained in music. And one among them was noted as a painter of pictures.

After the feast in honor of their departure, the Magi gathered together the gifts that had come down from the days of Adam and started out on their long journey, guided by the star.

See Notes on Sources *for additional material on the Magi.*

3. *The Gold of the Magi*

The gold the Magi carried with them, we are told, consisted of thirty pieces. This gold had been carried unminted in Noah's ark through the flood and was later buried with Adam's remains in the center of the earth, in Jerusalem.

Terah, father of Abraham, coined the gold into thirty pieces; and with this gold Joseph was purchased by the Ishmaelites, when he was sold into slavery by his brothers. When Joseph became Governor of Egypt, his brothers paid the same thirty pieces of gold to Pharaoh as tribute; and Joseph used the money to buy ointment from the Kingdom of Sheba for the embalming of his father.

The Queen of Sheba presented the thirty gold coins to Solomon on her visit to Judea. And during the Babylonian captivity the coins fell into the hands of the Persian king.

Now, along with the frankincense and myrrh, these thirty coins of gold were secure in the hands of the Magi, on their way to Bethlehem.

4. *The Magi in Herod's Court*

From the land of Asshur, where the Magi started, to Bethlehem in the land of Israel, was a journey of two years by camel. But just as Abraham's steward, Eliezer, made the seventy-day journey from Hebron to Nahor miraculously in three hours; so also did the twelve Magi of Asshur complete their two-year journey in a single day. And the nearer they came to Bethlehem, the brighter shone the star that guided them.

The Magi arrived in Jerusalem with the splendor of kings, and soon crowds gathered about them asking in astonishment: "What has brought you here, and what is the meaning of the bright star which moves before you?"

The Magi replied: "Has no one told you? Have you seen no sign?"

"Told us what? Seen what?" the people asked in confusion.

And the Magi told them of the star of the East and the birth of the Messiah.

Several of King Herod's men were in the crowd and they hurried off to tell the king what they had heard from the mouths of the strangers from Asshur. Herod called together his wise men and asked:

"What have your prophets foretold about the Messiah?" For the Idumean king was unlettered in the Hebrew prophets.

The advisors to the king opened the Book and read to him:

"But thou, Beth-lehem Ephratah, though thou be little among the thousands of Judah, yet out of thee shall he come forth unto me that is to be the ruler of Israel; and whose goings forth have been foretold from of old, from time everlasting. And he shall stand and feed in the strength of the Lord, in the majesty of the name of the Lord his God; and they shall abide. For now shall he be great unto the ends of the earth."

Herod repeated to himself: "Ruler of Israel! King of the Jews! Ruler of Israel!" Then he demanded that the Magi be brought before him.

Herod knew exactly what he was going to do. For Herod had come to the throne of Israel treacherously like a fox, and he had murdered everyone he suspected might dethrone him. He had killed his brother-in-law, the High Priest Aristobulus, because he was a Hasmonean and rightful heir to the throne; he killed the beautiful Mariamne, his queen, in a jealous rage; and he killed his sister's husband when he suspected him of siding with Mariamne. He had killed many of his friends in fits of suspicion, many of his faithful servants in fits of anger. And he had even caused the death of three of his own sons.

Now he resolved to destroy the child who, it was foretold, would become ruler of Israel!

"Bring the Magi to me!" he commanded.

And when the Magi were brought before him, Herod spoke softly to them, and asked: "What sign have you seen regarding this new-born king?"

And the Magi replied: "We have come to fulfill what was written in prophecy by Seth, son of Adam, who foretold that there shall be a child born in Judah whom the greater part of the world shall serve; and he gave us a sign of his coming; and our Prophet Zoroaster commanded us to come with gifts to the babe when he is born. We are here to witness Seth's prophecy and to fulfill our Prophet Zoroaster's command."

"Go and find the child," said Herod cunningly. "When you have found him, and you are certain that it is he whom you seek, bring me word so that I, too, may go and worship him."

The Magi promised to do the king's bidding, and continued on their journey. They followed the star until it came to the cave where Mary and her child were resting. And there the bright star stopped above the entrance. The Magi knew that they had reached their destination.

(At that very moment the star fell into a well in Bethlehem from which water was drawn for Mary's needs. And to this day, it is believed, the pure in heart who look down into that well can see the wonderful star that guided the Magi.)

5. *The Exchange of Gifts*

The Magi entered the cave and they found that it was as bright as if the sunlight streamed into it. In the center of the cave they could see Mary seated with the infant in her lap. She had long fingers and delicate features. Her face was round and her hair was bound up, and the color of her skin was that of ripened wheat. The infant, though still so small, was clearly in the likeness of his mother.

The Magi explained the purpose of their visit; then each in turn took the infant in his arms and presented the gifts that he had brought. There were gifts of gold (signifying the respect shown to a king), of frankincense (the offering made on an altar), and myrrh (symbolizing incorruptibility). Then they presented the many gifts they had brought for Mary and for Joseph.

"It is meet that I should send a gift in return," said Mary.

She looked about her, but could see nothing they could spare. So she picked up one of her son's swaddling bands and gave it to the honored guests. The Magi gratefully received the gift and asked that the painter in their company be allowed to paint a likeness of the mother and the child to take to their king.

And when the painting was completed, the Magi took their leave and departed.

6. The Magi Return Home

That night the Magi started out for Jerusalem and King Herod's court, as they had promised. But when they stopped to rest and fell asleep, an angel appeared to them in their dreams; and all twelve dreamt the same dream, saw the same angel, and heard him say the same thing: that Herod plotted to kill the infant they had just left and they should therefore avoid the king and return home by a different route.

The Magi immediately awoke. They departed secretly and with great haste. And they did not rest until they were safe in their own country.

The King of Persia and all his priests and advisors came to greet the Magi and plied them with questions about their adventures. The painting of the mother and her child was passed from hand to hand in adoration.

"We have received a gift in return, the meaning of which we do not know," said the Magi. And they brought forth the swaddling band that Mary had given them.

The king examined the gift and then placed it as an offering upon the holy fire which they worshiped. But when the sacrificial fire had gone out, behold, the swaddling band lay upon the altar as if it had not been touched by fire. And the band was placed in the royal treasury, along with a golden tablet upon which was inscribed all that had transpired, so that the mission of the Magi would be forever remembered in Asshur.

7. *The Circumcision*

Eight days after Mary's child was born, Joseph took him to a synagogue in Bethlehem for the circumcision.

As Joseph entered with the child in his arms the congregation arose and called out: "Blessed be he that cometh!"

And Joseph responded: "Here I am ready to perform the commandment to circumcise my son and to bring him into the covenant of the Lord, as it is written."

The child was placed on the Throne of Elijah, and after the rite had been performed, the mohel asked: "What do you intend to name this child?"

"His name is Jesus," Mary replied.

"What kind of name is that?" asked the mohel.

"It is the name," answered Mary, "that in the mouth is honey; in the ear, music; and in the heart, joy."

"O give thanks unto the Lord, for he is good, for his loving kindness endures forever!" The mohel went on with the ritual. "This little child Jesus, may he become great!"

The wine was blessed; the godfather placed a drop of the wine on the infant's lips; and the Cup of Blessing was given to the mother.

The ceremony was over.

And after they returned from the synagogue, Joseph went to register for the census; and inscribed in the book: "Joseph, the son of Jacob, and Mary his wife, and Jesus their son, who are of the House of David and of the Tribe of Judah."

Then Joseph took his family and went up to Jerusalem.

8. *Jesus in the Temple*

Joseph and Mary would not leave for home before Mary had completed her forty days of purification; nor before they had brought the child for presentation in the temple.

Joseph and Mary came to the temple at the prescribed hour with two white turtledoves bought in the outer court.

As they appeared before the priest, Mary said: "What can I render unto the Lord for all his benefits toward me? Because he has inclined his ear toward me, I will call upon him as long as I live!"

There was in the temple at that time a man named Simeon, called the Righteous. Simeon had reached the age of three hundred and fifty, it was said, yet he came to the temple each day to look upon every male infant. For the Lord had promised Simeon that he would not taste of death until his eyes had seen the child born of a virgin who would be the Messiah as foretold by the Prophet Isaiah.

As soon as Simeon saw Mary and the child in her arms, whose infant face shone like a pillar of light, he cried out: "The Lord has fulfilled his promise to me! For today my eyes have seen the salvation of the nations and the glory of the people of Israel."

And with these words Simeon the Righteous gave up his ghost.

The people who heard Simeon's words and saw him pass away, looked with awe and adoration upon Mary and her son.

The sacrifices over, Joseph put Mary and her child on Thistle, their faithful old donkey, and started out on the long journey back to Nazareth, with Simon leading the ass, and Joseph and James following closely behind.

CHAPTER SEVEN

Flight to Egypt

1. *The Massacre of the Innocents*

King Herod waited for the Magi to return. He waited and waited and waited. And with each passing day his rage mounted. When he could wait no longer, he sent out his guards to search the roads east and west and north and south. And he ordered that wherever the Magi were found, there they should be slain.

The guards searched the roads east and west and north and south, but they failed to find the Magi. They returned to the king with the report that strangers answering the description of the Magi had made their way to Tarshish, seeking passage for Persia by sea. Herod, in his fury, ordered all the ships of Tarshish to be destroyed by fire, so that the Magi, in whatever disguise, would be destroyed.

Even if the Magi were destroyed by fire or drowned in the sea, thought he, the infant they had come to see was still alive. And Herod conceived a new plan: he would decree that every male infant in Bethlehem, as well as in the rest of his kingdom, must be slain, and in that way he would surely destroy the infant the Magi had come to worship as the future King of the Jews.

For such an edict Herod needed permission from the Roman Emperor. Herod gathered together great gifts of gold and silver and journeyed to Rome to convince the Emperor of the justice of his decree. And his gifts were so great that Rome agreed. But by the time Herod returned to Judea, two years had passed since the visit of the Magi, and the edict therefore went out that all male children in the kingdom, two years or under, should be massacred.

Some say that the king's cruel henchmen slew two thousand infants; and others say that they killed twelve times twelve thousand infants.

And those who passed Rachel's grave said that they heard her weeping and lamenting the slaughter of the innocents.

In religious lore there are several instances of tyrants who condemned all infants to be slain so that a particular child might perish with them. The tyrant Nimrod, builder of the Tower of Babel, issued a similar decree when informed by his stargazers of the appearance of a bright star in the east which announced the birth of Abraham, son of Terah, who, they predicted, would grow up to destroy their idols and depose King Nimrod.

2. Joseph's Escape

On the night Herod's wicked decree was issued, an angel came to Joseph in a dream and said: "Arise, Joseph, and take Mary and her child and leave your home and your kindred! Go down to Egypt by way of the desert and remain there until a sign is given you to return."

Joseph arose before dawn, at the hour when the cock crows and the horse neighs in the stable. He placed Mary and her child on one ass, and he mounted another, and three boys and one girl followed closely behind them, as well as the old midwife Zelomi, who had attached herself to the family. They did not stop to prepare provisions for the long journey, for they carried with them to provide for their needs the gold brought to them by the Magi. Under cover of night they left Nazareth without taking leave of their kin or their neighbors, and started out in haste for the hill country and the desert leading to the borders of Egypt.

They had not gone very far when the sun came up, and they knew that Herod's men would be out upon the roads. But they did not know where to hide. At that moment they saw a laborer sowing wheat in a field along the road. The child Jesus picked up a handful of the seed and threw it by the wayside. Instantly it grew before their eyes and ripened, ready for reaping. In this tall wheat Joseph and his family hid themselves.

Soon Herod's men came by and asked the farmer: "Have you seen a woman pass here carrying a child in her arms?"

"Yes," said the farmer. "I saw her as I was sowing the wheat."

"The wheat is grown and ripening," said Herod's henchmen. "It must have been sown many months ago."

And they went away.

3. *The Palm for Victory*

On the third day of the journey, Joseph and his family reached the desert. In the heat of the day Mary grew faint and, seeing a tree, she asked that they stop and rest in its shade.

As they were sitting in the shade of the tall palm tree, Mary looked up at the fruit on its top and said: "I wish it were possible to get some of that fruit."

"The fruit is out of our reach," said Joseph. "I think of our need for water. The waterskins are empty and we have none to refresh ourselves and our beasts."

Jesus, in his mother's lap, addressed the palm: "O tree, bow down and refresh my mother with your fruit."

The tree bent its top down and they all gathered fruit, with which they were refreshed.

Then Jesus said: "O palm tree, straighten yourself and be strong; and open your root to refresh us with the water of the spring hidden in the earth beneath you."

The palm tree straightened up, and from one of its roots there began to flow a stream of water, clear and cool and sparkling.

Then Joseph and all those who were with him rejoiced and gave thanks to God and sang: "Let us call upon the Lord who is worthy of praise; so that we shall be saved from our enemies."

The next day, before they left the generous palm, Jesus turned and blessed it: "O palm tree, may one of your branches be planted in paradise! And it shall be said of him who conquers in any contest: 'You have attained the palm of victory!'"

As he still spoke an angel appeared and took one of the palm branches to heaven.

(And since then the palm is the symbol of spiritual victory, just as the olive is the symbol of peace.)

4. *Adventures in Sotrina*

When Joseph began to despair as he thought of the thirty-day journey through the desert still before them, Jesus said to him: "Fear not, for I will shorten the distance to one day's journey."

And when Joseph lifted his eyes he could see in the distance the mountains and cities of Egypt. Before the day was over they entered the city of Sotrina, and there Joseph sought refuge for his family in the guest house of the great temple of that city.

In the temple there were three hundred and sixty-five idols, to each of which sacrifices were made one day in the year. And above them all was an idol to whom the other idols paid homage. The people of Sotrina worshiped a god called Abraxas; and their word of power and of magic was *abracadabra.*

And it came to pass that as Mary and Jesus entered the guest house of the temple, all the idols fell upon their faces, and the great idol lay prostrate amongst them. The priests in the temple rushed to their great idol to learn the meaning of the commotion and prostration, and they were told that one greater than all the gods in their land had just arrived in Egypt, and that they were exceedingly afraid.

Now the high priest of the great temple had an only son, three years old, who was beset by demons. And when the demons took hold of him, he would scream and shout, tear off his clothes, run naked into the streets, and throw stones at the people. And there was no power to restrain him.

This afflicted boy came to the guest house where Mary was bathing her son, and picked up one of the swaddling bands which Mary had washed and placed to dry. When he touched the cloth that belonged to Jesus, the demons came rushing out of the boy's mouth in the form of ravens and serpents.

Healed and whole again, the boy ran to his father to tell him what had happened.

The news of the self-abasement of the idols and the healing of the high priest's son reached the ears of Affrodosius, the governor of the city. He gathered his army and brought it to the temple. The priests thought that he had come to avenge the idols; but instead, the

Governor of Sotrina came before Mary, who was carrying Jesus in her arms, and he said:

"I do not want to have happen to us what happened to Pharaoh, who, not believing in the warning of Moses, was drowned in the sea with his hosts. Unless we take care to do what we have seen our gods do, we may run the risk of his anger."

And the governor and his men paid homage to Mary and her son.

5. *The Possessed and the Leprous*

Joseph and his family left Sotrina and went on until they came to another city. And there, at the crossroads, they were stopped by a naked young woman who threatened them with stones.

This girl had gone out one night alone to fetch water from the well; and there Satan, disguised in the form of a young man, had come toward her. She tried to drive him off, but was unable to touch him. He entered into her and dwelt in her. And ever since that time she could neither bear clothes upon her, nor dwell in a house. She fled naked into the streets. When put in chains she would break them; and when locked in her room she would escape through the window to the crossroads and the graveyard to throw stones at every passer-by. The inhabitants were sorry for the poor girl and prayed that she might die.

When Mary saw the bewitched girl she pitied her and threw one of the child's swaddling bands to her. The girl caught it. And straightaway Satan, in the form of a jaunty young man, left the young woman. He fled and was seen no more.

The cured woman blushed at her nakedness. She covered herself with the swaddling band; and, shunning the sight of men, fled to her home to get dressed. There she gave an account of all that had happened to her. And the girl and her family went out to receive Joseph and Mary with great hospitality.

The next day the grateful girl prepared scented water for Mary in which to bathe her son. And after the child was washed, the girl took the water to a poor young orphan, living in her father's courtyard, who was white as snow with leprosy. The afflicted girl washed herself in the water in which Jesus had been bathed, and at once she was cured of her disease and was whole again.

The orphan came to pay homage to Joseph and Mary, and said to them: "I have neither father nor mother, and I entreat you to let me become as a daughter and as a serving maid to you, and let me come with you wherever you go."

Joseph and Mary granted her wish, and she joined their household.

6. *The Shame of the Father*

They went on their way until they came to another city in which an illustrious prince maintained a lodging house open to the needs of strangers. Joseph and all the members of his family came to lodge there for the night.

It was customary for the guests to visit their host, and Mary sent the girl who had been cured of leprosy to visit the princess.

The young girl whom Joseph and Mary had adopted found the princess weeping and sorrowing.

"Why do you weep, mistress?" she asked.

"I weep because of a sorrow that cannot be revealed," the princess replied.

"If you confide in me, perhaps I can find a cure for your grief."

"If you promise not to tell it to anyone," said the princess, "I will reveal to you my secret sorrow."

The girl promised.

The princess then confided: "I married the prince and we lived happily together for many years, saddened only because we had no son. Then I gave birth to a son. But, alas, he was leprous. The prince turned away with loathing and shame from our child. And he said to me: 'Either you send him away with a nurse to a distant place where no one would know he is our child; or kill him. If you refuse, I will never live with you again.' And my grief is beyond endurance. For I do not want to give up my husband, and I cannot give up my unfortunate son."

"I, too, was a leper," said the young girl, "and I was cured."

"Where is he who cured you?" asked the princess with sudden hope. "And what must I do?"

"He is in your courtyard, in the lodging house for strangers. And I will tell you what to do."

The princess rose up and prepared a great banquet for Joseph and his family and invited all the great men of the city. And the next day she prepared scented water for Mary in which to wash her child. The princess washed her son in the water in which Jesus had been bathed. Immediately the young prince was cleansed of leprosy, and his father was no longer ashamed of him.

The prince and the princess praised God, and gave thanks to Mary and her son. The princess bestowed great gifts upon all of them, and sent them on their way with great honor.

7. *The Bewitched Bridegroom*

The following day, at sunset, Joseph and his family reached a city where they saw three weeping women coming out of a cemetery. Mary sent her adopted daughter to find out what had befallen them to cause them to weep so bitterly. But the women refused to reveal the cause of their sorrow. Instead they asked:

"Where do you come from, and where are you going so late in the evening?"

"We are wayfarers," the young girl replied, "and seek a place where we may spend the night."

"Come and spend the night with us," said the three women.

Joseph and his family were taken to a handsome house, and made welcome in quarters furnished with great splendor.

Late in the evening Mary heard loud weeping and lamenting coming from the chambers where the three women had retired. She sent her adopted daughter to find out what troubled them.

The young girl went to their chamber, and there the strangest sight met her eyes. She saw the three women prostrate beside a mule decked out in costly silks. And they were feeding him sesame.

"This mule," explained the women in tears, "is our only and beloved brother, born of the same father and the same mother. When our parents died, and left us great wealth, we tried our best to arrange for our brother's marriage. But a jealous woman bewitched him. One night, a little before daybreak, when the door to our house was shut, we saw that this our brother had been turned into a mule, as you see him now."

"Could you not take the curse off him?" asked the girl.

"We called upon every wise man, every magician, every enchanter in the world and offered a great reward for his cure. But none could restore him. And so, when our grief is great, we go to the cemetery to weep upon the graves of our parents, but we return unconsoled."

The young woman said: "I was a leper and I was cured. And the same woman who cured me may be able to restore your brother also."

"Where is this good woman?" the sisters asked.

"She is a guest in your house, and her name is Mary."

The women went straightaway to Mary and revealed to her the cause of their grief, and implored her to help them. Mary pitied them. She took her child and placed him upon the back of the mule, saying:

"My son, play with this mule and take the curse away from him."

As Mary uttered these words, the mule turned into a young man before their eyes. And the young man and his sisters fell upon their knees and thanked Mary, and they held Jesus in their arms, kissing him tenderly.

Then the three sisters said to each other: "Our brother has been restored because of this young woman who came and told us about Mary and her son. It is meet that our brother, who has no wife, should take this young woman and marry her."

They asked Joseph and Mary for their consent, and it was given to them. The sisters prepared a great marriage-feast to which all the elders of the city were invited. And their tears were turned into joy; and their sorrow into song.

Joseph and Mary stayed with them for ten days, spent in celebration. And when they finally left, the three sisters and their brother and the bride accompanied them a great distance. And when they parted, they parted in tears, especially the young woman who had been cured of leprosy and was for a while Mary's adopted daughter.

The belief in demons, the possession of a living soul by an evil spirit or the soul of one dead, and the transformation of human beings into animals was so firmly established among the Jews in the days of Jesus that we find repeated discussion on this topic in the

Talmud. Prescriptions by the rabbis on how to avoid such calamities and, when stricken, how to cope with them, indicate that even the most learned and enlightened of that day never doubted their reality. Certain foods eaten at certain times were prescribed as a protection against demons and evil spirits. It was even believed that no man ever commits a sin unless an evil spirit first enters into him and induces him to do the evil thing.

Many theories were evolved on the origin of the demons. According to one theory: "The male hyena after seven years becomes a bat; the bat after seven years becomes a vampire; the vampire after seven years becomes a snake; the snake after seven years becomes a demon."

Since demons and evil spirits were normally invisible, means were devised to detect, and even to see them. This was the formula as given in the Talmud: "Who wishes to perceive their footprints should take sifted ashes and sprinkle them around his bed. In the morning he will see in the ashes something resembling the footprints of a cock." He who wishes to see evil spirits and demons with his naked eye "should take the after-birth of a black she-cat, the offspring of a black she-cat, the firstborn of a firstborn, roast it in the fire, pulverize it, then fill his eye with it, and he will see them. He must seal the powder into an iron tube and seal it with an iron signet, lest he come to harm."

In the days of Jesus these beliefs were held not only in Judea but throughout the world. One unknown Greek poet of that time declared: "All the air is so crowded with them [demons] that there is not one empty chink into which you could push the spike of a blade of corn."

Nor have these beliefs entirely disappeared. They are implicitly believed in by millions of people, and have survived in their ancient form to the present day.

8. *The Good Robber*

Joseph and Mary were passing through desert country infested with thieves and robbers. And as they journeyed one night, they came upon two thieves, Demas and Gestas, who had been posted by their companions to patrol the road.

When Demas saw Joseph and Mary coming toward them he said to Gestas:

"I see that the woman carries in her arms a child with a shining countenance. Let them pass on their way without our plundering them. And I will give you as your share forty dirhams if you say nothing about it to our companions." And he gave his belt to Gestas as a pledge of the money he had promised him.

And Mary said to Demas, "Because of your kindness to us, the merciful God will forgive your sins."

(In the Arabic Gospel of the Infancy of the Savior the names of the robbers are given as Titus and Dumachus; and the story ends with the infant Jesus saying to his mother: "Thirty years hence, O my mother . . . these robbers will be raised upon the cross along with me, Titus on my right hand and Dumachus on my left, and after that day Titus shall go before me into Paradise.")

9. *Sea-Bitter and Bethaven*

Joseph and his family came to a city where there were two women, wives of one man, and each had a sick child. One of the women was called Miriam or Sea-Bitter, and her son's name was Cloopas. The other woman's name was Bethaven the Troublesome, and her son's name was Yohid. Bethaven's son died, and she buried him. Sea-Bitter's child, too, was dying, but she had heard about Mary and Jesus and she took her son in her arms and carried him to Mary.

Sea-Bitter brought with her a beautiful scarlet and purple mantle for a child, and she said: "O Mary, please exchange with me this cloak for one of your son's swaddling bands."

Mary understood what the mother wanted and she made the exchange. Sea-Bitter took the band, made it into a little shirt, and put it on her son. And the child was immediately cured.

From that day on a great hatred sprang up in Bethaven's heart toward Sea-Bitter whose son was cured, while her own child lay in his grave.

One day, when the oven was ready for the bread to be baked, and Sea-Bitter went out to fetch the rising dough, Bethaven seized

Cloopas and shoved him into the blazing fire. When Sea-Bitter returned, she found her son, who was wearing the shirt made of the swaddling band, playing in the midst of the flames and laughing as if there were no fire there.

Sea-Bitter took her son out and hurried to Mary to tell her what had happened.

"Divulge to no one what Bethaven has done," Mary advised. "Trust in God to judge between you."

Sea-Bitter returned home and said no word to her husband of what had happened nor uttered a word of reproof to Bethaven.

Not long afterwards, Bethaven was drawing water at the well when she saw Cloopas near her and no one else nearby. She seized the child, threw him into the well, and went home. Later in the day others came to draw water from the well, and when they looked down, they saw Cloopas, wearing the shirt made of the swaddling band, sitting on the surface of the water unhurt. They drew him out and returned him to his mother.

Once again Sea-Bitter ran to Mary in tears, saying, "What shall I do, my lady, for Bethaven will sooner or later destroy my son in her hatred."

"Fear not," said Mary. "For it is written that he who digs a pit for others, shall fall into it himself. And he who lives by hatred shall be destroyed by hatred."

A few days later Bethaven, unrepentant, went again to the well to draw water. Her foot became entangled in the rope and she fell into the well. When they drew her out, her skull was fractured, every bone in her body was broken, and she died a miserable death.

The custom of exchanging cloaks with a person held in reverence has persisted among the Jews for many centuries. A garment, usually new, was given to the person considered holy, and in return an old garment was accepted, one worn by the holy person, who, in wearing it, endowed the garment with the power of a blessing. The exchange might be made of any article of clothing, except shoes or anything else made of leather; for it was not right to expect the Lord to bless that which came from the hide of a living thing. The custom still exists among the remnant of the East European Jewish sect known as Chassidim.

10. *A Boy Named Bartholomew*

There lived in those days a woman who had twin boys. They were stricken with a deadly disease, and one child died and was buried. The other lay drawing his last breath. The mother took her dying son in her arms and ran to Mary and pleaded:

"O Mary, have pity on me! For I who have been blessed with two sons am now cursed with two deaths, and my sorrow is greater than I can bear. One of my sons is dead and the other in my arms is on the point of dying. Pray for me to God, our God, the Compassionate, the Merciful, the Affectionate, to save my son for me!"

And Mary said to her: "Fear not, and have faith. Place your child in my son's bed and cover him with my son's covers."

And though the child had already closed his eyes in death, as soon as he was placed in the bed and covered, he opened his eyes and called out:

"Mother, I am hungry!"

The grateful mother praised Mary for her goodness and took her hungry son home.

The name of the boy so rescued from the brink of death was Bartholomew, who grew up to be known as Saint Bartholomew.

11. *Jesus Before Pharaoh*

Word of the miracles wrought by the infant Jesus reached the ears of Pharaoh, ruler of Egypt. He was distressed by the news, remembering Moses many generations earlier, and he ordered his henchmen to bring Joseph and his family before him as soon as they reached Memphis, the capital of the kingdom.

Jesus was two years old when he was brought with Joseph and Mary before the mighty ruler. He stood in front of his mother with a stem of lilies in his hand. And the king addressed himself, not to Joseph nor to Mary, but to the child:

"Another Hebrew boy, named Moses, came to our kingdom many generations ago, and he brought us much suffering. Are you not like Moses?"

"I came after Moses as the dawn comes after the night," said Jesus in a clear voice. "I bring neither anger nor vengeance. Wherever I go, gardens will grow, where only nettles grew before."

And Pharaoh said: "I see you have a wand in your hand. Moses with his wand turned the water in our rivers and our wells into blood for seven days. Will you do the same with your wand?"

Jesus stretched out his hand and waved the lilies toward the river; and the river flowed with sweet milk.

"There is your answer," said Jesus.

And Pharaoh asked: "Next time you stretch our your hand, will the land be filled with frogs and the dust with lice as they were in the days of Moses?"

Jesus waved the lilies in his hand and the air became filled with seeds which the brisk breeze scattered over the fields to make them fertile.

"There is your answer," said Jesus.

And Pharaoh said once again: "If you can cause good seed to fly over our fields, will you also cause us to be plagued with flies, as our ancestors were plagued in the days of your ancestor, Moses?"

Jesus again waved his lilies as if they were a wand, and the air became filled with buzzing bees that gathered in oblong swarms on the branches of trees, and they built many hives and the land was made rich with wild honey.

"There is your answer," said Jesus.

And the king asked: "Will you, like Moses before you, plague our cattle in the field, and our horses, and our asses, and our camels and our oxen and our sheep with grievous murrain, so that they will not multiply and they will die?"

Jesus was tired and climbed up into his mother's arms. And while he rested, all the animals in Egypt brought forth young.

Still Pharaoh was not reassured. He said to Jesus: "Will you now scatter the ashes of our fires and cause man and beast to be covered with boils, and bring great sickness upon our land?"

Jesus just uttered a word, and all those who had ailments in Egypt on that day were instantly cured.

"Will we be threatened with hail that will destroy our crops and ruin our fruit trees?" asked Pharaoh.

Jesus pointed his stalk of lilies into the air, and hail began to fall.

It fell gently, and each hailstone clung to the trees like rosebuds. Then came thunder that tilled the fields. And the entire land of Egypt prospered.

"Of all the plagues of Moses," said Pharaoh, "the people remember the locusts with greatest horror. The locusts came in like dark clouds, and settled over our land. And when they rose, there remained not a blade of grass nor a green leaf. Will you bring this plague upon us?"

Jesus waved his hand, and the air became filled with birds of many colors. They nested in the trees and filled the air with song.

"I know," said Pharaoh, "you plan to plague us with darkness so thick that it may be touched with the hand, and no man can see another, nor take one step in safety."

"I bring you light, not darkness," said Jesus.

And, behold, the land was filled with a brightness unknown in Egypt before, so that even the caverns where there had never been any light were now as bright as a field in the noonday sun.

"There is one last question," said the king. "What about the first-born in Egypt? Will the Angel of Death come, as he came in the days of Moses, and slay them, from the first-born of the king who sits on a throne to the first-born of the handmaiden at her work in the mill, yet shall he pass over the houses in which dwell your people, the Hebrews?"

"The first-born shall live and they who are dead shall live," said Jesus.

And in that moment all the first-born in Egypt who were in their graves arose and were happy.

The tears rolled down the face of the ruler of Egypt, and he welcomed Joseph and his family to Memphis, inviting them to live there as long as they pleased.

12. *The Pledge of Lazarus*

In The Book of the Bee *we find an interesting variation of the story of how the child Jesus was saved from the wrath of Pharaoh.*

At the gates of the city called Hermopolis, leading into Egypt, there were two huge figures of brass made by master craftsmen, and these statues could speak like men. When Joseph the Carpenter and his family neared the gates, the two figures cried out in a voice that could be heard all over Egypt: "A great king has come!" And as the words rang out, all the idols in the land fell from their pedestals and were broken.

The King of Egypt, fearing that someone had come to wrest the kingdom from him, sent messengers to search throughout the land for the stranger of whom the idols had spoken. The heralds searched in the north and the south, in the east and the west, but could not find the one they sought.

Then the king commanded all the people to leave the cities and return to the city gates one by one, where each would identify himself. This the people did. And when Mary entered with Jesus in her arms, the idols of Hermopolis cried out, "This is the king you seek!"

Pharaoh resolved to slay the child. But one of the king's officials, named Lazarus, who was held in high esteem by the court, came forward and questioned Joseph.

"From what land are you?" asked Lazarus.

"From the land of Palestine," said Joseph.

When Lazarus heard that these people had come from the land where the wicked Herod ruled, he went before the king and said:

"O noble Pharaoh, may you live forever! Accept me as a pledge for this child! And should any deceit ever be found in him, behold, I am before you to do with me according to your will!"

And Pharaoh allowed Joseph and his family to enter Egypt to remain there unmolested, upon the pledge given for them by Lazarus.

And so began the love of Lazarus for Jesus.

13. *Miracles Without Number*

Joseph and Mary settled in Memphis for three years. And during these three years Jesus performed many miracles:

The Blooming Staff: One day Jesus stuck a dry staff into the ground, and at once it grew into an olive tree bearing fruit. That tree, we are told, still thrives and bears fruit in Buk, not far from Moharrak.

Three Staves of a Tub: One day Jesus met an old shepherd and his two sons, who were very, very poor. Jesus took three staves from a tub and stuck them into the ground as his gift to these good shepherds. Straightaway the three staves grew into three fruit-bearing trees. And in the time of Cyriacus it was reported that those trees were still blooming and bearing fruit.

The Dried Fish that Swam Away: One day Jesus was playing with some children. He took a dried and salted fish and put it into a basin of water, and commanded the fish to throw out the salt and swim. And the fish did as it had been commanded.

Many of the miracles in the Infancy Gospels are repeated in diverse forms, and frequently are attributed to the apostles in the apocryphal Acts. In the Acts of Peter, for instance, the apostle commands a dried salt herring to swim, and it obeys his command.

The Fountain of Heliopolis: Mary and her son once came near a very old sycamore tree, called Matarea, at the outskirts of Heliopolis. When they discovered that they were being pursued by robbers, the sycamore opened up to receive them and shelter them until the robbers passed. Meanwhile Mary became very thirsty, and Jesus caused a fountain to flow to quench his mother's thirst. Now up to that time the waters of Heliopolis were salty and unfit for man or crop; but after Jesus opened that fountain the waters of Heliopolis turned sweet, and any sick person who drank of them was instantly cured.

The Choicest Balm: One day Mary washed her child's clothes and poured the water out on the ground. And immediately on that spot there appeared an apursam tree, a species of the balsam not found anywhere else in Egypt. The oil of the tree had many wonderful qualities. If iron was dipped into it and then brought near a fire, shone like wax; if some of the oil was thrown upon water, it sank to the bottom; and if a drop of the balsam fell into the palm of a man's hand, it passed through the hand to the opposite side. And the oil of the apursam had a sweeter fragrance and greater healing power than any other balsam.

The Guilt of the Blind and the Lame: Dahman, in whose house Joseph and his family were staying, was robbed one day, and no one could find the thief. Now Dahman had two servants; one was blind and the other was lame. And when they were accused, the lame man pleaded: "How could I have robbed you? I am lame." And the blind man pleaded: "How could I have robbed you? I am blind."

Jesus spoke and said: "The lame man could be the eyes, and the blind man the legs, and together they might have robbed their master."

(The Arabic Gospel of the Infancy of the Savior records: "And the Lord Jesus did in Egypt very many miracles which are recorded neither in the Gospel of the Infancy nor in the perfect Gospel.")

14. *A Double Holiday*

At last the day arrived when the heartless murderer, Herod the Idumean, had to die. He suffered from an incurable distemper. When he tried to sit up, he could not breathe; when he tried to lie down on his back, he suffered unbearable pain; and whatever position he took, new sufferings assailed him. Yet, though he was only a hair's breadth from his grave, he still plotted murder and schemed bloodshed.

He called Salome, his sister, to his bedside. "I know that my end is near," he said to her, "and when I die the people will sigh, but not with sorrow. Yet do I want to make the day of my death a day of great mourning. Therefore, I have ordered all the leaders beloved in Israel gathered in the great hippodrome and accused of treason. When I die, command the executioners, in my name, to kill them all and let not one escape, as did escape that child of which the Magi spoke! Announce their execution with the announcement of my death. And in that way, Salome, the day of my passing will be turned into a day of great sorrow."

Then Herod fell back upon his pillow and died.

His sister commanded the executioners to kill the men held prisoner in the hippodrome. But they refused unless she could bring them an order in the king's hand. And Salome was compelled to admit that the king was dead.

The executioners ran and told the guards of the hippodrome, who opened the gates and released the prisoners.

And the day on which Herod died was turned into a double holiday: the people celebrated their leaders' escape from death; and they rejoiced that the Idumean tyrant was at last dead.

And that very night an angel of the Lord came to Joseph and to Mary, and said: "The wicked King Herod who sought your child's life is now dead and you may return to Judea, even to Nazareth, your home."

PART III

Boyhood in Nazareth

Jules Lamberton, in his devout *Life and Teachings of Jesus Christ,* assures us that from the time Joseph and his family returned from Egypt to Nazareth, "No one in the circle in which the Holy Family lived suspected the existence of any mystery. The early years went by and then childhood, boyhood, youth, without anyone noticing anything superhuman about Him. His parents kept their secret to themselves."

The lore does not reflect this secrecy. The apocryphal works concerning this period in the life of Jesus are filled with public miracles and cures, and the revelation of astounding knowledge and wisdom. Among the most touching stories in the lore are those showing the tender relationship between the child Jesus and the aging Joseph.

The legends selected for the following section have been arranged chronologically to cover the period from the early childhood of Jesus to the time he reached the age of thirteen.

CHAPTER EIGHT

The Little Boy Jesus

1. *The Clay Sparrows*

One day a group of small boys was playing on the banks of a stream and Jesus was amongst them. They kneaded the soft clay and molded with their fingers many figures of birds and beasts. Each time one of them finished shaping an animal or a bird, he would shout:

"Look, boys, look! Isn't my horse beautiful?"

Or, "My dove is like the dove on the throne of Solomon!"

All of them boasted, but Jesus.

After some time, when they had made many clay birds and animals, Jesus said quietly: "My animals are really the best. For I can order mine to move, and they will move."

The boys looked at him with derision and said:

"Your animals are made of clay like ours; how can they move?"

"Adam was made of clay," said Jesus.

"Only God, blessed is he and blessed is his name, can do that," said the boys.

Jesus turned to his clay creatures and said: "I command you to arise and move!"

At once the sparrows stirred, shook the dust out of their wings, and flew away. And the asses and the oxen rose and went down to the water's edge to drink.

When this happened the boys became frightened and ran to their homes to tell their parents what they had heard and what they had seen.

And the parents warned them: "Stay away from Mary's son. Avoid him, and do not play with him after this."

For they could not decide whether there was good or evil in the child.

2. *The Kids and the Goats*

The next time Jesus came out to play with his companions they ran away and hid themselves. Jesus came to the courtyard of one house, where a number of women, mothers of his companions, were standing in a circle and talking.

"Have you seen the boys who were playing here a little while ago?" Jesus asked.

"No," said they, "we don't know where they are."

The children in their hiding place began to snicker. And Jesus asked again: "What are those sounds I hear?"

And the mothers replied: "O those sounds! It is only the neighing of the goats and the kids!"

Jesus called out loud: "Goats and kids! Come to your shepherd and let us play!"

Out scampered several goats and kids, running to Jesus.

The women began to weep and begged Jesus to have mercy on them and change the goats and the kids back again into human children.

"Come, boys, let us go and play," said Jesus.

And before the eyes of the mothers, the goats and kids turned back into boys.

Later the mothers said, each to her own child: "See that you do everything that Jesus, Mary's son, tells you to do, and never disobey him."

For they now believed that the child Jesus had great powers.

3. *If You Could Make a Wish*

Jesus was playing one day in a courtyard with a group of boys. And when they finished their game, some of the mothers called to the children and asked:

"If you could make a wish, what would you like to be when you grow up?"

"I would like to be a dyer," said one, the son of a mason. "For I love bright colors and I would dye the wool gay red and yellow and purple."

"I would like to be a jeweler," said another, "for I like the sparkling jewels and, also, they would make me rich."

"I would like to be a soldier," said the son of the miller, "for then I would wear a soldier's garb, and everyone would fear me."

"And I would like to be a sailor," said the son of the tailor, "for then I would sail over the seas to many strange lands and have many great adventures."

"And I would like to be a beekeeper," said the well-digger's son, "for then I could eat all the honey I want."

"And I would like to be a doctor," said one, "for then I would heal all that are sick and I would become famous."

"What would you like to be, son of Mary?" the women asked Jesus.

"I know what I will be," he answered. "I will be the King of the Jews; and all the nations of the earth will worship me."

The women laughed and asked: "And what will your throne be made of, can you tell us? Will it be made of gold, or of silver, or of ivory?"

"None of these," said Jesus. "My throne will be made of wood. And if you come with me I will show you the tree from which it will be made."

He led them to a brook nearby and pointed to a young oak growing at the edge of the bank.

"There is the tree from which will come my throne," said Jesus. And he began to cry.

And the women could not understand why he wept.

4. *The Boy on the Roof*

One day Jesus and a group of boys climbed up on a roof to play. In their game, one boy pushed another who fell down to the ground and was instantly killed. All the children climbed down and fled. Only Jesus remained near his dead companion.

The news soon reached the dead boy's parents, and they came running in anguish and in tears. When they saw Jesus beside the body of their son, they assumed that he was the cause of their child's death.

"Why have you killed our son, Zeno?" they asked.

"You should first ask whether or not I have killed him, before you ask why," said Jesus.

"If you did not kill him, who did?" the parents demanded.

"My mother says that God hates the talebearer as he hates the murderer," said Jesus, and refused to reveal the name of the boy who had caused their son's death.

The parents ran to Joseph and Mary saying: "Your son refuses to tell us who threw our son Zeno down from the roof, and we believe he did it himself."

Mary came and put her arms about her boy and asked softly: "Now, my son, tell me, did you throw Zeno down?"

"I did not do it," said Jesus. And seeing that the dead boy's grief-stricken parents did not believe him, he added: "Let us ask Zeno and he will tell you that I didn't."

"But Zeno, our son, is dead," wailed the parents.

Jesus bent over his friend's body and called out in a loud voice: "Zeno! Zeno! Tell your parents whether it was I who threw you down from the roof!"

Zeno opened his eyes and said: "No, it was not Jesus, but another."

Those standing by were amazed to hear the dead boy speak. And because Zeno did not betray the boy who had accidentally thrown him down, Jesus said to him: "Arise from the ground, Zeno!"

The boy arose. And they all went to his parents' home to praise God for the miracle that had been performed before their eyes.

5. Satan, the Mad Dog

There lived in those days a woman who had an only son who was tormented by Satan. When Satan took possession of the boy, he would bite anyone who came near him. And if he could find no one else to snap at, he would bite his own hands until they were covered with wounds.

When the mother heard of the cures effected by Jesus, she brought her son to Mary and begged for help.

While the mother was pleading with Mary, the demented boy

wandered out of the house and sat down beside Jesus who, with Joseph's other children James and Justus, sat watching a group of boys at play. Satan took possession of the sick boy and, as he was accustomed to, the boy tried to bite the person nearest to him. But as soon as he touched Jesus, Satan jumped out of the possessed boy in the form of a mad dog, and fled.

And the name of that demented boy, out of whom Satan issued in the form of a mad dog, was Judas Iscariot.

6. *The Boy With a Crown*

One day Jesus was out in the fields, playing with his friends, and they said: "Come, let us play the game of kings."

The boys spread out their garments on the ground and seated Jesus upon them as on a throne. They gathered flowers and wove a garland for his head, and then they stood about him in a ring, like a royal guard about a king. Whenever anyone passed by on the road, the boys would ask them to offer a salutation to their king.

A group of people came up the road carrying a boy of about fifteen who looked as if he were dying. The boy had been bitten by a venomous snake when he tried to rob a partridge's nest of its eggs; and he was being carried to a physician in the city.

The boys who were playing with Jesus and acting as the king's guard, surrounded the passers-by, demanding: "Come and offer a salutation to our king!"

The parents and the relatives of the poisoned boy were too distraught to take part in the children's game; but the small boys would not let them pass until they had paid homage to their king.

Jesus asked them: "Why do you carry this boy?"

And the parents told him what had happened.

"Let us go and kill that snake," said Jesus. "Then your son will be whole again."

At first the parents refused to go back, eager to reach the physician in the city. But the boys surrounded them and made them obey the king.

When they came near the nest, Jesus commanded the serpent to come out of its hiding place and suck out all the poison with which it had infected the boy. The snake crawled out of its hiding place and did as Jesus commanded.

Then Jesus said to the serpent: "This boy meant you no harm yet you tried to kill him. May the harm you intended for him come upon you!"

At these words the snake burst asunder. Then Jesus stroked the hand of the bitten boy, and he was instantly healed. The boy began to weep in gratitude, and Jesus said to him:

"Weep not, for we shall meet again and you shall be my disciple."

And the name of that boy was Simon Zelotes, whom the Apostles later called Simon the Canaanite.

7. *The Miraculous Cloak*

When Jesus was seven years old, his mother sent him to the fountain one day to fetch a pitcher of water. After he had filled the pitcher, a boy accidentally bumped into him and the pitcher fell to the ground and was broken.

Jesus unfolded his cloak and in it carried home to his mother as much water as there had been in the pitcher.

Some time later, Jesus was sent by his mother to fetch hot coals from a merchant. But the servant in the merchant's house was a wicked fellow, and he said: "I have heard that you can carry water in your cloak; you cannot have any coals unless you show me that you can carry them also in your cloak."

Jesus unfolded his cloak and put the hot coals in it, as if they were pears and citrons. He carried them home safely to his mother, and the coals remained hot, yet the cloak did not burn.

These two stories of the cloak from which the water would not seep out, and which fire would not burn, are apparently intended to show that Jesus came to bring peace to the world, since fire and water are symbols of peace when they behave other than is their nature.

8. *The Lily at the Doorstep*

Mary noticed that every time Jesus brought water from the well and she used it to wash the walls, they shone like gold. If she washed the doorsteps with this water, they appeared like marble.

Once, when she poured into the yard the water she had used in the cleaning of the house, there sprang up beside the doorstep a stately lily.

On another day when some of the water emptied into the garden fell upon a poisonous snake, the serpent curled up in the grass and writhed and squirmed until it died.

Mary noticed all these things. And she saw that whenever her son helped her with the work in the house, wonderful things always seemed to happen. The washing dried and folded and was placed in the proper drawer, without her hands touching it. The fire kindled itself when it was needed; and went out when the need for it was over. The beds made themselves before she could touch them. And all her daily chores were accomplished as soon as she thought of them.

This often confused Mary, the mother; and Jesus, her son, would laugh at her confusion.

9. *The Seventh Birthday*

Jesus was seven years old when his grandparents, Joachim and Anna, prepared a great feast to celebrate his birthday. And they invited all their kin and friends, and many honored and learned guests.

At the feast Jesus arose before the guests and said:

"I have dreamt a dream. And in my dream I stood alone upon the sandy beach before a stormy sea. With the wand in my hand I touched the sand, and each grain turned into a living thing, full of beauty and song. Then I touched the raging waves, and they turned into trees full of blossoms and singing birds. And all about me were praising God."

Anna, the grandmother, came forward and placed her hand tenderly on her grandson's head, and said:

"My child, I know the meaning of your dream. For I saw you stand beside the sea; I saw you touch the sand and waves; I saw them turn to living things.

"The sea of life rolls high and stormy; the multitude of men are waiting idly like the dead sand on the beach. Your wand is truth. What you touch with truth brings them all to life; and the very winds burst into song.

"And the meaning of your dream is this: There is no death. Because the wand of truth can change the dry bones to living things; it can grow flowers in the most stagnant pool; it can turn the most discordant notes into harmony and song."

Joachim, the grandfather, then came forward and said: "My beloved child, today you are seven years old, and your grandmother and I wish to give you a gift by which to remember this day. Ask for the thing you want most, and it shall be yours."

And Jesus replied: "There are many boys and girls in Nazareth who are hungry. And it would please me most if they could share with us this great feast. That is the gift I should like most."

"Go and invite them yourself," said Joachim. "And it shall be as you say."

Jesus ran happily through Nazareth, inviting the children to the feast. And when he returned to the house of his grandparents, one hundred and threescore children gaily followed him.

Places at the banquet tables were cleared for the children, and Jesus and his mother served the young guests.

And that was the birthday gift Jesus chose when he was seven years old.

10. *Jesus in the Lions' Den*

When Jesus was eight years old he went with his family on a pilgrimage that led them from Jericho to the River Jordan. This was the road the Children of Israel had traveled when they came from Egypt to Canaan, from slavery to freedom.

Near the Jordan the pilgrims reached the place where the Ark of the Covenant had rested, and there they also rested, telling stories of the days of the Judges and the Kings, when the wilderness near the Jordan was infested with lions and other wild beasts, and it was not safe to pass any cave along the banks of the river.

Suddenly they heard a great roar which seemed to come from a cave nearby. The pilgrims listened with fear in their hearts; and the fear turned into panic when they heard the lions' roar again. But Jesus was not afraid, and he walked without faltering right into the lions' den.

The pilgrims exclaimed: "His sin and the sin of his parents must be very grievous, or else the boy would not of his own accord have offered himself up to be devoured by the lions."

And all the people were filled with pity and sorrow.

In the midst of their sorrowing, Jesus came out of the cave surrounded by the lions, with the cubs playing about his feet. Afar off he saw his parents bowed down in grief, and the rest of the pilgrims deep in sorrow. Their sadness turned to joy and astonishment when they saw Jesus at the mouth of the cave, but they dared not come near for fear of the lions that surrounded him.

Jesus said to them: "How much better are these beasts than you, seeing that they recognize their master, while you who are made after the image and likeness of God, do not recognize him!"

Then Jesus walked toward the Jordan, to the exact spot where Joshua, the son of Nun, had led the Children of Israel across on dry land. The river parted and the waters piled up to a great height, and the river bed was as dry as it was on the day the prophets Elijah and Elisha crossed it. Jesus and the lions, in the sight of all, crossed the Jordan. And Jesus said to the lions: "Go in peace! Hurt no one; neither let any man hurt you!"

The lions turned and ran off to the desert whence they came. And Jesus returned to his parents and the other pilgrims, and they continued on their way.

11. *Jesus and the Old Woman*

One day Jesus wandered out of Nazareth and came to a place at the outskirts of the town where an old woman was making earthen pots. Jesus stopped to watch her, and the old woman said to him angrily: "Aren't you ashamed to loiter here? Go away!"

Jesus waited until the woman left her workshop. Then he took all the pots that had not yet been fired and smashed them into bits, and he went home.

When the old woman returned and saw what had happened to all her work, she remembered Mary's son loitering before the workshop. She ran to Mary in tears, complaining: "Your son has done me a very grave injury!" And she told Mary about the broken earthen pots.

"Did you see him break them?" asked Mary.

"No," said the old woman. "But there was no one else nearby who could have done it."

Mary called her son and asked him whether he did the old woman an injury.

"Go to her shop and see for yourself," said Jesus.

Mary said to the old woman: "Let us go and see. And if my son has done you an injury, I will pay you for it."

They went to the old woman's workshop and found it full of the most beautiful pots ever made; nor could twelve potters have made so many in thirty days.

The old woman fell upon her knees and she thanked Jesus and his mother, Mary.

12. *Jesus in the Tile Factory*

One day Jesus walked out of town along the river until he came to a factory where a large number of workmen were making tiles. First he watched them and then he asked permission to help them. And he worked with them all day long.

At the day's end the workmen looked about them at the work done, and were pleased to find that they had accomplished in that day more than in any preceding five days.

As they were all leaving for home, one old potter said: "I wonder what became of the little boy who helped us today. I feel badly about him, for we gave him neither food to eat nor anything for his labor."

"If we find him," said the others, "we shall show our gratitude."

But Jesus, angered by their failure to offer him food, or to thank him for his help, hid in the factory until the workers had gone. Then he broke all the tiles, and he left.

By that time it was very late in the evening and Joseph and Mary had gone out in search of him. They met him coming from the outskirts of town, overwhelmed with fatigue. They brought him home and asked him whether he wanted to lie down, and Jesus said:

"I am hungry, for I have not eaten anything all day."

The next morning, when the tilemakers and the master of the factory came to work, they were astonished to find the work of the preceding day completely destroyed. And one of them said: "This havoc must be the work of the boy who helped us yesterday, because he was angry that we gave him nothing."

"I believe," said another, "that the boy who was with us yesterday was Joseph the Carpenter's son. Let us go and tell him what damage the boy has done."

But when the men went and told Joseph, he would not believe that Jesus would do such a thing.

"If you do not believe us," said the master tiler, "come with us and see for yourself."

They returned to the factory with Joseph and, to their great astonishment, they found nothing broken.

The workers said: "Forgive us, Joseph, we beseech you; for we are repentant."

"May God forgive you," said Joseph. "He is better able to do it than I. And remember never to let anyone go hungry, not even the stranger in your midst."

13. *The Avenger and the Healer*

Among the countless legends about the boyhood of Jesus, there are some which have been called "the Destructive Miracles." These legends concern themselves with the vengeance Jesus visited on those who kindled his wrath or tried to do him harm. The stories, "Jesus and the Old Woman," and "Jesus in the Tile Factory," in this chapter, scarcely belong in the "destructive" category, since it is clear that they were only intended to teach a lesson to a grouchy old woman and heedless men, but meant them no harm.

There are, however, some stories in the lore, more particularly those of Arabic origin, which demonstrate a vengefulness not consistent with the character of Jesus at any time in his life, and of which the following are typical examples.

Son of Iniquity: One boy, who was envious of the skill with which Jesus created pools at the river's edge, destroyed them with his foot. In his anger, Jesus cursed the boy; and the boy fell down dead. The parents of the dead boy went to Joseph and to Mary and cried out: "Your son has cursed our son, and now he is dead."

And Mary said to Jesus: "My son, what has he done to deserve death?"

Jesus said angrily: "He deserved death because he destroyed the works that I made."

Mary then pleaded with her son; and not wishing to grieve his mother, Jesus kicked the hinder parts of the dead boy and said:

"Rise, you son of iniquity!"

And the dead boy arose and went home.

The Plague of Blindness: One day when Jesus was walking with his father Joseph through the village, another boy came running with malicious intent and bumped into Jesus with such force that he knocked him down.

Jesus arose in anger and said to the boy: "As you have thrown me down, so shall you fall down, and never rise again."

And immediately the boy fell dead to the ground.

His parents came to Joseph and Mary and pleaded: "Go away from this city and take Jesus with you. For every word he utters is accomplished while he is still speaking, and he has the power to destroy our children with his anger."

A large crowd gathered, joining with the parents of the dead boy, and Jesus, fearing they might harm Joseph and Mary, said:

"May the angels smite these people with blindness as the angels who visited Lot smote the Sodomites seeking to do him harm, and as the Prophet Elisha smote the army sent to apprehend him."

And the people were smitten with blindness.

The Foolish Sodomite: Jesus was playing with his companions at the water's edge, damming up pools of water. The son of Annas the high priest took a willow branch and willfully destroyed what Jesus had constructed.

Jesus turned on him and said: "O, wicked and impious and foolish Sodomite! O workshop of Satan! What harm have my pools done to you that you destroyed them? You shall dry up like the willow branch with which you destroyed my work!"

Immediately the boy withered like a dead branch, within the sight of all the other children. And some who saw what had happened ran to tell the priest Annas; and he came and took his withered son to Joseph and said:

"See what your son has done!"

Joseph and Mary then pleaded with Jesus; and for their sake he healed the withered boy. But he left one of the boy's arms withered and useless so that he would remember all his life not to destroy the works Jesus had wrought.

The stories of Jesus as an avenger are few; the stories of Jesus the healer and comforter are many. Even in the "destructive" legends, Jesus is portrayed as forgiving the repentant, including those he had called the "workshop of Satan." In the innumerable legends about the boy Jesus as healer and comforter, all his acts stem from a constant spring of love and compassion for the poor, the sorrowing, the afflicted, and the downtrodden. And here are examples of such legends.

The Healing Breath: One day Joseph sent his son James into the garden to gather vegetables for a broth; and Jesus went along with him. While James was gathering the vegetables, a viper darted out of its hole and struck his hand.

James cried out in pain and in fear of death. Then Jesus took his brother's hand and blew upon it where it had been bitten. And immediately James was healed. When they looked down on the ground, there lay the viper at their feet, dead.

The Healing Touch: One day a neighbor of Joseph the Carpenter was cutting wood, and the axe came down and clove the sole of his foot in two. His cry brought a crowd running to him where he lay on the ground bleeding to death.

Jesus pressed his way through the people and took hold of the woodcutter's foot. At his touch the wounded man's blood stopped flowing.

"Arise," said Jesus to the young man, "and finish cutting your wood."

The Healing Word: One day a man working on a building fell down from the scaffolding and was instantly killed. Jesus, who had followed the crowds to the scene of the accident, made his way to where the dead man lay. He said quietly:

"Man, arise, for your work is not yet done."

The man arose, revived and healed by the words.

CHAPTER NINE

Student and Apprentice

1. *Jesus Before the Teacher*

There was an old schoolmaster in Jerusalem named Levi. Every morning Rabbi Levi went to the synagogue for his morning prayers, and when he returned home, he gathered around a long table his twenty-five students (the greatest number any one teacher was allowed to teach), and he taught them the Hebrew letters and the Laws of Moses.

The old schoolmaster recited a letter, or a word, or a sentence, and the pupils repeated it after him many times, until they remembered it. The teacher would point to the first letter of the alphabet and chant: "Aleph."

And the children would chant after him: "Aleph."

"Again," Rabbi Levi would say.

"Aleph."

"And again."

Again the children would chant: "Aleph!"

Often Rabbi Levi would describe the shape of a letter by comparing it with an article of clothing or some household tool, to impress the letter upon their minds.

"The gimel is like a boot with a high heel and a thick sole," he would say. And his pupils would look with surprise at this letter and discover that their rabbi was right; and after that they always remembered the shape of the gimel.

Or Rabbi Levi would say: "The daleth is like a door standing open, and that is why daleth is the word for door." And the children looked with surprise at the letter and saw that it looked exactly like an open door; and they always remembered the shape of the letter daleth.

After they had learned all the letters, and repeated them aloud one hundred and one times, Rabbi Levi taught them words, beginning traditionally with the first sentence in Leviticus: "And Jehovah called to Moses and spoke to him from the established tabernacle, saying . . ."

If the teacher noticed a listless child who did not open his mouth to repeat a word or a phrase, he would stop and point his accusing finger, and say: " 'He who studies in his head only and does not repeat it aloud, forgets all he has learned within three years.' So it is written. 'Open your mouth and learn the Scriptures; open your mouth and study the Mishnah, so that it may remain with you.' So it is written."

The teacher also had a storax rod for those pupils who were not attentive, or those who whispered during their studies. But he used the rod sparingly. And when their interest flagged he told them a legend or a parable. And when they became restless, he quoted a proverb that was both a lesson and a scolding. He would say to them: "If you have acquired knowledge, what do you lack? And if you lack knowledge, what have you acquired?"

One day Rabbi Zacchaes, a doctor of law, said to Joseph the Carpenter: "Your son, Jesus, is seven years old. Why do you not send him to Rabbi Levi that he may learn the letters and the Scriptures?"

"We by no means wish to hinder him from being taught," said Joseph, "if anyone can teach this child."

"Rabbi Levi can teach him," said Zacchaes.

"I shall speak to Mary about it," said Joseph.

And the next day they brought Jesus to Rabbi Levi to be taught by him.

When all the pupils were in their places, the teacher said to Jesus: "Say after me: Aleph."

And Jesus said: "Aleph."

"Now say after me: Beth," instructed Rabbi Levi.

"Tell me first the meaning of aleph," said Jesus, "and I will then repeat beth."

The teacher became angry and threatened to whip the boy with his rod for refusing to repeat each letter. And Jesus said:

"I can tell you the meaning of aleph and of beth and of gimel and of daleth and of all the letters down to resh, sheen and tov."

"What else can you tell me?'" asked the astonished teacher.

"I can tell you the meaning of the shapes of the letters; why some are straight and others oblique; why some have points and others have none; why one letter goes before the other; and why some have double figures and appear different at the end of a word than elsewhere. Do you want me to go on?"

"Go on," said the amazed rabbi.

"This I have learned from my father," said Jesus. "Aleph and beth come first for they are the first letters of the words meaning 'gain understanding.' Gimel and daleth come next for they stand for the words meaning 'be benevolent to the poor.' The face of daleth is turned away from gimel to teach us that charity should be given in secret so that he who receives it is not shamed.

"Hey and vov signify the Name of God.

"Zain, cheth, teth, yod, coph and lamed stand for: He who is good to the poor, him God will bless, he will sustain him, be gracious to him, give him an inheritance and weave a crown for him in the World to Come.

"There is an open mem, and a closed mem for the ends of words to denote that some doctrines are open to reason and others are not. There is a curved nun and a straight nun at the ends of words, implying that they who are faithful in time of adversity will certainly be faithful in normal times.

"Samech and ain stand for the words meaning 'support the poor.' The letter peh means mouth. There is an open peh and a closed peh. The letter tzadik means 'the righteous'; and there are two kinds of tzadik: those who are righteous when all goes well; and those who are righteous even in times of adversity. Kiph is the first letter of the word 'holy' and resh is the first letter of the word 'wicked'; and that is why the face of kiph is turned away from the face of resh. Sheen is the initial of the word sheker, meaning 'falsehood'; and tov, the last letter in the alphabet, is the last letter of the word ameth, meaning 'truth.'

"*Sheker* consists of three consecutive letters in the alphabet: sheen, kiph and resh, to show that falsehood rests on a weak foundation. But *ameth* consists of aleph, mem and tov, the first, the middle, and the last letter of the alphabet, to show that truth has a firm foundation and shall survive forever."

When Jesus had finished, Rabbi Levi said: "I believe this boy was born before Noah to have gained so much knowledge."

Then he turned to Joseph and Mary and said: "Take this boy away, for I thought you brought me a pupil, and instead you have brought me a master. Now I shall have to depart from this place, because an old man like myself has been taught by a child, and I can find neither beginning nor end to his wisdom."

Jesus smiled and said: "Let the unfruitful bring forth fruit, and let the blind see the living fruit of the true judgment."

And he returned home with his parents.

2. The Meaning of Alpha

Joseph watched Jesus grow vigorous in mind and body, and increase in stature. And it seemed wrong that he should grow up without instruction in human learning. Joseph therefore took him to another teacher.

"What do you want me to teach your boy?" asked the teacher.

"First teach him the Greek letters," said Joseph. "And after that you can teach him the Hebrew."

"It is written: 'Cursed is the man who has his son taught Greek philosophy,'" said the Rabbi.

"I do not ask you to teach him Greek philosophy, only the Greek alphabet," said Joseph. "And it is written: 'Let the words of Japhet (Greek) be in the tents of Shem (Israel).'"

The teacher knew of the attempts that Rabbi Levi had made to teach the boy, and he was afraid. He did not even argue that it was allowed to study Greek only in those hours that were neither day nor night. Instead he wrote out the Greek alphabet, and showing it to Jesus he said: "Come, say after me alpha." And with a pointer he pointed to the first letter.

But Jesus would not respond.

The teacher then said to the boy: "Say after me beta."

"If you will tell me the power of alpha," said Jesus, "I will tell you the power of beta."

The teacher did not know what to answer him.

And Jesus said: "If you do not know the mystery of the first letter, I will tell you what it is. Look at it and you will see that it consists of three common lines. Two lines are brought together, supported by a cross line; and they form a triangle with three points of intersection. Now tell me, why has this letter triangles that are gradate, subacute, mediate, obtuse and prostrate?"

The teacher, on hearing this, cried out: "My heart is astonished. I do not think any man can understand his words, unless God is with him."

Jesus then took a book that lay on the teacher's desk, opened it, and began to read. But he did not read what was in the book. He spoke with the spirit of prophecy; and the words came out of his mouth like a fresh stream from a living fountain. And he spoke with such certainty and such force, that all those present were astonished. A crowd gathered to listen to the boy who spoke with the readiness of words and the ripeness of wisdom.

And when Jesus stopped, they urged him to go on and teach them more with the inspiration of the spirit.

Then Jesus went home to his mother and to his father. And Joseph said to Mary:

"My soul is sorrowful even unto death on account of that child. For if any should offend him, he has the power to cause death, in his anger."

And Mary said: "Fear not, Joseph, and do not believe it possible that Jesus will cause any wrong. For he who sent him to me will himself guard him from all mischief and preserve him from all evil."

And Jesus remained at home and was not sent again to be taught by any schoolmaster.

3. *Hillel's Pupil*

Jesus was ten years old when he went up with his parents and kin to Jerusalem for the Passover Feast. And there, to his great dismay, he saw the butchers killing pure white lambs and turtle doves for the sacrifices.

"Why do you kill these creatures and burn their flesh in the name of God?" he asked.

"These are our vicarious sacrifices," the priests answered.

"Did not King David say that God does not require sacrifices for sin?" asked Jesus. "And did not Isaiah say that it was sinful to bring burnt offerings before the Lord?"

The priests looked at the little boy with amazement, and asked in turn: "Little boy, are you wiser than all the priests in Israel?"

Jesus was not content with their response and went to Hillel the Gentle, Chief of the Sanhedrin, and said:

"Rabboni, you are wise. Can you tell me why the temple, the house of God where love and kindness should dwell, is filled with the bleating of slaughtered lambs and the stench of burnt flesh? Can man be kind and just after committing such cruelties?"

Hillel put his hand gently upon the boy's head and said: "There is a God of Love, and if you will come with me I shall help you find him."

But Jesus said: "Why need we go anywhere? Isn't God everywhere?"

Rabbi Hillel then sought out Mary and Joseph and asked them to leave Jesus with him for a while so that he might teach the boy the precepts of the Law.

They gave their consent; and Jesus lived with Hillel the Gentle in Jerusalem. Hillel taught his new pupil daily. And daily the master learned from his pupil.

Jesus remained with Hillel for a year, and then he returned to his home in Nazareth; and there he worked with Joseph as a carpenter.

4. Jesus and Joseph

When Jesus was old enough, Joseph the Carpenter took him along as he went through Nazareth and the neighboring places looking for work.

Joseph's daughters, Assia and Lydia, and his two elder sons, Judas and Justus, were married and had established families of their own. There remained in Joseph's house only his wife Mary, and his two sons, Simon and James, and the youngest of them all, Jesus. And Joseph the Carpenter loved the youngest member of his family most of all.

Sometimes Joseph was called in to mend chests, doors, beds, milk pails and water buckets. More often the people ordered benches, or new ox yokes, or plows and other wooden tools; and these Joseph made in his workshop. As he worked, Joseph talked to Jesus, calling him "deliverer of my soul" and "apple of my eye" and "my beloved son" and "sweetest name in my mouth" and many other endearing names. And Joseph taught Jesus all he knew of the Law and the Prophets.

Often Joseph made a mistake in cutting the wood or in joining the planks and it grieved him. But after young Jesus began to help him, Joseph's grief lifted like the early morning clouds of summer. For whenever Joseph made a mistake Jesus rectified it with a word of his mouth or the touch of his hand. And the skill of Joseph's hands grew as long as Jesus was with him in the workshop.

Joseph, who had been known in Galilee as a good and righteous man, though not so gifted as a carpenter, began, in his old age, to gain fame for his great skill.

5. *The Tools of the Mind*

Jesus was in his father's workshop on Marmion Way in Nazareth helping with the work one day, when he said: "These carpenter's tools we use remind me of the tools of the mind."

"In what way?" asked Joseph.

"Take this square, for instance," said Jesus. "We use it to measure out all the lines and to straighten out all the uneven places. In that same way we square the corners of our conduct."

"What of the compass?" asked Joseph.

"We use the compass to draw circles around our desires and to keep them within bounds."

"And what of the axe?" asked Joseph.

"We use the axe to cut away the useless parts and in that way make our character symmetrical."

"How would the plane come in?" asked Joseph.

"We use the plane to smooth out the rough, uneven surface of the board that goes into the building of our Temple of Truth. And in the same way we use the chisel, the plummet and the saw in the workshop of our minds, just as in this workshop here."

Then Jesus saw a small ladder leaning against the wall, and he said: "Even this ladder of three steps is like the ladder of faith, hope and love on which we climb to reach the dome of the good life."

Joseph embraced him and said: "My beloved son, you are the deliverer of my soul."

6. The Rich Man's Couch

One day a certain rich young man came to Joseph and ordered a couch six cubits long, which he wanted to be both useful and beautiful. Joseph, who had never before made a couch, undertook this task with trepidation and foreboding.

After considering the measurements given him by the rich patron, Joseph went out into the field to get the wood. He selected two beams, cut them with an iron saw, and smoothed them with an axe. But when he placed the planks together he found that one was too short and the other too long. Joseph was exceedingly grieved. He was about to go out to look for another beam to cut, when Jesus stayed him, saying:

"Put these two pieces of wood together so as to make both ends on your side even."

Joseph was puzzled yet did as he was told.

"Hold both ends firmly and keep them even," said Jesus.

Joseph was still puzzled, but again he did as he was told.

Jesus took hold of the uneven ends and pulled the shorter plank toward him until the ends on his side were also even.

"Grieve no more," said Jesus to Joseph. "Now they are ready for the couch you promised to make."

And Joseph said: "Blessed am I, because God has given me such a boy!"

That evening when Joseph told Mary what had happened in his workshop, she rejoiced with him; but they said nothing about it to their neighbors.

As might be expected, this theme has many variations. The circumstances differ, but in each case a beam or a plank or a piece of furniture is lengthened or shortened, with Joseph holding one end and Jesus holding the other. There is even one legend in which Joseph cut a cedar board too short and could not afford to buy another. Jesus tells him not to be grieved and pulls it out so long that Joseph has more than an ell of wood left over.

Some commentators on this lore are distressed, not by the repetition, but by the disregard for geography, history, and, at times, logic. Yet a measure of the great charm of the lore resides in the very fact that in the folk imagination there are no time or space restrictions. Rivers appear regardless of geography, for Jesus to walk by, on the outskirts of Nazareth; Roman kings appear who rule over Jerusalem, though none are to be found in the history books; members of the Tribe of Judah become high priests, though this was forbidden by the Law. The lore creates its own fact and its own logic. But it never does violence to the purpose — the lesson it wishes to impart and the point it wishes to underscore about the beneficent powers of the young Jesus.

CHAPTER TEN

Jesus in the Temple

1. *The Visit to Jerusalem*

When Jesus was twelve years old, he went up with his family and their kin and their neighbors to celebrate the Feast of the Passover in Jerusalem.

Though the holiday commemorated an event that took place many centuries earlier, the people rejoiced as if their emancipation from Egyptian slavery had just happened. And though this pilgrimage was taken every year, its luster, especially for the young, was never diminished.

On arriving in Jerusalem, Joseph took Jesus with him to the temple courts where he purchased the paschal lamb. They waited amid the multitude of pilgrims until their turn came to make the offering. And as they waited, they could hear, above the sounds in the court, the music in the temple and the singing of the Levites.

"What ails you, O sea, that you flee, you Jordan that you turn back, you mountains that you skip like rams and the hills like lambs?"

"All nations and all peoples, praise the Lord: for his loving kindness is mighty and his truth endures forever!"

With these songs still ringing in their ears, Joseph and Jesus took the paschal lamb to the home of a kinsman where it was roasted over an open fire. And as soon as night came, all gathered around the festive table, young and old, and the ritual began.

The wine was blessed; the hands were washed; they dipped a green sprig of parsley in salt water and ate it in remembrance of the tears of those who had been enslaved; they welcomed the guests in the prescribed manner; and then the youngest boy in the gathering asked:

"How does this night differ from any other night?"

And Joseph, being the oldest at the table, answered: "We were slaves unto Pharaoh in Egypt, and the Lord redeemed us with a mighty hand — "

After the meal they recounted all the events that had happened long ago, in the days of Moses and Aaron.

The ceremony at the table began almost as soon as the first star appeared; and it lasted until the cock crowed and the morning star shone in the paling sky.

After the Feast of the Passover the pilgrims streamed back from Jerusalem to their homes in all parts of Judea. The men traveled in groups; and the women in separate companies. The dust of the road rose up in clouds, and the spirits of the returning celebrants rose even higher.

Joseph, in the company of his sons and kin, did not see Jesus around but assumed that he was with Mary and the women of the household. And Mary, who did not see Jesus, assumed that he was with Joseph and the men of Nazareth.

After a day's journey from Jerusalem, Joseph's family gathered together for the evening meal; and Jesus was not among them. Joseph and Mary and all the members of the family began to seek him among their kin and neighbors. With mounting anxiety they went from camp to camp, asking:

"Have you seen our boy, Jesus?"

But no one had seen him all day long.

Then Joseph said to Mary: "No one has seen Jesus since we left Jerusalem. Let us return and seek him there."

They returned to Jerusalem with heavy hearts, and they searched for him in every place where they thought he might be found. But no one had seen him since the Feast of the Passover. And on the third day Joseph and Mary went to the temple to reveal their grief to the rabbis.

They went up to the temple courts and asked the guards: "Have you seen about these courts our son Jesus, a fair-haired boy, with deep blue eyes, twelve years of age?"

The guards replied: "Yes. He is now in the temple disputing with the doctors of the Law."

They entered, and there they found a great assembly of the learned, the priests and the teachers, the rabbis and the scribes, questioning a young boy before them on the mysteries of the Law and the sayings of the prophets.

And the boy before the learned assembly was their son Jesus.

2. Who Is That Boy?

When Mary and Joseph discovered their son at the temple, the rabbis were in the midst of a discussion about the Messiah.

"Have you read the books?" one of the teachers asked Jesus.

"Both the books, and the things contained in the books," Jesus replied.

"Can you explain them?" asked a rabbi.

And Jesus explained to them the Law and the Prophets; the precepts and the statutes; and the hidden meaning behind them all.

"What can you tell us of the spiritual kingdom that the Messiah will establish?" they asked.

"The world was created in six days, each day representing a millennium," said Jesus. "Just as at the end of six days comes the Sabbath, so also at the end of six thousand years from the days of Adam, the world will come to an end and the Messiah will arrive. And the Messiah, son of David, will reign forever." Then he explained that that kingdom will be like the kingdom of the Ten Lost Tribes beyond the River Sambatyon, where all the people live in justice and in peace.

The learned men turned in astonishment and asked of each other: "Pray, who can that boy be?"

3. Jesus and the Astronomer

A learned astronomer was present in the assembly at the temple, and he arose and asked Jesus:

"What do you know about astronomy?"

Jesus, without hesitation or faltering, explained the number of spheres and the heavenly bodies, and the meaning of their numbers; he expounded on their different natures and operations; he defined their aspects, triangular, square or sextile; he interpreted their course, direct and retrograde; he gave the motion of the planets each day, and each hour of the day; and he ended with a commentary on the intrastellar mysteries beyond the reach of reason.

And the astronomer turned and asked: "Pray, who can that boy be?"

4. Jesus and the Physician

A physician skilled in the natural sciences was one of those in the assembly at the temple. He arose and asked Jesus:

"Have you studied medicine and the related sciences?"

And Jesus, without perplexity or irresolution, explained the relationship of physics to metaphysics; and hyperphysics to hypophysics; then he enumerated the members of the body and their functions; the number of the bones, veins, arteries and nerves, and all the intakes and outlets of the body; he explained the effects of heat or dryness on the human body, or heat and cold; and the disturbances created in the body by variations of moisture and temperature. From the physical body of man he passed over to the soul and its powers; the perceptions and the faculties; human emotions, their conjugation and disjunction; and he concluded with a discourse on the relationship between soul and body, beyond the reach of any mortal mind.

The physician then turned and asked: "Pray, who can this boy be?"

5. Are You the Mother?

The assembly at the temple was still discussing all the things Jesus had said, when Mary came forward, saying:

"My son, my beloved son! Your father and I have sought for you everywhere with troubled hearts."

And Jesus said to her: "Why did you seek me everywhere? Did you not know I would be in the temple, which is the house of our Father in Heaven?"

"What have you eaten these three days?" asked the mother.

"The teachers in the temple bid me to their table," said Jesus, "and they would not let me go hungry."

The teachers, the scribes, the Pharisees and all those assembled, surrounded Mary and asked:

"Are you the mother of this boy?"

When Mary said that he was indeed her son, they said: "Blessed are you to be the mother of such a son, and blessed is the fruit of your womb! Such knowledge and such wisdom we have not heard from the mouth of any boy; nor have we ever heard of any record of such wisdom in a boy!"

6. *Life in Nazareth*

After his return from Jerusalem Jesus helped his father in the carpenter shop and studied the Law and the Prophets.

At home he called Joseph "father" and Mary "mother," and he obeyed them in all their commands; and did nothing to displease them. To all their kin and neighbors he appeared an obedient and loving son, like any other worthy son.

Often he walked out alone into the peaceful hills surrounding Nazareth. As he passed the fields of wheat and barley and the groves of fig and pomegranate trees, he would observe the men cultivating their plots and groves. From the top of a hill, on a sun-lit day, he could glimpse beyond the long stretch of low-lying hills the waters of a blue and silver sea; and to the north he could discern the mountains receding as far as the peaks of Lebanon. And he would smell the fragrant air, heavy with the citron in bloom, or the lilies in the field, or the ripening fruit.

At the family gatherings and the feasts celebrated in the home, Jesus, though the youngest of them all, was always asked to preside at the table. No one ever sat down to eat or drink before he had taken his place and blessed them. And if Jesus were detained, they waited for him.

After the ritual Washing of the Hands and the Blessing of the Bread, they sat down to eat with decorum. At the meal no one ever spoke a word of anger or rancor. And when the simple meal ended, Jesus would say:

"With the sanction of the master of the house and all those present, let us bless him of whose bounty we have partaken!"

And all present at the table would respond in a low voice: "Blessed is he of whose bounty we have partaken, and through whose goodness we live!"

Then the lengthy aftermeal grace would continue, varying with the holidays and the circumstances, uttered hardly above a whisper, only the lips moving for the words spoken in unison. Toward the end Jesus would lift his voice above the others, half chanting the words of the ritual:

"Young lions may lack and suffer hunger; but they who seek the Lord know no want. Blessed is the man who trusts in the Lord, and whose trust is the Lord. He gives strength to his people; and he will bless his people with peace. Amen."

Then they returned each to his task.

CHAPTER ELEVEN

The Death of Joseph the Carpenter

1. *Joseph's Illness*

At the age of one hundred and eleven years, Joseph the Carpenter reached the limit of his days.

In mind he did not wander, and in physical strength he suffered no weakness. He walked erect like a boy and with the vigor of youth. His limbs were unimpaired and free from pain. His eyesight was clear and sharp; nor had he lost a single tooth from his mouth. And to the last days of his life he worked each working day as a carpenter.

But one day an angel of the Lord came to Joseph to remind him that all men made of earth must return to the earth. And Joseph rose up and went to the temple in Jerusalem for the last time. When he reached the altar, he poured out his heart in prayer and confession, saying:

"O God of my soul, my body and my spirit! Now that my days on earth are coming to an end, I beseech you to send the prince of your holy angels to be with me when my soul departs, that my soul may leave this wretched and afflicted body without great terror. Since fear and sadness seize all living things at the hour of their death, let not the face of your angel be turned from me until the soul is severed from the body. I beseech you, O God, let not the demons of diverse faces come near my soul; nor the keepers of the gates hinder my soul from entering paradise! Let not the lions rush in upon me; nor the waves of the fiery river overwhelm my soul! O God of my fathers, author of all compassion and consolation, have pity on my soul, and console me in this hour! Here, at the gateway of all prayer, I pray to you who are the fountain of all glory for evermore. Amen!"

Then Joseph arose and returned to his home in Nazareth, and

went to bed with the disease of which he was to die. And the gold of his wisdom and the silver of his understanding lost their luster. He could neither eat nor drink, nor could he center his attention on anything, and the disease was hard for him, who had never been ill from the day of his birth.

And all in Joseph's household knew that his end was very near.

2. *The Last Visit*

It was a hot summer's day when the righteous Joseph prepared to give up his unquiet soul to his Creator. First he uttered a groan, then he clapped his palms three times, and in a resolute voice he repeated the Prayer of the Departing Soul.

As Joseph was praying, Jesus came to his bedside, troubled in soul and spirit.

"How do you feel, my beloved father?"

"The agony of death has already surrounded me, my beloved son. But as you entered my chamber, my soul was consoled."

Then Joseph began to recall the day he first saw Mary in the temple, and all the events that had taken place since then. He spoke of the days Jesus had spent with him in the workshop, and all the miracles the boy had performed for his sake. And as Joseph spoke the tears streamed down over the ridges of his cheeks.

Jesus could not refrain himself from weeping when he heard the dying man's words, and he left the chamber and went out into the courtyard. There he found his mother, who asked him: "O my beloved son, how is the pious and honorable Joseph?"

And Jesus answered: "Who is there of the race of men who have worn the flesh, who will not taste death? Death holds sway over the entire human race. Even you, O my virgin mother, must look for the same end of life as other mortals. Even I must taste death because of the flesh that I wore in you. Though a man attain the age of Adam, in the end he must die."

Mary began to weep, and Jesus said to her again:

"Come, let us go in and be with Joseph in these last moments of his understanding."

They entered the dying man's chamber and saw the signs of

death already manifest on Joseph's face. Mary sat down at her husband's feet, and Jesus sat near his head.

Joseph opened his eyes and fixed them on the boy. He made an effort to speak, but the silence of death was already upon his tongue. He lifted his right hand and made a sign. And Jesus went out and called Joseph's children, his sons and his daughters, to come to their father's bedside. They surrounded the dying man, lamenting, and Mary and Jesus wept with them; knowing that this was their last hour with the good Joseph.

3. *Jesus and the Angel of Death*

Jesus lifted his eyes toward the south and saw the Angel of Death enter the house, surrounded by many attendants, armed with swords of fire, with brimstone and smoke issuing from their nostrils and their mouths. Unnoticed by the others in Joseph's room, Jesus commanded the Angel of Death and his hosts to leave the chamber. And they fled.

Jesus prayed, and the angels Michael and Gabriel, and a choir of angels, entered the death chamber and surrounded the head of Joseph's bed.

Then Jesus arose and left the room, so that the Angel of Death could return and administer to Joseph the drop of gall from the tip of his sword, that the dying man's soul could separate from his body and be taken up to heaven by the angels.

After a short time Jesus returned and he saw Joseph's body lying still like an empty vessel. And he said to his mother:

"Where are now the skill and all the works this man has wrought since the days of his youth? They have all passed away in this hour as though he had not been born into the world at all."

4. *Lamentation for Joseph*

When it became known in Nazareth that Joseph the Carpenter had passed away, the neighbors and friends assembled in the courtyard, lamenting and weeping. And when they saw a member of Joseph's family, they omitted the customary greetings and said instead: "The Lord has given and the Lord has taken away. Blessed be the name of the Lord!"

And all within hearing responded: "Amen!"

The neighbors lifted Joseph's body from his bed and washed him. They poured the cleansing water over him and chanted:

"He is clean! He is clean! He is clean!"

And when his body had been anointed and wrapped in linen, Jesus approached and placed his hands upon the body and prayed:

"Let not the evil smell of death have dominion over you; nor a worm come forth from your body. Let neither flesh nor shroud rot in the earth until the day of the banquet of a thousand years. Let this day of the twenty-sixth of the month of Ahib be remembered, and he who on this day helps the poor, the widow and the orphan, shall suffer no lack in this world all the days of his life. And he who begets a son and names him Joseph, glorifying your name, famine and pestilence shall not be known in his house for your name's sake."

And all those who heard Jesus pray, said: "Amen!"

5. Joseph's Burial

The pallbearers, the chiefs of the city, lifted Joseph to carry him to his resting place. To their amazement they found that his shroud had no seams, nor entrance, nor any binding edges, and that Joseph's body was sealed within like a fruit within its skin.

They carried the body to the burial cave where Joseph's ancestors were interred, to bury him beside his fathers.

As the men were opening the gates of the burial ground, Jesus stretched himself out on Joseph's body and wept for a long while.

Then they opened the tomb, took up Joseph's body, and placed it near his father Jacob. And the cave was sealed.

Those present washed their hands and said: "God makes death vanish in life eternal; he wipes away the tears of all mourners; and he shall take away the reproach of his people all over the earth: for the Lord has spoken."

And as they left the burial ground, each in turn stooped down

and plucked a few blades of grass; and as they scattered them in
the breeze, they said with a sigh: "He remembers that we are nothing but a little dust."

*According to the Aquarian Gospel, Jesus was in India, preaching
on the shores of the Ganges, when a traveler from the West brought
him the tidings of Joseph's death and told Jesus that Mary, griev-
ing, "wonders whether you are still alive or not; and she longs to
see you once again."*

*Jesus wrote to console his mother, and sent the letter by the hand
of a merchant going to Jerusalem. And this, in brief, is what Jesus
wrote:*

My mother, noblest woman of womankind! A man just from
my native land has brought me word that father is no more in
the flesh, and that you grieve and are disconsolate.

My mother, all is well — for father and for you. His work
on earth is done, nobly done; and in all the walks of life man
cannot charge him with deceit, dishonesty, nor wrong intent.
Why then should you weep? Tears cannot conquer grief. There
is no power in grief to mend a broken heart. When grief comes
trooping through the heart, plunge deep into the ministry of
love, and grief will leave you. Strive to be content; and I will
come to you one day with richer gifts than gold and precious
stones.

*The letter in full, as given in the Aquarian Gospel, dwells in this
vein on the power of good deeds to conquer sorrow. That Jesus
was away from home when Joseph the Carpenter died is a unique
episode in the lore.*

PART IV
The Unknown Life of Jesus

About the years between the age of thirteen to the time Jesus appeared at the Jordan, sixteen or eighteen years later, we have in the New Testament only the cryptic statement: "And Jesus increased in wisdom and stature, and in favor with God and man" (Luke 2:52).

The New Testament and most of the accepted Apocrypha of the New Testament offer no clue to Luke's recondite statement. The events of the infancy and childhood of Jesus are given in detail; then the record breaks off abruptly, until it begins again with the announcement: "Then came Jesus from Galilee to the Jordan, to be baptised by John" (Matt. 3:13).

The lore, however, delves heartwarmingly into the great mystery of what some scholars call "the hidden years" in the life of Jesus.

Several diverse legends undertake to record all that happened to Jesus during these "hidden years," and in the following section several of these accounts are presented. The documents from which they are taken may have little historical value for the scholar who seeks factual data that can withstand the test of higher criticism; but as legends and as lore they rank high in portraying the importance that every phase of the life of Jesus assumed in folk imagination the world over.

CHAPTER TWELVE

The Life of Saint Issa

The most colorful account of the "hidden years" is to be found in a strange book, called The Unknown Life of Jesus Christ, *by Nicolas Notovich, who, after the Russo-Turkish War of 1887–1888, traveled through India well equipped with gold, firearms and wine. After a brief visit to Srinagar, capital of Kashmir, he proceeded to Ladakh in the upper valley of the Indus. On the way, at the Monastery of Moulbeck, near the town of Wakkha, the adventurous Russian heard a Tibetan lama refer to a Grand Lama, or Dalai Lama, named Issa (Jesus). Upon inquiry, Notovich was told that a chronicle of the life of Issa was preserved among the sacred scrolls of the Convent of the Himis.*

After many adventures, Notovich reached the town of Leh, capital of polyandric Ladakh, and from there he went up to the great Convent of the Himis, situated high above the town on a picturesque rock with a commanding view over the valley of the Indies, to witness a religious festival. After the dramatic ceremonies, Notovich sought an explanation of their meaning from the chief lama, and at this time he was told that among the thousands of sacred scrolls detailing the lives of the Buddhas and their saints, there was one about the Prophet Issa who preached the same doctrine in India as he later preached in Israel, where he was put to death by the pagans.

The original scroll on the Life of Issa, the chief lama explained, was written in Pali and later translated into Tibetan. The Tibetan translation was kept in the Convent of the Himis and the original remained in the library of Lhassa.

After a number of adventures, Notovich finally received permission to have the scroll on the life of Issa taken out and translated to him, while he carefully transcribed it in his traveler's note-

book "*according to the translation made by the interpreter.*" *And when the translation was finished, the scroll was returned to its place in the library, high in the mountains of Tibet, guarded by high temple doors, painted in bright colors and decorated with huge copper rings.*

Notovich tells us that the account, as literally translated to him, was "disconnected and mingled with accounts of other contemporaneous events to which they bear no relation," and he took the liberty to arrange "all the fragments concerning the life of Issa in chronological order and [I] have taken pains to impress upon them the character of unity, in which they were absolutely lacking" — a step no reputable scholar would have taken. But strangely enough, the very statement may add credence to the author's claim.

However unconvincing this document may be as an ancient record, approached as lore it compares favorably in literary expression and sublimity of sentiment with the best of the vast New Testament apocryphal works.

The document — the Life of Saint Issa, "Best of the Sons of Men," — is presented here in abridged form, beginning with Chapter IV; but the wording is that of the original.

(IV) . . . When Issa was thirteen years old, the age at which an Israelite is expected to marry, the modest house of his industrious parents became a meeting-place of the rich and illustrious, who were anxious to have as a son-in-law the young Issa, who was already celebrated for the edifying discourses he made in the name of the All-Powerful. Then Issa secretly absented himself from his father's house; left Jerusalem, and, in a train of merchants, journeyed toward the Sindh, with the object of perfecting himself in the knowledge of the word of God and the study of the laws of the great Buddhas.

(V) In his fourteenth year, young Issa, the Blessed One, came this side of the Sindh and settled among the Aryas, in the country beloved by God. Fame spread the name of the marvellous youth along the northern Sindh, and when he came through the country of the five streams and Radjipoutan, the devotees of the god Djaine asked him to stay among them. But he left the deluded worshippers

of Djaine and went to Djagguernat, in the country of Orsis, . . .
where the white priests of Brahma welcomed him joyfully. They
taught him to read and to understand the Vedas, to cure physical
ills by means of prayers, to teach and to expound the sacred Scriptures, to drive out evil desires from man and make him again in
the likeness of God. He spent six years in Djagguernat, in Radja-
griha, in Benares, and in other holy cities. The common people
loved Issa, for he lived in peace with the Vaisyas and the Sudras
(farmers and merchants), to whom he taught the Holy Scriptures.
But the Brahmins and the Kshatriyas (priests, warriors and rulers)
told him that they were forbidden by the great Para-Brahma to
come near to those who were created from his belly and his feet;
. . . Issa . . . declaimed strongly against man's arrogating to himself the authority to deprive his fellow-beings of their human and
spiritual rights. "Verily," he said, "God has made no difference between his children, who are all alike dear to Him." . . . The Vaisyas and the Sudras were filled with great admiration, and asked
Issa how they should pray, in order not to lose their hold upon
eternal life.

"Pray not to idols, for they cannot hear you; hearken not to the
Vedas where the truth is altered; be humble and humiliate not your
fellow-man. Help the poor, support the weak, do evil to none;
covet not that which you have not and which belongs to others."

(VI) The white priests and the warriors, who had learned of
Issa's discourse to the Sudras, resolved upon his death, and sent
their servants to find the young teacher and slay him. But Issa,
warned by the Sudras of his danger, left by night Djagguernat, gained
the mountain, and settled in the country of the Autamides, where
the great Buddha Sakya-Muni came to the world, among a people
who worshipped the only and sublime Brahma. When the just Issa
had acquired the Pali language, he applied himself to the study of
the sacred scrolls of the Sutras. After six years of study, Issa, whom
the Buddha had elected to spread his holy word, could perfectly
expound the sacred scrolls. He then left Nepaul and the Himalaya
mountains, descended into the valley of Radjipoutan and directed
his steps toward the West, everywhere preaching to the people the
supreme perfection attainable by man; and the good he must do to

his fellow-men, which is the sure means of speedy union with the eternal Spirit.

"He who has recovered his primitive purity," said Issa, "shall die with his transgressions forgiven and have the right to contemplate the majesty of God. . . . Even as a father shows kindness toward his children, so will God judge men after death, in conformity with His merciful laws. He will never humiliate his child by casting his soul for chastisement into the body of a beast. . . . Man is naught before the eternal Judge; as the animal is before man. Therefore, I say unto you, leave your idols and perform not ceremonies which separate you from your Father and bind you to the priests, from whom heaven has turned away. For it is they who have led you away from the true God, and by superstitions and cruelty perverted the spirit and made you blind to the knowledge of the truth."

(VII) The words of Issa spread among the Pagans, through whose country he passed, and the inhabitants abandoned their idols. Seeing which, the priests demanded of him who thus glorified the name of the true God, that he should, in the presence of the people, prove the charges he made against them, and demonstrate the vanity of their idols.

And Issa answered them: "If your idols, or the animals you worship, really possess the supernatural powers you claim, let them strike me with a thunder-bolt before you!"

"Why dost not thou perform a miracle," replied the priests, "and let thy God confound ours, if He is greater than they?"

But Issa said: "The miracles of our God have been wrought from the first day when the universe was created; and are performed every day and every moment; whoso sees them not is deprived of one of the most beautiful gifts of life. . . . But woe to you! . . . if you demand that He attest His power by a miracle! For it is not the idols which He will destroy in His wrath, but those by whom they were created; their hearts will be the prey of an eternal fire and their flesh shall be given to the beasts of prey."

. . . When the Pagans saw that the power of their priests was naught, they put faith in the words of Issa. Fearing the anger of the true God, they broke their idols to pieces and caused their priests to flee from among them. Issa furthermore taught the Pagans that they should not endeavor to see the eternal Spirit with their eyes; but to perceive Him with their hearts, and make themselves worthy of His favors by the purity of their souls.

"Not only," he said to them, "must ye refrain from offering human sacrifices, but ye may not lay on the altar any creature to which life has been given. . . . Withhold not from your neighbor his just due, for this would be like stealing from him what he had earned in the sweat of his brow. Deceive no one, that ye may not yourselves be deceived; . . . be not given to debauchery, for it is a violation of the law of God. That you may attain to supreme bliss ye must not only purify yourselves, but must also guide others into the path that will enable them to regain their primitive innocence."

(VIII) The countries round about were filled with the renown of Issa's preachings, and when he came unto Persia, the priests grew afraid and forbade the people hearing him. Nevertheless, the villages received him with joy, and the people hearkened intently to his words, which, being seen by the priests, caused them to order that he should be arrested and brought before their High Priest, who asked him: "Of what new God dost thou speak? Knowest thou not, unfortunate man that thou art, that Saint Zoroaster is the only Just One, to whom alone was vouchsafed the honor of receiving revelations from the Most High? . . . Who, then, art thou, who darest to utter blasphemies against our God and sow doubt in the hearts of believers?"

And Issa said to them: "I preach no new God, but our celestial Father, who has existed before the beginning and will exist until after the end. . . . As the new-born child in the night recognizes the mother's breast, so your people, held in the darkness of error by your pernicious doctrines and religious ceremonies, have recognized instinctively their Father, in the Father whose prophet I am. The Eternal Being says to your people, by my mouth, 'Ye shall not adore the sun, for it is but a part of the universe which I have created for man. It rises to warm you during your work; it sets to accord to you the rest that I have ordained.' . . . Ye pretend that man must adore the sun, and the Genii of Good and Evil.

But I say unto you that . . . the sun does not act spontaneously, but by the will of the invisible Creator, who has given to it being."

"Who, then, has caused that this star lights the day, arms man at his work and vivifies the seeds sown in the ground?"

"The Eternal Spirit is the soul of everything animate, and you commit a great sin in dividing Him into the Spirit of Evil and the Spirit of Good, for there is no God other than the God of Good. And He, like to the father of a family, does only good to His children, to whom He forgives their transgressions if they repent of them. . . . Therefore, I say unto you: Fear the day of judgment, for God will inflict a terrible chastisement upon all those who have led His children astray and beguiled them with superstitions and errors; upon those who have blinded them who saw; who have brought contagion to the well. . . . Your doctrine is the fruit of your error in seeking to bring near to you the God of Truth, by creating for yourselves false gods."

When the Magi heard these words, they feared themselves to do him harm; but at night, when the whole city slept, they brought him outside the walls and left him on the highway, in the hope that he would not fail to become the prey of wild beasts. But, protected by the Lord our God, Saint Issa continued on his way, without accident.

(IX) Issa — whom the Creator had selected to recall to the worship of the true God, men sunk in sin — was twenty-nine years old when he arrived in the land of Israel. Since his departure therefrom, the Pagans had caused the Israelites to endure more atrocious sufferings than before; and they were filled with despair. . . .

"Children, yield not yourselves to despair," said the celestial Father to them, through the mouth of Issa, "for I have heard your lamentations, and your cries have reached my ears. Weep not, oh, my beloved sons! for your griefs have touched the heart of your Father and He has forgiven you, as He forgave your ancestors. Lift up those who are fallen; feed the hungry and help the sick, that ye may be altogether pure and just in the day of the last judgment which I prepare for you."

The Israelites came in multitudes to listen to Issa's words; and they asked him where they should thank their Heavenly Father,

since their enemies had demolished their temples and robbed them
of their sacred vessels. Issa told them that God cared not for temples erected by human hands, but that human hearts were the true
temples of God. . . .

"Therefore, I say unto you, soil not your hearts with evil, for
in them the Eternal Being abides. When ye do works of devotion
and love, let them be with full hearts, and see that the motives of
your actions be not hopes of gain or self-interest." . . .

(X) Issa went from one city to another, strengthening by the
word of God the courage of the Israelites, who were near to suc-
cumbing under their weight of woe, and thousands of the people
followed him to hear his teachings. But the chiefs of the cities
were afraid of him and they informed the principal governor,
residing in Jerusalem, that a man called Issa had arrived in the
country, who by his sermons had arrayed the people against the
authorities, and that multitudes, listening assiduously to him,
neglected their labor; and, they added, he said that in a short time
they would be free of their invader rulers. Then Pilate, the Governor of Jerusalem, gave orders that they should lay hold of the
preacher Issa and bring him before the judges. In order, however,
not to excite the anger of the populace, Pilate directed that he
should be judged by the priests and scribes, the Hebrew elders,
in their temple.

Meanwhile, Issa, continuing his preachings, arrived at Jerusalem,
and the people, who already knew his fame, having learned of his
coming, went out to meet him. . . . And Issa said to them: "The
human race perishes, because of the lack of faith; for the darkness
and the tempest have caused the flock to go astray and they have
lost their shepherds. But the tempests do not rage forever and the
darkness will not hide the light eternally. Soon the sky will become serene, the celestial light will again overspread the earth, and
the strayed flock will re-unite around their shepherd." . . .

The priests and the elders who heard him, filled with admiration for his language, asked him if it was true that he had sought
to raise the people against the authorities of the country, as had
been reported to the governor Pilate.

"Can one rise against strayed men, to whom darkness has hidden their road and their door?" answered Issa. "I have but forewarned the unhappy, as I do here in this temple, that they should no longer advance on the dark road, for an abyss opens before their feet." . . .

Then the elders asked him: "Who art thou, and from what country hast thou come to us? We have not formerly heard thee spoken of and do not even know thy name!"

"I am an Israelite," answered Issa, "and on the day of my birth have seen the walls of Jerusalem, and have heard the sobs of my brothers reduced to slavery, and the lamentations of my sisters carried away by the Pagans, and my soul was afflicted when I saw that my brothers had forgotten the true God. When a child I left my father's house to go and settle among other people. But, having heard it said that my brethren suffered even greater miseries now, I have come back to the land of my fathers, to recall my brethren to the faith of their ancestors, which teaches us patience upon earth in order to attain the perfect and supreme bliss above."

Then the wise old men put to him again this question: "We are told that thou disownest the laws of Mossa, and that thou teachest the people to forsake the temple of God."

Whereupon Issa: "One does not demolish that which has been given by our Heavenly Father, and which has been destroyed by sinners. I have but enjoined the people to purify the heart of all stains, for it is the veritable temple of God. As regards the laws of Mossa, I have endeavored to reestablish them in the hearts of men. And I say unto you that ye ignore their true meaning, for it is not vengeance but pardon which they teach. Their sense has been perverted."

(XI) When the priests and the elders heard Issa, they decided among themselves not to give judgment against him, for he had done no harm to any one, and, presenting themselves before Pilate — who was made Governor of Jerusalem by the Pagan king of the country of Romeles — they spoke to him thus: "We have seen the man whom thou chargest with inciting our people to revolt; we have heard his discourses and know that he is our countryman. But the chiefs of the cities have made to you false reports, for he is a just man, who teaches the people the word of God."

The governor thereupon became very angry, and sent his disguised spies to keep watch upon Issa and report to the authorities the least word he addressed to the people.

In the meantime, the holy Issa continued to visit the neighboring cities and preach the true way of the Lord. . . . And all the time great numbers of the people followed him wherever he went, and many did not leave him at all, but attached themselves to him and served him.

And Issa said: "Put not your faith in miracles performed by the hands of men, for He who rules nature is alone capable of doing supernatural things: while man is impotent to arrest the wrath of the winds or cause the rain to fall. One miracle, however, is within the power of man to accomplish. It is when his heart is filled with sincere faith, he resolves to root out from his mind all evil promptings and desires, and when, in order to attain this end, he ceases to walk the path of iniquity. . . . Put not your faith in oracles. God alone knows the future. . . . The secrets of nature are in the hands of God; the whole world, before it was made manifest, existed in the bosom of the divine thought, and has become material and visible by the will of the Most High. When ye pray to Him, become again like little children, for ye know neither the past, nor the present, nor the future, and God is the Lord of Time."

(XII) "Just man," said to him the disguised spies of the Governor of Jerusalem, "tell us if we must continue to do the will of Caesar, or expect our near deliverance?"

And Issa, who recognized the questioners as the apostate spies sent to follow him, replied to them: "I have not told you that you would be delivered from Caesar; it is the soul sunk in error which will gain its deliverance. There cannot be a family without a head, and there cannot be order in a people without a Caesar, whom ye should implicitly obey, as he will be held to answer for his acts before the Supreme Tribunal."

"Does Caesar possess a divine right?" the spies asked him again, "and is he the best of mortals?"

"There is no one 'the best' among human beings; but there are many bad, who — even as the sick need physicians — require the care of those chosen for that mission. . . . Mercy and justice are the high prerogatives of Caesar, and his name will be illustrious if he exercises them. But he who acts otherwise, who transcends the limits of power he has over those under his rule, and even goes so far as to put their lives in danger, offends the great Judge and derogates from his own dignity in the eyes of men."

Upon this, an old woman who had approached the group, to better hear Issa, was pushed aside by one of the disguised men, who placed himself before her.

Then said Issa: "It is not good for a son to push away his mother, that he may occupy the place which belongs to her. Whoso doth not respect his mother — the most sacred being after his God — is unworthy of the name of son. Hearken to what I say to you: Respect woman; for in her we see the mother of the universe, and all the truth of divine creation is to come through her. She is the fount of everything good and beautiful, as she is also the germ of life and death. Upon her man depends in all his existence, for she is his moral and natural support in his labors. In pain and suffering she brings you forth; in the sweat of her brow she watches over your growth; and until her death you cause her greatest anxieties. Bless her and adore her, for she is your only friend and support on earth. Respect her; defend her. In so doing you will gain for yourself her love; you will find favor before God; and for her sake many sins will be remitted to you. Love your wives and respect them, for they will be the mothers of tomorrow and later the grandmothers of a whole nation. Be submissive to the wife; her love ennobles man, softens his hardened heart, tames the wild beast in him and changes it to a lamb. Wife and mother are the priceless treasures which God has given to you. They are the most beautiful ornaments of the universe, and from them will be born all who will inhabit the world. Even as the Lord of Hosts separated the light from the darkness, and the dry land from the waters, so does woman possess the divine gift of calling forth out of man's evil nature all the good that is in him. Therefore I say unto you: after God, to woman must belong your best thoughts, for she is the divine temple where you will most easily obtain perfect happiness. . . . Suffer her not to be humiliated, for by humiliating her you humiliate yourselves, and lose the sentiment of love, without which nothing can exist here on earth. Protect your wife, that she may protect you — you and all your household. All that you do for your mothers, your wives, for a widow, or for any other woman in distress, you will do for your God."

(XIII) Thus Saint Issa taught the people of Israel for three years, in every city and every village, on the highways and in the fields; and all he said came to pass. All this time the disguised spies of the governor Pilate observed him closely, but heard nothing to sustain the accusations formerly made against Issa by the chiefs of the cities. But Saint Issa's growing popularity did not allow Pilate to rest. He feared that Issa would be instrumental in bringing about a revolution culminating in his elevation to the sovereignty, and, therefore, ordered the spies to make charges against him. Then soldiers were sent to arrest him, and they cast him into a subterranean dungeon, where he was subjected to all kinds of tortures, to accuse himself, so that he might be put to death. . . . When the principal priests and wise elders learned of the suffering which their Saint endured, they went to Pilate, begging him to liberate Issa, so that he might attend the great festival which was near at hand. But this the governor refused. Then they asked him that Issa should be brought before the elders' council, so that he might be condemned, or acquitted, before the festival, and to this Pilate agreed.

On the following day the governor assembled the principal chiefs, priests, elders and judges, for the purpose of judging Issa. The Saint was brought from his prison. They made him sit before the governor, between two robbers, who were to be judged at the same time with Issa, so as to show the people he was not the only one to be condemned. And Pilate, addressing himself to Issa, said: "Is it true, Oh, Man! that thou incitest the populace against the authorities, with the purpose of thyself becoming King of Israel?"

Issa replied, "One does not become king by one's own purpose thereto. . . . I have only preached of the King of Heaven, and it was Him whom I told the people to worship." . . .

At this moment the witnesses were introduced, one of whom deposed thus: "Thou hast said to the people that in comparison with the power of the king who would soon liberate the Israelites from the yoke of the heathen, the worldly authorities amounted to nothing."

"Blessings upon thee!" said Issa. "For thou hast spoken the truth! The King of Heaven is greater and more powerful than the laws of man, and His kingdom surpasses the kingdoms of this earth. And the time is not far off, when Israel, obedient to the will of God, will throw off its yoke of sin. For it has been written that a forerunner would appear to announce the deliverance of the people, and that he would re-unite them in one family."

Thereupon the governor said to the judges: "Have you heard this? The Israelite Issa acknowledges the crime of which he is accused. Judge him, then, according to your laws and pass upon him condemnation to death."

"We cannot condemn him," replied the priests and the ancients. "As thou hast heard, he spoke of the King of Heaven, and he has preached nothing which constitutes insubordination against the law."

Thereupon the governor called a witness who had been bribed by his master, Pilate, to betray Issa, and this man said to Issa: "Is it not true that thou hast represented thyself as a King of Israel, when thou didst say that He who reigns in Heaven sent thee to prepare His people?"

But Issa blessed the man and answered: "Thou wilt find mercy, for what thou hast said did not come out from thine own heart." Then, turning to the governor he said: "Why dost thou lower thy dignity and teach thy inferiors to tell falsehood, when, without doing so, it is in thy power to condemn an innocent man?"

When Pilate heard his words, he became greatly enraged and ordered that Issa be condemned to death, and that the two robbers should be declared guiltless.

The judges, after consulting among themselves, said to Pilate: "We cannot consent to take this great sin upon us, to condemn an innocent man and liberate malefactors. It would be against our laws. Act thyself, then, as thou seest fit." Thereupon the priests and elders walked out, and washed their hands in a sacred vessel, and said: "We are innocent of the blood of this righteous man."

(XIV) By order of the governor, the soldiers seized Issa and the two robbers, and led them to the place of execution, where they were nailed upon the crosses erected for them. All day long the bodies of Issa and the two robbers hung upon the crosses, bleeding, guarded by the soldiers. The people stood all around and the relatives of the executed prayed and wept. When the sun went down, Issa's tortures ended. He lost consciousness and his soul disengaged itself from the body, to re-unite with God.

Thus ended the terrestial existence of the reflection of the eternal Spirit under the form of a man who had saved hardened sinners and comforted the afflicted.

Meanwhile, Pilate was afraid for what he had done, and ordered the body of the Saint to be given to his relatives, who put it in a tomb near to the place of execution. Great numbers of persons came to visit the tomb, and the air was filled with their wailings and lamentations. Three days later, the governor sent his soldiers to remove Issa's body and bury it in some other place, for he feared a rebellion among the people. The next day, when the people came to the tomb, they found it open and empty, the body of Issa being gone. Thereupon the rumor spread that the Supreme Judge had sent His angels from Heaven, to remove the mortal remains of the saint in whom part of the divine Spirit had lived on earth. When Pilate learned of this rumor, he grew angry and prohibited, under penalty of death, the naming of Issa, or praying for him to the Lord. But the people, nevertheless, continued to weep over Issa's death and to glorify their master; wherefore, many were carried into captivity, subjected to torture and put to death.

And the disciples of Saint Issa departed from the land of Israel and went in all directions, to the heathen, preaching that they should abandon their gross errors, think of the salvation of their souls and earn the perfect bliss which awaits human beings in the immaterial world, full of glory, where the great Creator abides in all his immaculate and perfect majesty. The heathen, their kings, and their warriors, listened to the preachers, abandoned their erroneous beliefs and forsook their priests and their idols, to celebrate the praises of the most wise Creator of the Universe, the King of Kings, whose heart is filled with infinite mercy.

CHAPTER THIRTEEN

The Aquarian Gospel

Among the many New Testament apocryphal works, the Aquarian Gospel of Jesus the Christ is one of the most remarkable. For while most of the apocryphal gospels are, or claim to be, of great antiquity, this work is of proximate recency both in "revelation" and publication. This gospel, we are told, was revealed to Dr. Levi H. Dowling early in our century. It was first published in Europe and in America in 1908. Since then it has given rise to the sect whose church is known as the Church Universal; not to be confused with the Universalist church.

The title of the gospel is derived from the astrological concept of time, and in this concept we are living in the age of Aquarius and are therefore Aquarians.

The title page of the gospel bears the legend: "Transcribed from the Book of God's Remembrances, known as the Akashic Records." And we are told that since the beginning of time, every sound, every color, every word and every thought that goes out on the ether is registered as if on a sensitized film (called Akasha); and all these recorded sights, sounds, thoughts and words are to be found in the Book of Remembrances, which is the Memory of God.

Dr. Dowling tells us that he prepared himself for forty years and then was able to transcribe and translate from the Akashic Records the life and the lessons of Jesus the Christ. And these constitute the Aquarian Gospel.

The work bears the name of Levi, but no indication is given whether this symbolizes the kinship of Jesus (Luke 3:24) or has reference to one of the teachers of Jesus' childhood.

As lore and as ethics, this strange work compares favorably with any of the extracanonical and apocryphal works of the New Testament. Some of the legendary material drawn from this source will be found in other parts of this book ("The Seventh Birthday," "The

Tools of the Mind," "John and His Teacher, Matheno," and others).
In this chapter are given some of the adventures ascribed to Jesus
during the "hidden years."

1. The Golden Cord

One day Rabbi Barachia of Nazareth came to Mary and said:
"Your son, Jesus, is now twelve years old. Let him come to my
synagogue and study with me."

"It shall be as you say," said Mary.

And one morning, after the service in the synagogue, the rabbi
said to Jesus: "Tell me, my son, which of the Ten Commandments
is the greatest?"

And Jesus replied: "I cannot see any one of them apart from the
others, for I see a golden cord which runs through all the Ten Commandments and binds them into one."

"And what is the name of that cord?" asked Rabbi Barachia.

"Love," said Jesus. "For God is love. If one is full of love, he cannot covet, he cannot kill, he cannot testify falsely, he cannot do anything forbidden by the Ten Commandments."

"Your words are seasoned with the salt of wisdom," said Rabbi
Barachia. "Who is the teacher who opened this door of truth to
you?"

"No one ever has to open the door of truth, for it is never closed,"
said Jesus. "If we open the windows of our minds, truth enters and
makes itself at home."

"And what strong hand can open the windows of our mind?"

"Love is that strong hand," said Jesus.

Then Rabbi Barachia and his pupil discussed the Ten Commandments, each in turn; and the rabbi tried to explain why they were
given to Israel.

That evening, when Mary asked her son about his studies with
Rabbi Barachia, Jesus replied: "The rabbi thinks that God has
favorites among the sons of men and that the Jews are his favorite
children. But I cannot see how God can have favorites and remain
just. Do the flowers grow only on this side of the walls of Jerusalem?
Are the seasons of seeding and reaping only for the Jews? It seems

to me that all God's children are greatly blessed. And when I grow a little older it is my wish to go out into the world and meet with my kin in other lands."

2. Jesus in India

Ravanna of Orissa, Prince of India, was in Jerusalem and in the temple court when Jesus confounded the rabbis and the doctors with his wisdom and his knowledge on so many matters. The prince went to Rabbi Hillel and questioned him concerning the boy; and Hillel the Gentle spoke with admiration of the wonderful youth and of the prophecies concerning him.

"Where does he live and where can I find him?" asked Ravanna.

"He lives with his father, Joseph the Carpenter, and you can find him in Nazareth, which is in Galilee."

The Prince of India went to Galilee with a retinue of men and asked directions to Marmion Way where Joseph's home and carpentry shop stood side by side. For many days the Prince of India remained in Joseph's house, talking to Jesus and his parents. And finally he asked Joseph and Mary to let Jesus return with him to India as his honored guest.

"Let him come with me to my palace in Orissa, and let him enter the temple of Jagannath to study the Vedas and the Laws of Manu from our wise priest, Lamaas Bramas," Ravanna pleaded. "And he, in turn, can teach the wisdom of his people to Lamaas."

Joseph and Mary consented to Ravanna's request. And Jesus left with the prince, crossing the Sind into India.

The priest Lamaas loved the boy Jesus the moment he came into the temple; and Jesus liked Lamaas above all the others in Jagannath. They often walked together in the temple grounds, discoursing on many matters.

Once Lamaas asked the young Jesus: "What is truth?"

"In all the world there are two things: one is truth; the other falsehood. Truth is that which is and changes not; falsehood is that which seems to be, yet never seems the same. Truth abides; falsehood perishes."

"You answer well, my Jewish master," said the graying priest to the young boy. "Now, tell me, what is man?"

"Man," said Jesus, "is truth and falsehood strangely mixed. And they strive in him."

"Man strives to attain power," said Lamaas. "What do you say of power?"

"Power," said Jesus, "is an illusion and nothing more. It is to be seen in the winds of the air and the waves of the sea and the arm of man. It spends itself and is no more. He who understands, understands the difference between power and force which is the Will of God."

"Wherefrom then comes understanding?" asked the priest.

"Understanding is the knowledge which can determine between truth and falsehood."

"How does wisdom differ from understanding?" asked Lamaas.

"Wisdom is the consciousness that God and man are one; that power is but an illusion; that heaven and earth and hell are not above or below, but within; and that God is all."

"Then what of faith?" asked the old man.

"Faith is the bridge that reaches from the heart of man to the heart of God. And that is salvation."

And so they discoursed; Lamaas questioning Jesus to gain from him greater wisdom; and Jesus questioning the priest to learn of the beliefs of the people of Orissa.

3. *Udraka the Healer*

Benares was a city rich in learning and famed for its knowledge of the healing arts. Lamaas took Jesus to Udraka, the greatest of all Hindu healers, that he might learn how to cure the sick.

Udraka taught Jesus and said: "Remember that the laws of nature are the laws of health. The human body might be likened to a harpsichord: When the strings are too lax or too taut, the instrument is out of tune — the man is sick. In nature there are many remedies for all the ills of man; but man's own will power is the greatest medicine of them all. At will a man can make a tense cord become lax, and a lax cord to become taut; and thus he can heal himself."

"How then can one heal another?" asked Jesus.

"The healer is the man who can inspire faith," said Udraka. "The tongue speaks to the ear; but the soul speaks to the soul. There are a thousand different ills; and a thousand different remedies to make men well: but that which may be a medicine for one man may be poison for another. The true healer knows which remedy is good for the particular illness of the particular man who is ill."

And Jesus remained with Udraka until he had learned from him all there was to be learned of the Hindu art of healing.

4. *Parable of the Nobleman and the Unjust Sons*

One day a great multitude of oppressed Sudras (the lowest of the four Hindu castes) came to hear Jesus preach by the river in Katak; and Jesus said to them:

"A certain nobleman, who owned a great estate, had four sons and he wanted them to grow strong by the talents they possessed. He called them together and gave each a share of his great wealth, then bade them leave and prosper.

"But the oldest son was very selfish and also very shrewd. He called his brothers to him one by one. And to the eldest of the three, he said: "I shall be your priest and leader. And you shall be the king of our estate." And he gave his brother a sword and charged him with the task of defending their estate.

"To the second brother he gave the right to graze the flocks upon their lands and to use the soil for crops and grain.

"And to the youngest of them all he had nothing left to give but toil. So he put the youngest brother in chains and commanded him to serve the older brothers as a slave.

"After some time the nobleman came to see his sons and how they fared. And when he saw what had happened, the father seized the priest, tore off his priestly robes, and placed him in a prison until he should atone for all his wrongs; the second son, the puppet king upon the throne in bright armour, he dethroned, broke his sword and flung his crown into the dust; then he called the farmer son to account for failing to rescue the youngest brother from the chains of slavery. Finally the father found the youngest son and with his own hands broke the cruel chains and set him free.

"After the sons had atoned for the wrong they had done, they returned to the father, each to receive an equal share in his estate; and they promised to live thereafter in peace and equality."

When the priests of India learned that Jesus was preaching against their caste system and advocated equality, they came in anger to drive him from their land.

Jesus left Benares at night to escape their wrath; and he did not rest until he reached the city of Kapivastu in the Himalayas, where the Buddhist priests welcomed him to their temples.

5. Jesus and the Buddhist Sage

Barato Arabo was a Buddhist priest who loved young Jesus as soon as he saw him. Jesus taught Barato the Psalms and the Prophets; and Barato taught Jesus the Vedas, the Avesta and the wisdom of Gautama the Buddha.

Arabo asked Jesus one day, "Do you know, my Jewish master, how man will reach a perfect state? Man is the marvel of the universe," he went on to say. "Time was when man did not exist. He was a bit of formless substance in the tides. By the universal law for all things to tend upwards, this substance tended upwards and evolved until it became a worm, then a reptile, then a bird and a beast, and at last it became a man. The time will come when everything in life will evolve to a state of perfect man."

"Barato Arabo, where have you learned all this?" asked Jesus.

"Our priests have taught us this from the time which no one any longer remembers; and that is how we know."

"Enlightened Arabo," said Jesus, "man may believe what others repeat. But thus he never really knows. Do you, yourself, remember when you were an ape, a bird, a reptile or a worm? And if not, what proof have you other than that the priests told you so? Time never was when man was not. For all forms of life on every plane are the thoughts of God that cannot change and cannot perish. In yonder kingdom of the soul this carnal evolution is not known. A beast, a bird, or a creeping thing is never man; and one does not change over from one to the other."

Barata was amazed to hear so young a sage speak with such authority and wisdom against the belief in the transmigration of souls. And all the priests who heard them converse, exclaimed: "This Hebrew prophet is the rising star of wisdom."

6. *Parable of the Rocky Field*

Jesus sat one day in meditation beside a flowing spring. A great multitude of Sudras had gathered there, for it was a Buddhist holiday. Jesus saw the hard lines of toil on every brow; but not a sign of joy in any face.

"Tell me," said Jesus, "why are you all so sad? Have you no happiness in life?"

"We do not know the meaning of that word," said the people. "We toil to live, and can hope for nothing else."

Jesus was moved by pity and love, and he said: "Toil should not make people sad. When there is hope and love in the toil of man, then all of life is filled with joy and peace; for that is heaven."

"We have heard of heaven," said one of the people. "But it is so far away."

"Brother," said Jesus, "you are wrong. Heaven is not far away."

"Then where is heaven?" the people demanded.

And Jesus told them a parable:

"A certain man possessed a rocky field. Even with constant toil upon this hard and poor land he could scarcely provide enough food to keep his family from starvation. One day a miner passing by saw the poor man in the arid field, and he said: 'Do you not know what lies below the surface of this barren field? Dig deep down into the rocky soil and see what you will find.' The poor man dug deep into the earth as he was told; and there he found a vein of pure gold."

Then Jesus explained: "Men toil on rocky soil, doing what their fathers did, not dreaming they can do anything else but toil in poverty. Behold, a miner comes along and tells them of the treasures that are theirs. In man's heart the greatest wealth abounds; if only the people would open their hearts and look for the treasures within. Then toil would no longer make them sad but would turn into joy."

7. Miracle in Leh

After many days and great peril, Jesus reached the temple of Lassa high in the mountains of Tibet. There the great sage Meng-ste welcomed him to the temple and showed him the library of manuscripts rich in ancient lore. Jesus studied the sacred manuscripts and discussed them with Meng-ste. And when he had completed his studies, he left for the city of Leh, in Ladak, to reside in the monastery.

Each day he would come down to the market place where the poor people gathered and he would preach to them.

One day a woman came to him in grief, carrying her son. The child was ill and the doctors had declared that there was no hope of saving him.

"Why do you bring him to me when the healers of your land have despaired?" asked Jesus.

"I have heard that you are a man of God," said the mother. "The healers despair; but I have faith."

Jesus placed his hand on the child's head, and said: "Good woman, your faith has saved your son."

And the child in her arms was well again.

After that the multitudes gathered in the market place of Leh to be healed by the young Hebrew sage, and to quench the thirst in their souls with his words. And when the day arrived for Jesus to leave their city, they grieved as children grieve when their mother is about to leave them.

8. Jesus in the City of Ur

From Lahore Jesus went to Persia; and from Persia he made his way to Assyria; and there he tarried in the city of Ur.

"Behold this land!" Jesus said to the people. "Two thousand years ago our Father Abraham lived in this place and worshiped one God. Then this land was rich and fruitful. Behold it now! The rains do not come as in former days; the vine does not bear; and withered are the figs before they ripen. This land that was once so fruitful has become as a desert. But if you follow good and shun evil, you will see this land of yours again filled with flowers."

Jesus went to visit the ruins of the once proud city of Babylon. He passed through the empty streets where the sons of Judah had been kept in captivity; and he walked along the banks of the river where the Levites had hung their harps upon the willows and refused to sing.

And Jesus said: "Behold the works of man! The King of Babylon destroyed the temple of the Lord and took his people captive in chains. Now see how the sun has gone down on Babylon! The songs in her streets have been hushed; and every unclean bird and creeping thing is at home in these ruins. Gaze upon the temple of Belus! Upon that altar of Baal beasts and birds and the children of men were sacrificed with great pomp. Now the gory priests are dead, and the place is desolate."

Then Jesus went his way, and after many days he reached his native land.

Jesus was thirteen years old when he left his home; and he was twenty-six years old when he returned to Nazareth.

He told his mother of all his days in the East, of the lessons he had learned and the works he had accomplished. And after six weeks at home, Jesus left again, this time going first to Greece and then to Egypt.

9. The Seven Degrees

Twenty-five years after Jesus had returned from Egypt to Nazareth with his parents, he came back again to that land. And he went to the city of Zoan and to the sages Elihu and Shalom.

"Why have you come back to Egypt and what wisdom can you gather in our halls?" they asked.

"I have come to enter the brotherhood in the temple of Heliopolis that I may learn of the heaviest sorrows, the deepest disappointments, and the direst temptations my brother may know, so that I may be able to help him in his need."

Jesus left for Heliopolis to take the secret vow. He was bathed in the fountain of the brotherhood and dressed in their garb. And the high priest of the temple gave Jesus the mystic name of *Circle-Seven-Logos,* to be his as long as he remained with them.

"The circle is the symbol of the perfect man; and seven is the perfect number; and logos is the perfect word that has the power to create and to destroy and to save," the high priest explained. "Now, go until you have explored the soul of man. Then return to me."

Jesus was led away into a chamber filled with a light like that of early dawn, the walls covered with mystic signs and sacred texts. There Jesus was left alone for many days.

One night, late past midnight, a secret door opened and a man in priest's garb entered. He wakened Jesus, and said: "Forgive me for coming at this unseemly hour. But I have come to save your life. The temple priests of Heliopolis are jealous of your wisdom and your fame, and they have devised this cruel plot to imprison you. If you wish to free yourself, follow my advice."

"And what is your advice?" asked Jesus.

"First you must make these jealous priests believe that you want to stay here all your life. After you have convinced them, I shall come and show you the secret passage that leads out of this prison."

And Jesus said: "Brother, I have not come here to learn deceit. And I shall not break my vow to the priests."

The tempter disappeared and Jesus was left alone. The next morning a white-robed priest led Jesus before a tribunal of the secret brotherhood. Not a word was spoken. But the high priest gave Jesus a scroll on which a single word was inscribed: SINCERITY.

And that was the first degree gained by Jesus.

After the first test Jesus was tried again and again until he had won the degrees of Justice, Faith, Philanthropy, Heroism and Love Divine.

After the six tests, Jesus appeared before the tribunal of the brotherhood on the day when the Children of Israel celebrated the Passover Feast. And the chief priest of the mystic order placed a diadem upon Jesus' brow: the diadem of the Seventh Degree.

And suddenly the bells of the temple began to ring of their own accord, while a dove, whiter than snow, descended from above and came to rest on Jesus' head.

Then a voice shook the temple walls, announcing the Seventh Degree: *This is the Christ!*

And all the living things on earth, man and beast, responded: "Amen!"

CHAPTER FOURTEEN

The Letter of Benan

In 1910 there appeared in Germany a work in five small volumes, edited by a fiction-writer Ernest Adler von der Planitz. Two of these volumes were devoted to a document presumably translated from the Coptic and the Greek, and the remaining three volumes were given to notes and editorial evaluations. The original documents and their translation into German were explained by von der Planitz in the following manner:

Fifty years earlier, in 1860, a certain scholar named Baron von Rabenau traveled through Egypt, and in a village on the ancient site of Memphis he met a merchant who owned a number of fifth-century Coptic papyri and other ancient fragments which, he claimed, were found in a tomb at Sakkara. Rabenau examined and acquired some of these documents, which were Coptic translations from the Greek in which they were presumably written in the year 83 A.D.

For fourteen years Rabenau labored on the translation of these documents without completing the task. In 1877 Rabenau met Ernest von der Planitz, then twenty years old, and interested him in the work he was doing. When Baron von Rabenau died two years later, von der Planitz continued the task alone for over thirty years, adding three parts of interpretation and comment to every two parts of text. Finally he published the work under the title: Der Benanbrief (*The Letter of Benan*).

When it was first published, Der Benanbrief *created a stir in theological circles and became the subject of a number of unfavorable critical estimates; for most of the critics were primarily concerned with the authenticity of the documents rather than their value as lore. The most learned of these criticisms appeared in 1921 under the title:* Der Benanbrief: Eine Moderne Leben-Jesu-Fälschung des Herrn Ernest Adler von der Planitz (A Modern Life-of-Jesus-Falsification), *by Dr. Carl Schmidt, Berlin University Pro-*

fessor of Theology and a noted authority on Coptic documents. Dr. Schmidt questioned the existence of Coptic and Greek documents such as von der Planitz described in his work and yet would not show to anyone; and even suggested that Baron von Rabenau and his experiences as described in Der Benanbrief *were more likely a fiction only remotely based on a fact.*

Whatever the critics may have proved about the authenticity of the original documents and whether, in fact, they ever existed, the legends in The Letter of Benan *are nevertheless an ingenious presentation, in the best folk manner, of the "hidden years" in the life of Jesus.*

The so-called letter, obviously a fictional device, is presented in traditional biblical form as to chapters and verses and numbered paragraphs, and is divided into two parts. The first part deals with the childhood and youth of Jesus, as related in a letter by the Egyptian physician and priest, Benan of Memphis, to his friend Straton (Strato) in Rhodes. The second part is given to Benan's travels through Italy, Gaul and Judea after the Resurrection of Jesus, his meeting with the Apostles John and James, his visit to Paul in prison, and his other adventures and wonderful experiences.

The following legends are based on Dr. Schmidt's summation of von der Planitz's work as contained in the first part of Der Benanbrief.

1. Jesus in Ranebchru's House

Soon after the whole of Egypt had become a Roman province, and the rule of the thirteen Ptolemies was at an end, there lived in Heliopolis a far-famed astronomer named Putiphra. There the wise man studied the heavens and practiced the art of forecasting by the stars.

One night, as Putiphra observed the stars in the evening skies to foretell the rise of the Nile and the crops of the coming year, there suddenly appeared a blue-white star, twenty times brighter than the sun; and it moved in the heavens until it came to rest directly over the land of the Hebrews. Putiphra at once named the new star *Siriu,* meaning "the scorching one"; and he dispatched the high

priest Ranebchru to the land of the Hebrews to learn the meaning of
the appearance of the new star.

Ranebchru traveled from Heliopolis to Bethlehem and there he
was told of a child born in a cave the very moment Siriu appeared
in the heavens.

"This child will surely grow up to greatness," said the Egyptian
high priest. And he went to the parents of the child, who were
very poor, to ask for permission to take their infant to Heliopolis.

"If you leave him in my care I shall rear him as if he were my
own son," said Ranebchru, "and he will be raised under the tutelage
of the great astronomer Putiphra."

"Would you promise us not to neglect his study of the Law and
the Prophets while he studies in Heliopolis?" asked the parents.

Ranebchru promised; and he returned with the child to his home
in Egypt. There the high priest cared for Jesus as if he were his own
son; and Putiphra taught the child all he knew of astronomy, divina-
tion, the meaning of numbers, and many other sciences. And Pinehas,
rabbi of the Jewish temple in nearby Onian, taught the boy the Law
and the Prophets and the lore.

For twelve years Jesus remained in the house of Ranebchru, and
he grew in knowledge and in wisdom. Then his beloved teacher
Putiphra died. And Jesus returned to his parents in Nazareth for
consolation.

He arrived just before the Feast of the Passover, and together with
his parents and their kin Jesus went up to Jerusalem to celebrate the
holiday. At that time there were gathered in the temple all the
learned doctors and rabbis, scribes and Pharisees, who discussed
the Law in all its interpretations. Jesus arose before them and
astounded them all with his great knowledge and his greater wisdom.

2. *The Physician of Anu*

Jesus soon returned to Anu-Heliopolis, the great seat of learning
in Egypt. There he met a boy named Benan, the son of a priest of
Memphis, who was studying the art of healing. Jesus resolved to
study medicine, and the two boys established a friendship that lasted
for many years. They went to the academies together, where Jesus

astonished his teachers and the people with his healing skill and wondrous cures.

During this time Jesus heard of a sect that rejected slavery and the sacrifice of living things. They ate no meat and drank no wine. And all they possessed, they owned in common; so that the rich man in their midst enjoyed no more than he who had nothing at all. All who ate worked, and worked willingly; and none was the servant of the other. Jesus went among them to heal their sick and there he learned of the Essene way of life.

Among the Essenes Jesus heard of another sect called the Healers. They devoted their lives to minister to the sick and the needy. This sect attracted many learned sons of Israel who dwelled in Egypt, and among them Jesus met Philo, whom he had known before only through his works of philosophy. Philo had heard of the youth, already known throughout Egypt as the Physician of Anu, who performed perplexing cures. Jesus and Philo spent many hours together, and Philo conveyed his distress for his people, accused by Apion the Greek before the willing listener Caius the Roman; and he wondered wherefrom the salvation of the people might come.

Then one day, when Jesus was twenty-six years old, Rabbi Pinehas summoned the Physician of Anu to Onias, and from his deathbed he said:

"My son, your fame as healer and teacher is known throughout Egypt. There are many healers in Egypt, but few in Judea. Promise me that you will return home to our people, for they are in need of you."

Jesus promised. And after Pinehas died, Jesus took leave of his many friends and admirers and returned to Nazareth.

Benan, now a physician, and Saites, also a young physician, and many others, amongst them Asartis, a young girl, all waited to hear from the Physician of Anu and hoped that he would return to them. But the weeks lengthened into months, and the months into years, and there was no word from Jesus.

When three years had passed, Asartis said to Benan: "Go you to Judea and find out what has happened to our friend. For it is three long years since Jesus left us, and we have had no word of him."

Benan and his friend Saites together traveled to the land of the

Hebrews, to the city of Jerusalem, and there they asked: "Pray can you tell us anything about the Physician of Anu?"

"We have never heard of the Physician of Anu," the people responded.

"Have you heard of Jesus the Healer?" they tried again.

"Do you mean Jesus of Nazareth whom people called the Messiah?"

"That must be he," said Benan and Saites.

"He was crucified only a few days ago on the Hill of Skulls with two others," they replied. "The Jews feared him because he called himself the Deliverer; and the Romans feared him because he was called the King of the Jews. So they crucified him."

Benan and Saites hurried to Golgotha in anguish. The place was deserted and the three crosses on top of the hill were all empty.

Benan and Saites returned sorrowfully to the city and began to ask many questions. Slowly they pieced together the many answers until they had learned what had happened to their friend, the Physician of Anu, from the day he returned from Egypt, three years earlier, to the day of the Crucifixion.

The Letter of Benan *goes on to tell, in the first person, how Benan witnessed the Resurrection; and how he brought back the news to Ranebchru in Egypt; and how Asartis died of grief when told of the trial and crucifixion of the beloved Physician of Anu.*

PART V
The Great Teacher

In the first three centuries of our era the church fathers
vied with each other in the effort to extol and sanctify, to
laud and magnify, to bless and exalt and honor each deed,
and each word of their Master. The result is a procession
of legends that have stirred every creative mind in Chris-
tendom, and compare favorably with the best religious
legends of the world. But when these are placed side by
side with the canonical Parables and Sayings of Jesus, how
utterly wanting they appear.

CHAPTER FIFTEEN

They Who Saw Jesus

1. The Death of a Priest

Long, long ago, when the temple of Jerusalem was first established and the priesthood selected to minister in it, the people appointed a College of Twenty-two Kohanim, one for each letter in the Hebrew alphabet. The twenty-two priests were given the power to keep their number forever intact. When one of them died, it was the duty of the others to select a successor and ordain him.

And it came to pass that when Jesus had attained the age of thirty and his name had become known throughout Judea for his knowledge of the Law and the Prophets, one of the twenty-two priests in the temple of Jerusalem passed away.

The College of Kohanim, dressed in their priestly garb, assembled to elect a successor after the customary days of mourning.

They took their seats in the order of their age. Each member had the right to name one candidate, whom he held to be most worthy to fill the office of the departed priest. And each candidate proposed was then examined according to the law.

They inquired into the candidate's antecedents; they asked whether he was old enough to hold this office; whether he was single or married; whether he earned his living by one of the forbidden trades; whether he was whole in body and without blemish; and they inquired into his daily habits, and whether he was pure in speech and eminent among his fellow men.

Twenty candidates were presented. Twenty candidates were examined. Twenty candidates were rejected. For none could meet all the rigid requirements for this high and honorable appointment.

The priests made their nominations in the order of their age, and the last to arise to present a name was the youngest of the Kohanim who said:

"Behold, many have been proposed by you and found unfit for this office in the priesthood. But I will tell you of a man who is worthy to be set in the place of the dead, and I think you will all agree with my choice."

The priests looked at each other in surprise, wondering who the man could be, and they said in one voice:

"Speak on, good man, for we are listening!"

"My choice is Jesus the Carpenter, son of Joseph the Carpenter. He is young in years, but within the age required by the Law. There is not another man in Judea his equal in learning and not another more worthy of this office. All of you who dwell in Jerusalem know of him, so that I need add nothing more to my nomination of Jesus the Carpenter, who dwells in Nazareth in Galilee."

Thereupon he sat down.

The others nodded their heads and looked at each other and, each in his own mind, wondered: "Why did not I think of Jesus?"

The questioning followed, and Jesus was found worthy in every respect.

After his ordination, Jesus ministered with the priests in the temple. And wherever he went he was given the Holy Scrolls in the synagogues so that he could read the Scriptures and interpret them.

And from that day forth they called Jesus Rabbi, wherever Hebrew was spoken; but in Galilee, where they spoke Aramaic, they called him Rabboni.

2. Rumors from Along the Jordan

Everywhere in Galilee there was talk of the coming of the Messiah, and the signs of his coming.

"Before the Messiah comes," said some, "the sea will rise fifty cubits above the height of a mountain and remain standing like a wall of stone. Then the sea will sink so low that the great fish, the whale-sharks and the leviathan, will appear on dry land and cry out to God."

"When the Messiah comes," old men told their grandchildren, "the stars shall fall down. A new heaven and a new earth shall appear, and all the dead shall be resurrected."

Scarcely a day went by in Judea without a rumor of war or rebellion, or the outbreak of a riot. Every day brought bloodshed caused by the Roman oppressor. And with the increase of their suffering the people dwelt on the hope of the coming of the Messiah who would bring deliverance from the yoke of tyrants, and who would establish a kingdom of justice, righteousness and peace.

In the fading light of the day, between the sunset and the evening prayers, men sick from the cruelty of the Romans opened their books of hope and deliverance, and read:

"I see Jerusalem rebuilt with sapphires and emeralds and other precious stones; the walls and the towers and battlements made of pure gold. And the streets of Jerusalem shall be paved with beryl and carbuncle and the stones of Ophir. And all her streets shall sing: Halleluiah!"

"In the days of the Messiah," people said, "a grain of wheat seed will produce ten thousand ears, each ear ten thousand grains, and each grain will yield ten pounds of clear, fine flour. And all the fruit trees of the entire earth will produce in like proportion. The animals feeding on the fruits of the earth will all grow peaceful, so that the wolf shall dwell with the lamb, and the leopard lie down with the kid."

They read Tobit and they read from those new and strange books of Esdras and the Book of Baruch, and the Book of Enoch, and the Book of Jubilees, and the Assumption of Moses, and all those other books that foretold the coming of their deliverance.

They repeated to each other the rumors that reached them from along the Jordan near the Dead Sea. There, at the very spot where Elijah the Prophet had crossed the river to ascend to heaven, among a sect variously called the Fearers of Sin, the Righteous, the Chaste, or the Healers (and whom the Talmud called the early saints), there had arisen one among them whose name was John, and he announced that the day of the coming of the Messiah, the Savior, was near at hand; and he exhorted the people to be baptized by him and prepare for the day.

Many young men left Galilee secretly to find out whether there was any truth in the rumors. Some never returned. And those who did return testified that there was no extravagance in the rumors.

Along the Jordan, near the Dead Sea, they reported, there dwelt a sect unlike any in Judea, who were called the Righteous. They ate little, and only that which they produced with their own hands. Their clothes were few and simple. Buying and selling was barred amongst them as a harmful occupation. There were no slaves among them; nor were any of them slaves to others. What they possessed belonged to them all equally, but they had no gold or silver among their possessions. No member of the sect ever took an oath, but their "yea" was "yea" and their "nay" was "nay," and as sacred as an oath. Most of the members of the sect were men, and all their members were unmarried. That their sect might not disappear, they adopted orphans to raise in their communities. They worked honestly from sunup to sunset, dividing their time between prayer and labor. Twice each day they bathed, holding the purity of the body next to the purity of the soul. Twice each day they ate their simple meal. They drank no wine, they used no ointments, and they did not permit a razor to touch their faces. Some refrained from eating meat or anything that came from a living being. And all awaited the coming of the Messiah.

The people listened to the reports in rapture. "Yes," they said, "and what of the man, John, who calls himself the Messenger?"

"They are despisers of wealth, and there is but one patrimony among all of them," the travelers continued. "They temper their passions as they temper their anger; and they speak always in low and calm voices. They are dedicated as much to the hatred of evil as to the love of the righteous. They have a greater affection for one another than anywhere else in Israel; and their habits are the habits of children who fear only their Master."

"Yes, yes," said the people impatiently, "but what of John who is called the Baptist?"

3. The Story of John the Baptist

Mary's father, Joachim, had a brother named Zacharias; and Mary's mother, Anna, had a cousin named Elizabeth. And these two were married. But they were not blessed with children.

Zacharias, who was a priest in the temple of Jerusalem, prayed one day: "O God, my bones have become feeble and my hair is white with age, but I have no son to succeed me, a son who would observe your commandments and be worthy in your eyes."

And an angel spoke to Zacharias, saying: "Grieve no more, for you shall have a son. You shall name him John, and he will grow up to be a prophet in Israel."

Zacharias said: "Lord, how can that be, since my wife and I are so very old?"

And the angel said: "The Lord can do that which pleases him. Nor shall your son be conceived as the other children of men. But by the chaste kisses that you will imprint upon the lips of Elizabeth your wife your son John shall be conceived."

"O Lord," Zacharias pleaded, "give me a sign that I shall really have a son!"

"The sign shall be given to you," said the angel. "From this hour until the hour your son is named, you shall be able to speak in signs only."

Zacharias opened his mouth to speak, but no sound came forth.

And, as the angel had foretold, Elizabeth gave birth to a son.

On the day of circumcision the guests arrived and Elizabeth told them she would name the child John.

"But there are none among our kin called by that name," her kindred protested. They turned to Zacharias, asking how he wanted his son named. And he wrote in answer: "His name is John."

And at that moment Zacharias's tongue was loosened, and he sang out:

"Blessed is the God of Israel, for he has visited us!"

And the guests whispered to each other: "What manner of child shall this be?"

4. *The Murder of John's Father*

When Herod issued the decree that all infants in Judea two years and under should be killed, the king's men came to Jutta and to the house of Zacharias and Elizabeth, seeking the infant John. But they found no one at home. For Zacharias had taken his son to the temple in Jerusalem and to the altar of God, and there he laid his hands upon the child and bestowed upon him the priesthood. Then

Elizabeth took the child and hastened into the hills to seek a safe hiding place.

But she could find no shield nor shelter anywhere, and she cried out: "O Dweller on High, give refuge to a mother and a child unjustly pursued by a tyrant king, as you gave refuge to the Prophet Isaiah in a cedar tree, when he was pursued!"

As she prayed the Archangel Uriel appeared beside her and commanded the hill upon which they stood to open, and the hill opened like a gate to let Elizabeth and her son enter. Then the hill closed again; and they dwelt within, nourished by a fountain and bread brought to them by angels.

Herod's men sought everywhere for John and could not find him. Finally they went to Zacharias in the temple and asked: "Where have you hidden your son?"

"I am a servant of God," said the high priest, "and I spend all my days beside the altar of the Lord. Therefore I do not know where my son is who dwells with his mother in the hill country."

The men reported Zacharias's answer to Herod, and the king said in rage: "Does Zacharias expect his son to grow up to reign over Israel? Tell him that if he does not show you where his son is hidden, his blood shall be upon his own hands."

When the king's men gave Zacharias the message from Herod, he answered calmly: "The Lord is my witness that my blood is innocent, and it shall be upon the hands of him who spills it."

Herod ordered his guard to go to the temple at dawn, when there would be none to prevent them, and to kill Zacharias wherever they found him.

The next morning, at the hour of the burnt-offering of propitiation, the priests arrived in the temple and waited for Zacharias to appear, to bless them and to lead them in prayer. But Zacharias did not come.

They waited for a long time; and the later it became, the greater became their fear. Finally one of them ventured into the inner chamber, and there, between the steps and the altar, he found Zacharias dead, his head lying in a pool of blood. And he heard a voice saying:

"Zacharias has been murdered and his innocent blood shall not disappear until the avenger appears."

The priest rent his clothes and went out to tell the others what his eyes had seen and his ears had heard. But when the other priests entered the chamber of the altar, the body of Zacharias had vanished, and his blood upon the steps had become hard like stone and could not be wiped away.

At the end of the days of mourning for Zacharias, lots were cast for the one to take his place. And the lot fell to an old man, named Simeon. They blessed Simeon and prayed that he should not taste of death until his eyes had seen the Messiah in the flesh.

In the legend of the Murder of Zacharias appears the very ancient belief that the blood of an innocent man cannot be wiped away until it has been avenged. An earlier legend of this nature is told about another Zacharias who lived in the days of the Babylonian Captivity, several centuries earlier, when Nebuchadnezzar's men pillaged the temple of Jerusalem and found one of the stones seething with the blood of a murdered priest.

5. John and His Teacher Matheno

In the hill country, where Elizabeth and her son were hiding, there lived a man in the cave of David whom everyone called the Hermit of Engedi. He was none other than the wise man Matheno who had come from the temple of Sakara to dwell in the desert and to meditate in solitude.

When John was seven years old, Elizabeth took him to the cave of David and said to the Hermit of Engedi:

"You are wise, Master Matheno, and you are learned. Will you take my fatherless boy and teach him knowledge and wisdom so that he will not grow up ignorant and without understanding?"

Matheno questioned the boy and John found favor in the hermit's eyes.

"It shall be as you say," said Matheno. "Leave your son with me, and I shall teach him whatever little I know."

And from that day forth John dwelt with the Hermit of Engedi. They lived on wild fruit and nuts, and on the wild honey and carob pods that were abundant in the desert. Their clothes were few. And the cave was their dwelling place. And all their waking hours they spent in study.

Elizabeth came to visit her son from time to time; and each time he seemed to have grown in stature and in wisdom. And John told his mother of his love for the wise and gentle hermit.

Matheno did not teach John out of books. John would ask questions and Matheno would answer them. The teacher would demonstrate his answers with legends and parables.

"What is sin?" John would ask.

And Matheno would reply: "Sin is the rushing forth of men into the fens of wickedness."

"Can sin be wiped out by sacrifices?" asked John.

"No," said Matheno, "sin cannot be blotted out with the blood of sacrifices of doves or lambs."

"How does one obtain forgiveness?" asked John.

"When the sinner pays the debt," the teacher replied. "No man can be forgiven by vicarious sacrifices. Nor can one man forgive or be forgiven for another."

"Can a man forgive himself?" asked John.

And Matheno would patiently explain the ways of true repentance which alone lead to forgiveness. "My son, remember that there is nothing greater than repentance. For repentance makes the coming of the Messiah nearer. The gates of prayer are sometimes open and sometimes closed, but the gates of repentance are ever open."

Another day Matheno taught his young pupil the golden rule. And that, said Matheno, was: "Do not do unto others what you do not want others to do to you."

On another occasion, Matheno explained to his young pupil why no strength is ever gained in idleness.

"Do not say, 'I did not seek, yet I found'; nor should you say, 'I sought but I did not find,'" said Matheno. "For they are not true. Say instead, 'I sought and I found.' For that is the truth."

In that way their days passed, the pupil asking good questions, and the teacher giving wise answers. And John grew in knowledge and in wisdom.

After John had been with Matheno for five years, Elizabeth died. Though John was twelve years old, and wise beyond his years, he wept and grieved for his mother like a small child who could not be comforted. Matheno put his arm around John's shoulders, and said:

"It is not well to weep because of death. For death is not the enemy of man; it is a friend who, when the work of life is done, cuts the cord that binds the human boat to earth, that it may sail away on smoother seas."

And after Elizabeth had been buried by her kin near Hebron, Matheno said to his pupil:

"There are no words that can describe a mother's worth; and your mother was tried and true. But she was not called away before her tasks were done. It is but selfishness that makes us wish to call again to earth those who have departed."

When time had healed John's wound and consoled him for his loss, Matheno said to him: "John, you must now prepare yourself. For you have a mission."

"What is my mission?" John asked.

"You have been called the harbinger, for you shall announce the coming of the Messiah."

"How shall I prepare myself?" asked John.

"There is but one way: Prepare yourself in your heart. Be pure in thought, in word, and in deed. The razor must not touch your face; nor shall wine enter your mouth. And when the time comes, you will point the way to the Messiah."

"How am I to point the way?"

"The man who stands at the crossroads and points the way, but does not himself go that way, is no better than a block of wood that can serve same purpose. The teacher must leave his footprints along the right path, so that those who come along in search of the road can see them and say: 'The Master went that way, and there we shall follow.'"

"And when they come to me what shall I do?" asked John.

"You must teach them how to purify their souls. And you must teach them by example. Wash your body before them, so that they may do the same. And as they cleanse their bodies, so shall they learn to cleanse their souls also."

"When shall I do that?" asked John.

"Now," said Matheno.

They went down together to the Jordan, east of Jericho, and there the hermit explained the inner meaning of the rite of baptism.

John remained with his teacher Matheno for a long time. Altogether he spent eighteen years with Matheno in the wilderness. And during that time John learned to conquer himself and to be the master of his mind as well as his desires.

Then he went down to the Jordan to carry out his mission as the Messenger of the Deliverer.

(There are other versions of John's life before he began his mission. *The Book of the Bee* states that "John the Baptist lived thirty years in the desert with the wild beasts; and after thirty years he came from the wilderness to the habitations of men. From the day when his father made him flee to the desert, when he was a child, until he came back, he covered himself with the same clothes both summer and winter, without changing his ascetic way of life. And he preached in the wilderness of Judea, saying, 'Repent, the kingdom of God draweth nigh'; and he baptized them with the baptism of repentance for the remission of their sins.")

6. *When Jesus Was Baptized*

One day Mary said to Jesus and his brothers: "I hear that John the Baptist, son of Zacharias and Elizabeth, baptizes for the forgiveness of sin. Let us all go that we, too, may be baptized by him."

Jesus replied: "What are my sins that I should be baptized of him, unless, perhaps, these very words which I now speak are my sin of ignorance?"

And he would not go down with them to the territory of Benjamin where John baptized multitudes in the Jordan, not far from the Dead Sea.

Instead, Jesus went to the city of Nain, and arrived there when the city was deep in sorrow. The Governor of Nain had died many years before and left an only son, still a child in his mother's arms. But the governor was of a noble and beloved family, and no one dared take his place. The people were ruled by the widow until the son could grow up. But when the youth was twenty-two years old and ready to assume the duties of the governor, he was afflicted by a strange ailment, and the physicians were unable to heal him. He died, and the people were carrying the bier through the gates of the city to the graveyard.

Jesus approached the mourners and said: "Put down the bier upon the ground."

Then Jesus took the dead man's hand and commanded: "Young man, arise! For you are only asleep; and now you must wake again!"

Straightaway the governor's son rose from his bier before the multitude of mourners, whose sorrow had turned into gladness.

Certain people who had witnessed what Jesus had done in Nain went down to John at the Jordan River and told him of what their eyes had seen. John then sent two of his thirty disciples to Jesus, asking: "Are you he for whom we are waiting; or must we look for another?"

And Jesus replied: "Go, and tell John everything you have heard and seen in this place. This is my answer." And he would say no more.

But the next time Mary spoke to her son about going down to be baptized in the Jordan, Jesus went with her and his brothers.

John could see with the eye of the spirit that Jesus was coming. And John waited, dressed in his cloak of camel's hair, girdled with a leathern girdle, and surrounded by his thirty disciples. Soon there appeared over the horizon a light like the light of a star; and it came from the shining face of Jesus as he approached. And soon the eyes of men were unable to look upon the splendor as Jesus drew nigh.

John said: "Rabboni, all of creation seeks your forgiveness and pleads for your mercy, how is it then that you should ask baptism from me?"

And Jesus replied: "For this I have been sent; and for this I have come."

Jesus undressed and an angel took his garments and held them for him in a cloud overhead. Then Jesus entered the waters of the Jordan. John stood on a rock in the water and placed his hand on the head of Jesus, ready to immerse him. At that moment the heavens opened and the Divine Splendor, in the form of a white dove, came down and rested on Jesus' shoulder. Then John took a shell and three times poured water over the head of Jesus.

And the waters of the earth, which had become polluted by the deluge in the days of Noah, were in that moment cleansed by the baptism of Jesus. And the Daughter of the Voice of Heaven was heard throughout the world, saying:

"Thou art my beloved son in whom I shall be blessed!"

7. Behold, the Man!

The people who were gathered at the Jordan when Jesus was baptized saw him as he emerged from the waters.

He was tall, seven spans high; and his wavy hair that had never been touched by shears was of the color of wine, golden at the root, and glossy, parted in the middle of the head after the manner of the Nazarites, and curled at the ends. His forehead was even and serene, and his face was without blemish, beautiful with the slight blush of the fair skin browned in the sun. His nose and mouth were without fault. His reddish beard was not long but abundant; and like the hair of his head, it was forked. His brown eyes were bright and sparkling, and reflected the moods of one who had often been in tears but never seen in laughter. And when he raised his hands, adding to the loftiness of his stature, the people saw that they were beautiful to look upon.

The lore has diverse descriptions of Jesus, particularly as to the color of his hair; and states that though two people may have looked at him at the same time, each saw him quite differently.

Strangely enough, there is a very early tradition that in his person Jesus was "little, ill-favored, ignoble." Clement of Alexandria, one of the early church fathers, assures us that "his form was without eminence, yea, deficient in comparison with the ordinary form of men."

There is one very ancient tradition that Jesus was a leper. And there are several others which make him appear without distinction, even homely, apparently to fulfill the statement in Isaiah about the appearance of the Messiah, "his visage was so marred, more than any man; and his form more than the sons of men."

8. *Two Heads on a Silver Charger*

Herod the Tyrant was told about John who ministered at the Jordan and baptized his followers saying: "The hour of deliverance is at hand!" And the tyrant's heart was uneasy.

One day word was brought to Herod that John had spoken harshly of the king's marriage to his brother Philip's wife, Polia, who called herself Herodias. The Baptist had proclaimed the marriage unlawful and called Herod and Herodias adulterers.

Herod caused him to be apprehended and when John was brought before him, he asked: "Are you John the son of Zacharias?"

"I am John, the son of Zacharias whom your father murdered in the temple of God. And you are Herod, the lawless, son of Herod the Idumean, who multiplies sin in Israel."

"What sin do you speak of?" asked Herod, seeing that this man was fearless of temporal powers.

"The sin you know of in your heart. For you have caused your brother's wife to commit adultery with you in defiance of God's law."

Herod feared to harm the Baptist because of his great following, and desired to let him go. But the wicked Polia demanded that he should be imprisoned in the dungeon of the fortress in Macheraus, near the Dead Sea. And she ordered that he be flogged there and tortured, so that he might repent his words against her and Herod.

But John suffered the torture and did not repent his words. Great multitudes of John's followers camped before the fortress, imploring Herod to let their leader go. But Herod stopped his ears and closed his heart to their pleas.

In the spring of that year, on his birthday, Herod gave a great feast for his nobles, and asked the beautiful Boziya, daughter of Herodias by a former marriage, to dance before him and his guests. And when she had pleased him with her dance, Herod said:

"Ask of me whatever you desire, Boziya, and it shall be given you."

"Whatever I desire?" asked the cunning Boziya.

"I swear it to you before all those assembled here," said Herod.

Boziya went to her mother's side and said: "You have heard Herod's promise. What shall I ask?"

"Ask for the head of John the Baptist," answered the wicked woman.

And Boziya said to the king: "You have promised on oath to give me whatever my heart desires. And my heart desires the head of John the Baptist on a silver charger."

Herod feared to do this. But Boziya kept him to his oath, and he fulfilled her desire.

When the daughter of Herodias received the head of John the Baptist on a silver charger, she carried it to her mother. Then she ran out to exult on the ice pond which was contrived for her to dance upon. But as she reached the center of the pond, the ice opened beneath her and she sank into the water up to her neck. And no one was able to deliver her.

Herod ordered that they should bring the sword with which John's head had been cut off and with it cut off Boziya's head also. And they placed her head on a silver charger and carried it also to Herodias, her mother.

The queen looked upon the two heads, and she instantly became blind. She touched John's head, hoping to be cured thereby, but her hand withered like a dry leaf in a hot flame. She wanted to cry out, but her tongue cleaved to her palate. Then Satan entered into her, and they bound her with fetters to restrain her in her madness. And she spent the rest of her days in darkness and misery.

CHAPTER SIXTEEN

The Wonderful Healer

1. Where There Is Faith

Word was brought to Mary from her half-sister Mary-Salome, that her only son, John, was to be married. And she and her husband, Zebedee, urgently invited Mary and Jesus and his brothers and his disciples to come to the wedding feast in Cana.

When they reached Cana, which was less than two parasangs distance from Nazareth, Zebedee, father of the groom, came to greet them and said to Jesus:

"Rabboni, come and sit at the head of the table, for you are our most honored guest."

But Jesus said: "He who exalts himself shall be abased; and he who humbles himself shall be exalted." And he took a seat at the table set for those who waited upon the guests.

The guests ate and drank and made merry. But in the midst of the festivities, Zebedee and his wife called Mary aside in great distress, and whispered: "Mary, our sister, what shall we do? For the wine has failed us, and we have no more to serve our guests. Great is the shame that has befallen us; and greater still because your son Jesus, of whose presence we are unworthy, is with us."

"Grieve not," said Mary.

Mary approached Jesus where he was reclining and said to him: "My son, my beloved son, whom my soul desires!"

And Jesus asked: "What do you wish, my mother?"

"There is distress in the house, for the wine has run out."

"My time has not yet come," said Jesus.

But Mary turned to those who were serving the guests, and she said to them, pointing to Jesus: "Do whatsoever he tells you to do."

Nearby there stood six large water pots made of stone, from which the wedding guests drew water to wash their hands, according to the Laws and the custom. And Jesus said to those who were serving: "Fill those water pots with water."

They hastened to do as they were told and filled each pot with three firkins of water.

Jesus then said: "Now serve this wine to the master of the feast first, and then serve it to the others."

The cup of the master of the feast was filled. He tasted it and said: "Never have I been to such a wedding before, where the wine is served as they do here!"

"What do you mean?" asked the bridegroom.

"I have always seen the best wine served at the beginning of the feast, but here it is given us at the end."

Then all the people drank of the wine from the water pots, and they all agreed with the master of the feast that it was the best wine. And there was enough for all the guests to the end of the feast.

When the festivities were over and the guests began to leave, Jesus called the bridegroom to him and said:

"John, leave your bride and your home and come with me; for I wish to bring you to a wedding grander than this. Come, and follow me!"

And John (who later became known as the Evangelist) arose and left his bride, and he followed Jesus.

The Wedding Feast at Cana is one of the best known canonical stories of the miracles of Jesus. In the gospels the name of the bridegroom is not given. But in apocryphal works the bridegroom is often identified as Simon the Canaanite. Some of the earliest apocryphal fragments identify the bridegroom as John, referred to as "St. John the Evangelist."

2. Jesus and the Sphinx

One day Jesus and his disciples came into a temple of the Gentiles, and the chief priest turned to the twelve disciples and said:

"O wretches, why do you follow this man who says he is the son of God? Is not this man the son of Joseph the Carpenter and his mother Mary? And are not James and Simon his brothers?"

The hearts of the disciples weakened when they heard these words. But Jesus, having looked to the right and to the left of the temple, saw two sculptured sphinxes on each side. And he said to the sphinx on the right:

"Come down from your place and answer the chief priest, that he may know who I am."

The sphinx left the pedestal and said in a human voice: "Do not say that I am a carved stone and that you alone have a name and are called the high priest! For though we are made of stone, it is you who have given us the name of a god. Then you purify yourselves seven days when you have intercourse with women, because of your fear of us. But I say to you that only the holy things can purify your temples."

The disciples turned to the chief priest and said: "Now even the stones have convicted you."

But the priest said: "By magic one can make the stones to speak. I will believe you only if you bring me the testimony of the patriarchs."

Jesus then said to the sphinx: "Go to the land of the Canaanites and to the cave in the field of Mamre, and cry out, saying: 'Abraham! Abraham! whose body is in this tomb and whose soul is in paradise, rise up! You and your son Isaac and his son Jacob, rise up, and come to this temple of the Jebusites, and convict the chief priest who does not believe that I am acquainted with you, and you with me!'"

The sphinx walked out of the temple and went to the cave of Mamre and cried out to the patriarchs as Jesus had commanded. Straightaway the three patriarchs set out for the temple of the Jebusites, and there they testified to all that Jesus had said, and convicted the chief priests. Then they returned to their resting place to await the time of the resurrection.

And Jesus said to the sphinx: "Return to your place."

The sphinx returned to its pedestal and was stone again.

Even so the chief priest did not believe in him.

This legend, which appears in the Acts of Andrew and Matthias, is told by the Apostle Andrew in the first person, long after the Crucifixion; and strangely enough, the story is told to Jesus who, as the pilot of a small boat, is not recognized by Andrew and his disciples. See: "Andrew and the Pilot," Chapter 27, pages 266–267.

3. *The Three Merchants*

Three merchants traveled along a road, and they found a great treasure. And they said to each other:

"Before we divide this between ourselves, let one of us go and buy some food, for we are hungry."

The one who went to get the food to eat said to himself: "If I were to poison the food and let the others eat it and die, then I would have all of the treasure for myself, and need not share it with anyone." And so he bought the food and sprinkled it with poison.

While he was gone, the other two conspired and said to each other: "Let us kill him when he returns with the food, so that we may divide his share of the treasure between us."

When their companion came back with the food, they pounced upon him and killed him. Then the two hungry merchants ate the food he had brought, and they, too, died.

Some time later Jesus and his disciples passed by that place, and Jesus said: "This is the way of the world! See how it dealt with these three. For he who longs to be rich is like a man who drinks sea water; the more he drinks, the more thirsty he becomes. And he never leaves off until he perishes."

4. *Veronica the Wise*

In the city of Paneas, in the land of Judea, there lived a very rich woman, named Veronica. She was wealthy and she was wise; but from childhood she had been afflicted with an issue of blood that could not be stopped. A great part of her fortune was spent on many physicians, yet she found no cure.

One day she heard of wonderful cures performed by a Rabbi of Nazareth. Veronica went in search of the healer; and she found him near a lake in Galilee, surrounded by a multitude of disciples and followers, the blind and the lame and the leprous who came to be cured; and many more who came to listen to his teachings.

Veronica was reluctant to approach the healer, lest he might turn away from her. And she thought to herself, "If only I could touch the hem of his garment, perhaps then I would be cured."

Slowly she made her way through the crowd, until at last she stood near the white-robed Healer of Nazareth. Then she touched his garment. And the fountain of her blood was stayed and she was well.

But Jesus cried out: "Who has touched me? For I feel the power gone out of me!"

Veronica fell at the feet of the healer, flooding the ground with her tears, and she confessed her daring.

Jesus said: "Arise, daughter. Your faith has cured you. Go home in peace."

Veronica returned home to Paneas, and petitioned King Herod for permission to build a great monument to him who had healed her so miraculously. King Herod was astonished when he read her petition and feared to refuse it. Whereupon Veronica erected a monument in the very heart of the city, made of brass, to which a portion of gold and silver had been added. And it represented a woman with her hands outstretched in prayer, and opposite her a man in a double cloak extending his hand toward her in benediction.

An unknown herb began to sprout in the ground around the monument. And it was discovered that this strange herb had great healing powers.

5. *The Rich Young Man*

A certain rich young man came to Jesus and said: "Good Master, what shall I do to inherit life eternal?"

And Jesus said: "Obey the Commandments, and fulfill the Law and the Prophets."

The young man replied: "I have kept the Commandments from my youth. What lack I yet?"

And Jesus said to him: "How do you say, I have fulfilled the Law and the Prophets, since it is written in the Law: 'You shall love your neighbor as yourself,' and lo! many of your brethren, sons of

Abraham, are clothed in filth, dying of hunger, and your house is full of many goods, and nothing at all goes out of it to them."

And turning to Simon, who was sitting by him, Jesus said: "Simon, son of Jonas, it is easier for a camel to go through the eye of a needle than for a rich man to enter into the kingdom of heaven."

Every recorded act and word of Jesus has, in the course of time, become the subject of voluminous commentary and interpretation. And the incident of the rich man received its share of attention at a very early date. In the ante-Nicene literature we find this opening to a lengthy sermon by Clement of Alexandria:

"Those who bestow laudatory addresses on the rich appear to me to be rightly judged not only flatterers and base . . . but also godless and treacherous. . . . Treacherous, because, although wealth is of itself sufficient to puff up and corrupt the souls of its possessors, and to turn them from the path by which salvation is to be attained, they stupefy them still more, by inflating the minds of the rich with the pleasures of extravagant praise, and by making them utterly despise all things save wealth, on account of which they are admired; bringing, as the saying is, fire to fire, pouring pride on pride, and adding conceit to wealth . . . a dangerous and deadly disease."

6. *King Abgar of Edessa*

In those days there lived in Mesopotamia, in the city of Edessa, an Armenian king, named Abgar. He was renowned among all the nations of the East for his great size and his valor. He was admired for his wisdom and prudence. But most of all he was loved by his subjects for his gentleness.

King Abgar ruled the happy people in the city which had been the home of Father Abraham, until the wicked Romans made Abgar's domain their tributary. And straightaway they established their statues and their many idols in the temples of Edessa. Abgar the Brave waged war against the invaders; and for many years he resisted them. During these wars he became victim of a painful disease for which there was no cure on earth.

One day King Abgar heard of the wonderful healer of Nazareth.

Abgar longed to leave his domain and travel to see Jesus and be healed, but strife kept him bound to his city. Whereupon King Abgar sat down and wrote this letter to Jesus:

FROM ABGARUS THE BLACK, *son of Archam, King of the Edesseans, an unworthy slave,*

TO JESUS CALLED THE CHRIST, *the good Savior and benefactor of men, who has appeared in the country of Judea,*

GREETINGS:

The account of the multitude of wonders accomplished by you has reached my ears. I have heard of the cures wrought by you without medicine and without herbs, but by the word of your mouth. And I listened to reports without number of how you make the blind to see and the lame to walk; how you have made the leper clean; and how you heal those who are tormented with lingering diseases and incurable ailments. And above all, how you heal those sick in spirit and possessed by demons.

And when I heard all this, I said to myself, this man is surely the Son of God, or he is God. On this account, I entreat you to come and heal me of the disease which afflicts me.

I have also heard that the Jews murmur against you and they wish to do you harm. Therefore come to Edessa. My city is small, but large enough for us both.

King Abgar called the painter Ananias and sent him with the letter to Jesus, enjoining him to observe the healer and to take accurate account of his appearance, his stature, the color of his hair, and in every detail, so that he might have a picture of him before his eyes.

Ananias traveled to Judea, but when he came before Jesus he was so dazzled by the splendor of the healer's countenance that he could make no accurate observation of him. That distressed the painter, knowing that he would fail in his mission for the king. But Jesus saw what was in Ananias's heart, and called for water and a towel. He washed and wiped his face, and gave the towel to the king's courier. And when Ananias looked at the linen towel, there, upon it, was the image of Jesus imprinted as if painted by a master painter! a long visage, and inclined, which is the sign of maturity and of ripe sadness.

"Take this towel to your king," said Jesus. And with his own hand Jesus wrote a reply to King Abgar, which said:

Blessed is he who believes in me, not having seen me. For it is written concerning me, that those who see me will not believe in me; and that those will believe who have not seen me, and will be saved. And because you have believed in me, the town in which you dwell shall be blessed. And if you will always keep this letter, the power of the enemies which rage against you shall not prevail; and your state shall, for your sake, be blessed forever. But touching that which you have written to me, that I should come to you, it is meet that I should finish here all that for the sake of which I have been sent, and, after I have finished it, then I shall be taken up to him that sent me. And when I have been taken up, I will send to you one of my disciples, that he may heal your disease, and give life to you, and to those who are with you.

Ananias brought the letter and the portrait on the towel to the king, and the king was cured of his illness. Abgar fell down on his knees and adored the image before him.

(The letter of Jesus and his image, we are told, remained in Edessa for many years, and protected the inhabitants from illness and invasion. When a barbarian horde attempted to conquer Edessa the people displayed the image on the city gate, and placed a child upon the tower of the gate to read the epistle from Jesus. The enemy would be seized with terror and flee, or would make peace.

Some claim that the letter and the image on the towel are now in the church of St. Sophia; others maintain that they are in the Armenian church of St. Bartholomew, where they are shown to the people once each year. But the Venetians claim that they secured the image and placed it in the church of St. Sylvester in Rome.)

7. Loaves and Fishes

An ever-growing multitude came to hear the teachings of Jesus; and wherever he went, the multitude followed him. Many of them were fishermen and vintners; many were simple sowers of seed and reapers of wheat and barley; and many of them were growers of

fruit and vegetables, from orach to carobs, and the balm of Ein Gedi;
but most of them were tailors and millers, masons and carpenters,
barbers and smiths, dyers and well diggers, potters and coopers,
carpet weavers and painters. Some were publicans and tax collectors;
some were armorers; and some were scribes and engravers. Most of
them were poor. And all of them sought deliverance.

Though many came to Jesus to be healed of a physical ailment —
the lame, the blind, the dumb, the maimed, the deranged, the leprous
— all were sick in spirit because of their oppression, and came for a
sign of deliverance from evil.

Jesus healed and he preached the Law, and he interpreted the
Law and the Prophets. And his words to the wounded in spirit
were more soothing than ointment and balm to the wounded in
body.

Once a great crowd gathered about him for three days and would
not leave. Jesus had compassion on them and would not send them
away lest they faint from hunger. And he told his disciples to feed
the multitude.

"But, Master," pleaded Andrew, "where shall we find bread in
this desert with which to feed thousands of men?"

One young man in the multitude came forward with five barley
loaves and two fishes and said to Jesus: "I have toiled much for
these, Rabboni, and they are yours, if you want them."

"Your reward shall be equal to your faith," said Jesus.

He took the loaves and fishes and pronounced the benediction.
Then he raised his eyes and hands heavenwards and prayed:

"O Lord, my Father, you know my heart and understand my
thought afar off! Bless these five barley loaves that they may fill the
multitude who came to hear your word! Let my prayer come before
you as incense and the lifting of my hands as the evening sacrifice!
Praise you the Lord, O my soul!"

And before those about him could whisper "Amen" there were
loaves and fish in abundance for all the five thousand hungry people
assembled there.

In his Christian Iconography, *Adolphe-Napoléon Didron points
out that the fish was the accepted symbol of Jesus Christ for many
centuries. The fish was sculptured upon Christian monuments, par-*

ticularly on ancient sarcophagi, and is found on stones, cameos and intaglios of Christian symbolical meaning. It is to be found on the obverse of medals bearing the name of Jesus, and on ancient Christian amulets which were placed about the necks of children to protect them from illness and evil. Baptismal fonts are frequently ornamented with fish. In paintings of the Last Supper, the fish is often shown on a dish placed prominently on the table.

8. *The Table from Heaven*

In Mohammedan lore the miracle of feeding the hungry multitudes is embellished with details reminiscent of The Arabian Nights. The following, an amplification on the feeding of the five thousand in the desert, is an example of Muslim inventiveness.

The apostles asked Jesus: "Son of Mary, is the Lord able to send down from heaven a table covered with food to satisfy us?"

And Jesus replied: "Whatever the Lord desires, that he is able to do. He stretched out his right hand and the heavens appeared. He stretched out his left hand and the earth was founded."

Then Jesus prayed: "O God, my Lord, cause to descend upon us from heaven a table covered with food, that this may be a day of rejoicing for us and those who come after. This shall be a sign of your omnipotence. Enrich us with your grace, for all treasures are yours. Amen!"

Thereupon two bright clouds descended from heaven bearing a golden table, upon which stood a covered silver dish.

Some in the multitude with little faith cried out: "Look, the magician has invented a new illusion!" And immediately they turned into swine whose eyes are always on the earth and never on the heavens.

But all the others watched Jesus wash his hands and then raise up the cover of the great silver dish upon the golden table. And they beheld an enormous fish, from which arose the sweet aroma of the fruits of paradise. The fish was seasoned with salt, pepper, parsley, ginger, capsicum, and other spices rare and fragrant. Surrounding the giant fish were five small loaves of barley.

"Is this fish the food of this world or of the other world?" asked Simon.

And Jesus answered: "Are not this world and the other world, with all they contain, equally the works of God?"

Jesus began to serve his guests, caring first for the old, the lame, the blind and the sick. As each portion of fish was served, it was instantly replaced by the great fish within the silver bowl. Thirteen hundred portions were served, and yet the fish remained whole, as if no one had touched it. And they who were served and ate of it were not only sated of their hunger, but they were also healed of their ills. The old became young, the blind recovered their sight, the deaf could hear, the dumb could speak, the lame could walk, and all their pains left them.

9. The Report of the Skull

Jesus and his disciples were walking along the shore of the Dead Sea, when they came upon a man's skull. The disciples wondered what the skull would report if it could tell them what it had found beyond death.

Jesus prayed, and at once the skull took on the form of a man, which stood upright, and spoke in the voice of a living man, saying:

"O Prophet of God, know that four thousand years ago I, a descendant of the Prophet Elijah, lived in pleasure. Until one day when I took a bath I was attacked by a fever that lasted seven days. Then the Angel of Death appeared, his head touching the heavens and his feet planted in the lowest depths of the earth. In his right hand he held a gleaming sword; and in his left, a cup with the bitter drink. With him were two other angels, who threw themselves upon me, held my tongue so that I could utter no cry, and pressed my veins to force my soul to depart."

"What happened then?" asked the disciples.

"Then I pleaded with the Angel of Death, and said: 'Spare me, and I will give you all I possess.' But this only angered him and he replied: 'God accepts no ransom!' And he raised the sword over my neck and gave me the cup, commanding me to drink it to the last drop."

And the disciples asked: "Then what happened?"

"I was bathed, wrapped in a shroud, and buried; but my soul had no knowledge of what transpired until my body was in the tomb and covered with earth. Only then did my soul return to my body, and I was seized with great terror and loneliness.

"After some time, two angels appeared with the scroll kept by the Recorder of the Deeds of Man, and they read to me all the good and evil that I had done during my life. And when they had finished they commanded me to sign the scroll and testify to the correctness of the record with my own signature. This record they hung upon my neck and left.

"Next there appeared two angels dark blue in color, and each held in his hands a column of fire so hot, one spark of it would suffice to destroy the earth. And they asked me: 'Who is your Master?' In my great fear of them I stammered: 'You are my masters!' And they replied: 'O enemy of God, you lie!' And they struck me with their columns of fire and caused me to sink to the lowest depth of the seventh earth. They said to the earth: 'Punish this man, for he does not know his Master.' And the earth said to me: 'O enemy of God, I hated you all the days that you walked upon my surface; and now I will avenge myself and reduce you to dust for all the evil you have done on earth.'"

"And then what happened?" asked the disciples.

"That was the end of the punishment of my body. But the punishment of my soul had just begun. For as soon as my body was reduced to dust, an angel opened the gates of hell, and called out: 'Take in a sinner who does not know his Master!' They bound me with a chain that was seventy ells in length, then they plunged me into the fires of hell. Soon the tormenting flames devoured my skin, and another was given me that I should suffer the torments again. My hunger was great, but when I asked for food they gave me the infernal fruit of the accursed Zaucum that looks like the head of a demon; and when I was writhing in thirst, they poured boiling water down my throat, and placed the end of the chain into my mouth with such force that it came out through my neck."

"How long did you suffer this?" asked the disciples.

"Those were the tortures of the first hell. There are seven hells, and each succeeding one grows more agonizing. The further one descends, the more crowded are they with men of evil deeds and of the figures of idols."

When the stranger described the torments of the evildoers of this earth, Jesus wept with compassion. And he said to the stranger:

"In all these years of your punishment, what did you desire most?"

"I longed that God would recall me to life so that I could serve him with all my heart and all my soul, that I might become worthy of paradise."

And Jesus said: "By the power of God, I now order you to become once more a perfect man; and remember who is your Master."

This man then lived sixty-six years after his resurrection by Jesus, and passed his days in fasting and his nights in prayer. He did not turn away from the ways of God for one instant until the day he died.

10. *Poor Man, Rich Man*

One day a disciple asked Jesus: "Master, how are you this morning?"

And Jesus replied: "Unable to forestall what I hope, or to put off what I fear, bound by my works, with all my good in the hands of another; there is no poor man poorer than I."

And on another day, Jesus said: "My condiment is hunger; my inner garment fear; my outer garment wool. I warm myself in the winter by the sun; my dainties are the fruits of the earth. Neither at eventide nor in the morning have I anything in my possession; yet no one on earth is richer than I."

11. *Doubting Thomas*

Thomas Didymus, of the Tribe of Benjamin and of the city of Paneas in Galilee, was a disciple full of doubts. And as he went with Jesus and the other disciples, he constantly asked for ever new miracles to dispel his doubts and the doubts of those in the multitude who were like him.

One day he said to Jesus: "Rabboni, there is one thing of which we wish you would assure us, and that is that no one ever dies, but sleeps, awaiting the resurrection."

"Thomas, my friend," said Jesus, "must you see with your own eyes before your heart is assured? And if a grain of wheat is buried, does it not rise to bear fruit?"

"My lord, our faith would be strengthened if we could see how bones in the tomb, which have been dissolved, are joined again and rise to testify before us."

Jesus turned to the other disciples and said: "Blessed are they who not having seen, yet believe; rather than they who having seen, yet believe not."

But Jesus could see that the doubt still rested in the heart of Thomas, and he said:

"Four days ago, the good soldier Lazarus, the son of Syrus and Emhasia, died in Bethany. And I have not yet gone to console his sisters Martha and Mary. Now we shall go there so that you, Thomas Didymus, may witness the eyes, from which all light has long since gone, see again; and the tongue, which has been stilled and corrupted, speak again."

Thomas grieved for the doubts he had uttered and said: "Rabboni, how can we go to Bethany, knowing that some of our brethren are set against you and are seeking to stone you?"

"Didymus," said Jesus, seeing how grieved was his disciple and wishing to comfort him, "he who walks in the light does not stumble."

So they walked together until they came to Bethany. And Mary came to meet them and said to Jesus amid her tears:

"Rabboni! Rabboni! Would that you had been here earlier; then my brother would not be in his tomb, for you could have healed him."

"Do you believe in me?" asked Jesus.

"Yes, Rabboni, I believe."

"Then come and see that your brother sleeps and I shall command him to waken."

They went to the tomb where Lazarus was buried, and Jesus asked his disciples to remove the stone from the entrance.

Thomas began to weep and said: "My lord, if you do this because of my unbelief, then may this tomb receive me unto the day of your resurrection!"

"Grieve not, Thomas," said Jesus. "Remove the stone that I may waken him who sleeps."

Thomas removed the stone, and out of the entrance came the stench of decaying flesh. Jesus came near the tomb and called out:

"Lazarus, come forth!"

And Lazarus, wrapped in his shroud, came out of the tomb, walking forth like a bridegroom leaving the bridal chamber, filled with exceeding fragrance. He kneeled before Jesus, and said:

"Blessed are you, Jesus, to whom belongs the voice of the resurrection!"

A crowd gathered out of Bethany to witness how the man they had buried on a Tuesday was resurrected four days later, on a Sabbath.

CHAPTER SEVENTEEN

The Master Storyteller

The parables of the Gospels are an integral part of the New Testament lore. The parable is the literary device used most frequently in the Synoptic Gospels to demonstrate a moral principle; and it is therefore necessary to understand its nature and peculiarities.

The word itself, parable, means to be likened or a comparison, and differs significantly from such literary forms as the fable, the myth, and the allegory. Whereas the fable deals with improbable and supernatural occurrences; the myth, with factual ideas based on fictitious events; and the allegory, with an extended, often very long, simile that may or may not be religious in nature; the parable is a distinct literary form that deals succinctly and sharply with actual or highly probable events of quite ordinary occurrences, implying or demonstrating an ethical truth. The parable has therefore been called: "An earthly story with a heavenly meaning."

The parable is encountered in all early religious teachings, and was used among the Jews of the five centuries before the Christian Era, when the majority of the people could neither read nor write and education was accomplished by "the teaching of the mouth."

Everyone acquainted with the Old Testament will remember the Parable of the Bramble that Would Be King (Judges 9 : 7–15), the Parable of the Ewe Lamb (II Samuel 12 : 1–4), the Parable of the Prisoner (I Kings 20 : 39–40), the Parable of the Vineyard (Isaiah 5 : 1–6), and the Parable of the Two Eagles (Ezekiel 13 : 2–10).

But it is not until we come to the great Rabbinic literature developed in Palestine and in Babylonia, known as the Talmud, that we find the parable in popular use, and its form highly stylized. The hundreds of parables to be found in Talmudic lore followed an almost fixed pattern, beginning with "a comparison" and often ending with a self-replying question.

Although Jesus used this contemporary literary form in his oral teaching, with all its fixed peculiarities and symbols, he lifted it to a height it had never attained before. And nowhere do we find so many, and, from a purely literary point of view, so lofty a group of parables as are to be found in the Gospels.

In addition to their teachings and the brilliance of their form, the parables of Jesus, when read collectively, give a vivid portrayal of life in Palestine in those days. They reveal a rural people, most of them poor, tending their sheep, cultivating their small vineyards, getting married, sorrowing in illness and bereavement; the young men craving adventure and sometimes leaving their father's fields to travel to distant lands. There are a few rich men among them, with the poor begging at their doors. Life is hard for the people, but not without its adornments and compensations.

Those who read the canonical parables must be struck by the extraordinary economy of words with which they are presented; and how crowded these miniature gems are with the reflection of the events of their times, the peculiarities of the general literature of that period, and the social and folk influences of other religions that infiltrated into Judaic life and thought during the three centuries preceding the ministry of Jesus.

In the best known of the parables, the Parable of the Good Samaritan, we find that Jesus drew freely upon the details of the then-current outrages against unidentified travelers who were attacked by highwaymen on the road between Jerusalem and Jericho and left prostrate by the wayside.

In other parables, Jesus restated with a new purpose stories and sayings popular in his times, retaining the familiar forms, but infusing them with new life. The parable about the Wise and Foolish Builders seems to be built on the assertion found in the Sayings of the Fathers According to Rabbi Nathan (Aboth d'Rabbi Nathan), which reads:

"A man who performs many good deeds and devotes much time to the study of the Holy Law, to what is he likened? To a man who builds a house of bricks upon a foundation of stone. When the rains come, the water stands about the foundation, but the walls remain in their place.

"But the man who studies much yet performs few good deeds, to what is he likened? To a man who builds a house of stone upon a foundation of bricks. When the rains come, the foundation weakens and the walls come tumbling down."

In the cryptic parable about New Wine in Old Skins we again find a new concept given to an old saying which exists in many forms, one of them appearing in the Sayings of the Fathers (Pirke Aboth), which states:

"He who learns from the young, to what is he likened? To one who eats unripe grapes or drinks wine from the vat. He who learns from the old, to what is he likened? To one who eats ripe grapes, or drinks old wine."

In the very old apocryphal work, the Story of Ahikar, we find a parallel to the parable of the Barren Fig Tree. In the form of a fable, Ahikar argues with his incorrigible adopted son:

"My son, you have been to me like the palm-tree that stood by the river and shed all its fruit into the water. And when the owner came to cut it down, it said to him: 'Let me alone this year, and I will bring forth carobs for you next year.' And the owner said: 'You have not been industrious before; how much more industrious will you be in the future?'"

In all the parables certain numbers are used figuratively and not literally, in accord with the lore of those days and as they appear throughout the lore of the Old Testament. The numbers one, two, three, five, seven, ten, twelve and seventy are particularly significant as symbols. One stands for "unity"; two, for "contrast" (because of the positive and negative Commandments in the two tablets of the Law); three stands for emphasis or "authority" (because of the Three Patriarchs); five stands for many good things and particularly "security" (because of the Five Books of Moses); seven represents "completion" or fullness (because of the Seven Days of the Week); ten stands for "the community" or the Law or the perfect number (because of the Ten Commandments); twelve stands for the Twelve Tribes and has other meanings; seventy is the number of the Sanhedrin, the highest court in ancient Israel. The squares of these numbers also carry symbolical meaning, and particularly three times three, seven times seven (the Jubilee number), and multiples of ten. Twelve, however, is multiplied by six (the Days of Creation) to reach the symbolical number seventy-two.

In the parables, as in the New Testament generally, the numbers were retained but given new symbols, such as: three symbolizing the Trinity; twelve, the Apostles; seventy, the Disciples, and so on. In practically all the parables of Jesus we find a number used for its symbolical rather than its literal meaning, as, for example, in the parable of the Wise and Foolish Virgins.

Quite different is the figurative use of numbers. The word often used in both the Old and the New Testament lore for "a very large number" is myriad (which means ten thousand), if used figuratively. In the parable of the Forgiven Who Do Not Forgive we find Jesus telling of a certain king who decides to take an accounting of his debtors and finds one who owes him ten thousand talents. The Hebraic talent was about two thousand American dollars, if in silver, and nearly five times that amount, if in gold. Obviously the figure could not possibly have been used literally but was intended to mean: a very large amount. When the selfsame debtor imprisons his servant for failure to pay a debt of one hundred pence, the number and the amount is again used figuratively, denoting: a very small amount.

In addition, the parables of the New Testament, like so many works of that period, reflect the new, outside influences, particularly Buddhist and Egyptian, unknown in very early Hebrew literature. The parables of the Two Men Who Prayed and of The Widow's Two Mites show the Buddhist influence. There exists a very ancient Buddhist story about a poor widow who had to beg for her bread, yet when she found two coins she brought them as an offering to the temple. The priest realized that her gift exceeded the rich gifts of those who could well afford them. In the Buddhist story the widow is rewarded by being taken in marriage by the king of the country. The Egyptian influence, noted in the Rabbinic literature of the period, is often characterized by the dead appearing to warn the living, or to serve them, and is shown in the parable of Dives and Lazarus.

More important than the influence of Hebraic, Buddhist and Egyptian concepts on the parables is the impact of the parables on subsequent Judaic literature and the literature of the Western world.

The parable of the Prodigal Son, as an instance, is reflected in a story in the Midrash Rabah, which may have followed it, telling of a king who had an only son. The son fell into evil ways and the king sent a tutor to him with the message:

"Repent, my son!" The son sent a message in reply, "How can I repent after what I have done? I am ashamed before you." Then the father replied: "Can a son be ashamed to return to his father? And if you decide to return, to whom will you return but to your father?"

In the Arabian A Thousand and One Nights, *the story about the king who built palaces for himself to enjoy in the ripeness of his age is clearly based on the parable of the Rich Man who hoarded his crops so that in the ripeness of his years he might sit back and "eat, drink, and be merry!" And in contemporary literature, the same parable seems to have inspired* A Gentleman from San Francisco, *by the Nobel Prize winner, Ivan Bunin, who uses the same theme in a contemporary setting and in a different literary form.*

In the folk imagination, the parables as a group are second only to the Sermon on the Mount.

CHAPTER EIGHTEEN

Letters, Discourses and Sayings

1. The Letters

The exchange of letters between Jesus and Abgar, King of Edessa, has been given in a preceding chapter. The record of this exchange of letters goes back at least to the third century A.D., and Eusebius, the father of church history, claims to have seen them in the archives of Edessa. Cedrenus maintains that Jesus wrote the letter to Abgar in his own hand, and sealed it with seven Hebrew letters which stood for: "The divine miracle of God is seen." Syriac, Greek, Latin and Arabic versions of these letters are recorded in St. Francis Xavier's Historia Christi, which appeared in the sixteenth century. The reader will find this exchange of letters in The Apocryphal New Testament, compiled and translated by William Hone, where they appear under the heading of "The Epistles of Jesus Christ and Abgarus, King of Edessa."

It is to be expected that anything supposed to have been written by Jesus should be believed to have healing powers and act as a talisman to ward off evil. The letter to King Abgar is written in the form of an ancient charm, specifying: "If thou wilt always keep this letter, the power of the enemies which rage against thee shall not prevail." And this letter has become the prototype of a number of letters attributed to Jesus, miraculously discovered in diverse parts of the world, and invested with the power of the amulet and the phylactery.

Perhaps the most recent and best-known letter is the one said to have been found under a stone near Iconium. The stone carried the inscription: "Blessed be he that shall turn me over." But no one seemed to have done just that for many years. One day a child of six or seven turned the stone over with ease, and there, to the astonishment of all, was the letter written by Jesus, in his own hand

and bearing the inscription: "The Commandments of Jesus Christ, signed by the Angel Gabriel ninety-nine years after our Savior's birth." The letter contains this significant paragraph:

He that hath a copy of this letter, written with my own hand and spoken with my own mouth, and keepeth it without publishing it to others, shall not prosper, but he that publisheth it to others shall be blessed of me. And if their sins be in number as the stars of the sky and they truly believe in me, they shall be pardoned. And if they believe not this writing and my commandments, I will send my plagues upon them, and consume both you and your children. . . . All goodness and prosperity shall be in the house where a copy of this letter shall be found.

In millions of homes throughout Europe, the Americas and even the Orient, copies of the "Letter of Jesus" are to be found, and are depended on as a tower of strength against evil.

2. Discourses

There are a number of apocryphal discourses attributed to Jesus. The most remarkable of these is to be found in The History of Joseph the Carpenter, *which runs into thirty-one chapters, and begins with: "It happened one day, when the Savior, our Master, God, and Savior Jesus Christ, was sitting along with his disciples, and they were all assembled on the Mount of Olives, that He said to them": Then follows the lengthy discourse.*

This work was originally written in Coptic about the fourth century A.D. and has gone through many translations and emendations. It is notable for its folk style. The second chapter begins with Jesus relating: "There lived a man whose name was Joseph, sprung from a family in Bethlehem, a town in Judah, and the city of King David." It is also remarkable for the quality and length of its prayers and confessions of the dead; and for the many strange folk beliefs it expresses, especially the belief in the power of names to ward off evil.

Given below in full is the twenty-sixth chapter of this work, as an indication of the nature of the discourses attributed to Jesus.

And I spoke to Joseph, and said: The smell or corruption of death shall not have dominion over thee, nor shall a worm ever come forth from thy body. Not a single limb of it shall be broken, nor shall any hair on thy head be changed. Nothing of thy body shall perish, O my father Joseph, but it will remain entire and uncorrupted even until the banquet of the thousand years. And whosoever shall make an offering on the day of thy remembrance, him will I bless and recompense in the congregation of the virgins; and whosoever shall give food to the wretched, the poor, the widows, and orphans from the work of his hands, on the day on which thy memory shall be celebrated, and in thy name, shall not be in want of good things all the days of his life. And whosoever shall give a cup of water, or of wine, to the widow or orphan in thy name, I will give him to thee, that thou mayest go in with him to the banquet of the thousand years. And every man who shall present an offering on the day of thy commemoration will I bless and recompense in the church of the virgins: for one I will render unto him thirty, sixty, and a hundred. And whosoever shall write the history of thy life, of thy labor, and thy departure from this world, and this narrative that has issued from my mouth, him shall I commit to thy keeping as long as he shall have to do with this life. And when his soul departs from the body, and when he must leave this world, I will burn the book of his sins, nor will I torment him with any punishment in the day of judgment; but he shall cross the sea of flames, and shall go through it without trouble or pain. And upon every poor man who can give none of those things which I have mentioned this is incumbent: viz., if a son is born to him, he shall call his name Joseph. So there shall not take place in that house either poverty or any sudden death for ever.

3. The Sayings of Jesus

Jesus often summed up observations and precepts in a memorable saying or proverb. The Sayings of Jesus are generally divided into: the Logia, the canonical sayings upon which the Gospels are based; and the Agrapha, the apocryphal sayings attributed to Jesus and which are of varying degrees of authenticity.

The number of these sayings, in both categories, is still growing.

*For surprisingly enough, some of them are of startlingly recent dis-
covery. The first collection of extracanonical sayings was not made
until late in the seventeenth century. And additions have been made
as new manuscripts were discovered, translated, and authenticated.*

*It was not until 1859 that the German scholar, Lobegott Friedrich
Constantin von Tischendorf, discovered the Codex Sinaiticus of the
Greek Bible in the Convent of St. Catherine at the foot of Mount
Sinai, with its treasury of Sayings. And as late as 1897 — only yester-
day, historically speaking — two British archaeologists, Dr. B. P.
Grenfell and Dr. A. S. Hunt, made a discovery at Behnesa, in Egypt.
Here, in their own words, is part of their report on the circumstances
under which their find was made.*

"On the edge of the Libyan desert, 120 miles from Cairo, a series
of low mounds, covered with Roman and early Arab pottery, marks
the spot where stood the capital of the Oxyrhynchite nome (province). The wide area of the site, and the scale of buildings and
city walls, where traceable, testify to its past size and importance;
but it declined rapidly after the Arab conquest, and its modern
representative, Behnesa, is a mere hamlet. A flourishing city in
Roman times, Oxyrhynchus offered a peculiarly attractive field
for explorers who, like ourselves, make the recovery of Greek papyri,
with all the manifold treasures they may bring, their principal aim.
. . . The ancient cemetery, to which for various reasons the first
three weeks' work was devoted, proved on the whole unproductive;
but in the rubbish-heaps of the town were found large quantities of
papyri, chiefly Greek, ranging in date from the first to the eighth
century, and embracing every variety of subject. . . . Among these
was a leaf from a papyrus book containing a collection of Logia or
Sayings of Our Lord, some of which were unknown before. These
must have been written between 150 and 300 A.D. And the likeliest
period of their writing is 200 A.D."

*The sayings found in the Oxyrhynchus papyrus are, at least in
part, taken from a very early Gospel According to the Egyptians,
mentioned by Origen but of which we have no copies, in full or in
part.*

*The small group of apocryphal Sayings of Jesus which follow
come from diverse sources, which are given in the* Notes on Sources.

In the Reading List, *a section is devoted to the Sayings of Jesus for those who wish to explore the topic further.*

(1) I am thou, and thou art I; and where thou art there am I also; and in all things am I sown. And from whencesoever thou gatherest me, in gathering me thou gatherest thyself.

(2) He who seeks will find; and finding, will wonder; and wondering, will reign; and reigning, will rest.

(3) The soul must be made to grow through faith and knowledge.

(4) Kind words are better than ointment; and a sweet saying than the perfume of love.

(5) A cheerful countenance is as the appearance of sweetness.

(6) Love rules willing hearts; fear the unwilling.

(7) The giver is happier than the receiver.

(8) Never be joyful, except when you have seen your brother in love.

(9) Love covers a multitude of sins.

(10) You see your brother; you see your God.

(11) There are those who stretch the warps and weave nothing.

(12) Blessed is he who also fasts for this, that he might feed the poor.

(13) You have dismissed the living, who were before you, and talk of the dead.

(14) When you fast, pray for those that are about to perish.

(15) A man not tempted is not proved.

(16) Anger destroys even the prudent.

(17) Where there are pains, thither runs the physician.

(18) Excepting for a few saints, men have always thought that they could atone for their crimes with money.

(19) You hear with one ear, but the other you have closed.

(20) If anyone does not work, let not such a one eat; for the Lord our God hates the slothful.

(21) The Heavenly Father desires rather the repentance than the punishment of sinners.

(22) The world shall be built up through grace.

(23) Show yourself a tried money-changer, in that you can distinguish between good and bad coin.

(24) Ask great things, and the small shall be added; ask heavenly things, and the earthly shall be added.

(25) He to whom more is forgiven, loves more.

(26) No one shall be called good who mixes evil with the good, for gall does not mix well with honey.

(27) Men must give an account of every good word that they fail to speak.

(28) If you cannot keep that which is small, who will entrust you with that which is great? For he that is faithful in very little, is also faithful in much.

(29) As you judge, so shall you be judged.

(30) Blessed are they who mourn the destruction of the unbelievers.

(31) Let us resist all iniquity and hold it in hatred.

(32) Beware how you sit with sinners.

(33) Take not the world for your lord; lest it take you for its slave.

(34) One day Jesus and his disciples passed a man who spoke evil of them in a loud voice; but Jesus spoke only good in return. And when his disciples asked him why he spoke good to him who spoke evil, he replied: "Each gives out of his store."

PART VI
From Mount Olivet to Calvary

Of all the tragedies in recorded literature, religious or secular, there is not another so profoundly moving as the trial
and crucifixion of Jesus of Nazareth. In the folk imagination
this tragic sequence of events retained its heartbreak un-
diminished, like a spring that is never muted. However
varied the legends, the events invariably arrange themselves into a fixed progression: the Conspiracy, the Trial,
the Crucifixion and Burial, and the triumphant Ascension.

The most beautiful legends about the trial, the sentence
and the crucifixion are to be found in the earliest Passion
Gospels; and some of the most appealing legends of the
Resurrection and the Ascension, in the comparatively recent Aquarian Gospel. From these early and late Gospels
were selected the legends in the following five chapters.

CHAPTER NINETEEN

The Conspiracy

1. *Carius' Report to Herod*

King Herod dispatched Carius, his trusted chief of Galilee, to find out all he could about Jesus and his works. For Herod had heard that Lazarus, brother of Mary and Martha, had been raised from the dead by Jesus, the Rabbi of Nazareth.

Carius went and soon returned.

"What have you learned about this man?" asked Herod.

"There is talk of him throughout the land," said Carius. "Some say he is John the Baptist come to life again. And some say he is Elijah the Prophet who has come to heal the sick and comfort the sorrowing. And there are some who say that he is the Messiah, a king and the descendant of a king."

"Do all the people believe in him?" asked Herod.

"No," said Carius. "Some believe in him and some speak against him. There are people who say that he is a magician like Jannes and Mambres before Pharaoh. They complain that he breaks the Sabbath and profanes the Law. They even say that he threatens to destroy in one moment, the temple which took Solomon forty-six years to build. But the poor, the sick and the sorrowful believe in him. They tell many stories about his miracles, and they tell of teachings even more wonderful than the miracles he performs."

"And what do you think of this man?" asked Herod.

"From what I have heard," Carius replied, "this man is worthy of being king over all of Judea and the countries of Philip."

What Carius had reported in private to Herod soon became known throughout Judea. And everyone began to refer to the Rabbi of Nazareth as "Jesus, the King of the Jews."

2. Herod's Plot

When King Herod heard Carius' report, his heart hardened and he said to himself: "My father killed twelve thousand times twelve thousand infants when this man Jesus was born, in order to destroy him, and Jesus escaped him; but I will not suffer him to escape me."

Herod took gifts in great numbers and gold and silver coins and dispatched them to his Roman rulers, with flattery for Caesar and false rumors about Jesus.

Then the king called together the rich men and the leaders among his subjects who depended on his favor, and said to them: "Have you heard what Carius has reported to me concerning Jesus being worthy to be made the King of the Jews?"

"We have heard," they said.

"Do you agree that he who is found consenting to this shall be destroyed by the sword, and all members of his household seized?"

And the men trembled before the tyrant and said: "We agree."

"Then you must find a way to testify against him before Pilate that he may be destroyed," said Herod.

The friends of Herod called a secret council to accuse Jesus of rebellion against Rome. At this meeting many spoke against Jesus, and among them were the high priests Annas and Caiaphas; but others at the meeting spoke for Jesus, and among these were Rabbi Nicodemus and Joseph of Arimathea.

3. The Secret Meeting

We might never have known what transpired at that secret meeting of the magistrates and the friends of Herod, who gathered to plot against Jesus, if we had no record of what was said by those who assembled. But during the alteration of a building in the Neapolitan city of Aquila in 1820, under a stone in the ground, was found a marble coffer. And in the coffer were a number of documents. One document contained the minutes of a meeting of a council of twenty magistrates, held in Jerusalem, concerning Jesus. The record lists the following of the assembled and their statements.

Simon Lepros: By what right is a rebellious man condemned?

Rabam: I know not why laws are made, when they are not kept.

Achias: One must first have a true and correct report before passing a sentence of death.

Subath: By virtue of divine and human statutes no one should be condemned, unless he is guilty. Therefore, what has this man done?

Rosnophin (*repeating what Rabam said*): Why are laws made, if they are not kept?

Phutiphares: An impostor who spreads sedition among the common people is not good for the country.

Ryphar: The laws punish none but the guilty; therefore, if he is a transgressor, let him first confess his own deed; but do not condemn him hastily.

Joseph of Arimathea: O how shameful it is that in a city not one should be found to be a defender of the innocent!

Joram: Should we allow a righteous man to die for his righteousness?

Ehiberis: Though he be righteous, yet should he be put to death; for his teachings stir the people to rebellion.

Nicodemus: Does our law, then, prejudge a man before he has been heard and before it is known what he has done?

Diarabias: Because he is accused before a council, he is worthy of death.

Sereas: A rebellious man is harmful to the country, therefore he must be removed from the people.

Rabinth: Whether just or unjust, because he is against our ancient laws, we can neither tolerate nor suffer him.

Josaphat: Then let us imprison him forever.

Ptolomaeus: Is he then neither righteous nor unrighteous? Why, then, do we delay so long before we condemn him to death, or banish him from our country?

Jeras: It would be much better and wiser that he be exiled and sent to the Emperor.

Mesa: If he is righteous, we ourselves will turn to him; if he is unrighteous, let us put him out from amongst us.

Samech: Let us use peaceful means so that he will not resist us; and if he still insists on going against us, we can then punish him.

CAIAPHAS: You do not know what you are saying: It is better for us that one man should die so that the whole nation should not perish.

4. *Judas Ish Sekharyut*

There lived a man in Jerusalem of the Tribe of Judah whose name was Reuben; and his wife's name was Cyborea, and she was of the Tribe of Issachar.

One night Cyborea dreamt that the child in her womb would be a boy who, when he grew up, would murder his father, marry his mother, and by his wickedness cause the destruction of his nation. Cyborea told her husband of her dreadful dream, and they decided that when their child was born they would name him Judas, place him in a waterproof basket and set him adrift on the sea. Then the fate of the child would be left in the hands of God.

And so they did.

But the wild waves did not destroy the child nor did the birds of prey devour him. His basket drifted to the shores of the Island of Sekharyut. And when the childless queen of the island came to bathe in the sea, she found Judas and took him home to her palace and claimed him as her own son.

Some years later the queen gave birth to a son of her own, and Judas, in a fit of jealousy, killed his foster brother, and fled to Jerusalem. He looked about him for employment, and went to Pontius Pilate to whom he offered himself in service.

5. *Pontius Pilate*

King Tyrus had a son by one of his handmaidens, Pilam, daughter of poor Atus. Pilam named her child Pilam-Atus, and he was called Pilate for short. The king wished to destroy the son of his error, and he sent Pilate off to the island Pontus, whose inhabitants were very cruel, hoping they would destroy him. But the youth, who began to call himself Pilate of Pontus or Pontius Pilate, proved a fair match for the cruel Pontians; and for every act of cruelty they performed, he performed two.

Pilate returned home after some time and he killed Tyrus' son, the prince and heir to the throne. For this crime Tyrus sent Pilate as a hostage to the Romans. But when Pilate arrived in Rome he killed the son of the King of France. And for this crime he was sent back to Pontus.

Herod the Brazen, who had usurped the throne of Judea, had a fondness for tyrants. When he heard of the wicked Pilate he asked Rome to proclaim Pilate procurator of Judea.

And to this Pontius Pilate came Judas Ish Sekharyut (called Judas Iscariot) and offered his services.

6. *Judas Repents*

One day the Roman Procurator, Pilate, passed a garden which had a tree covered with beautiful and tempting apples, but the tree was beyond his reach. On returning home, Pilate told Judas, who was in his service, about his craving for those apples. Whereupon Judas went out and killed the owner of the garden (not knowing that the owner was his father, Reuben), and confiscated the apples for his master.

In gratitude, Pilate commanded the rich widow, Cyborea, to marry Judas. And she did so — she not knowing that Judas was her son; nor he knowing Cyborea was his mother. But the red-bearded Judas soon discovered his true relationship to Cyborea, and he was stricken with remorse.

"Go to the Rabbi of Nazareth," Judas was advised. "Confess your sins, repent, and beg to be accepted among his disciples."

Judas did as he was advised. He professed his repentance so earnestly that he was made the twelfth disciple of Jesus, and appointed as purser for the rabbi and his followers.

For two years Judas remained a disciple of Jesus; but he was a disciple in name only, craftily supporting Jesus and secretly spying on him, hoping to hear his rabbi utter words of blasphemy against the Law of Moses or of rebellion against Rome.

When Caiaphas and Annas and their following began to contrive against Jesus, they drew Judas Iscariot into their conspiracy.

7. *Gestas and Demas*

In those days in which they conspired against Jesus, two robbers were sent up from Jericho to Jerusalem.

The first of these was named Gestas. He had become a robber in his youth. He had robbed travelers, and then slain them with his sword. Some he would strip of their clothes and leave them naked on the highway. Women travelers he hung up by their heels. He drank the blood of infants like a vampire. All the days of his life he disobeyed the laws of God and man; and he gloried in his deeds of violence. Such was Gestas.

The second of these robbers was named Demas. He was by birth a Galilean; but in his youth he joined Gestas and a band of robbers who terrorized the travelers on the highways to Egypt. Later he established an inn in which he robbed the rich who sought refuge in his place. He even set his hand to rob the temple in Jerusalem. There he stripped naked the priestess of the sanctuary, who was the daughter of the priest Caiaphas. And he stole from the temple the treasury of gold placed there by Solomon.

But, unlike Gestas, Demas was kind to the poor. In his youth he saved Joseph and Mary from being robbed during their flight to Egypt, and paid his companion Gestas forty dirhams of his own money to let them pass unmolested. He went out at night to take down the poor who had been crucified by the Romans and left to be eaten by the vultures. And, he secretly gave them burial in accord with the law of Moses and Israel. Such was Demas.

These two were brought to Jerusalem before Pilate.

8. *Thirty Pieces of Gold*

Early one morning Judas Iscariot entered the sanctuary of the temple in Jerusalem and said to the priests: "What will you give me if I deliver to you the plunderer of the Prophets and the robber of the Law?"

Caiaphas and the others thought Judas was speaking of the thief who had robbed the temple treasury and who had stripped the priestess of the sanctuary. They replied: "We will give you as a reward thirty pieces of gold."

(These thirty pieces of gold were the same that the Magi had brought among the gifts for the infant Jesus. Joseph lost them in the desert during his flight to Egypt, and a shepherd found them and brought them as an offering to the temple in Jerusalem.)

Judas left the temple with the thirty pieces of gold. He met Jesus on the street and followed him to the house of Simon the Leper, where the disciples were assembled. Then Judas returned secretly to the priests and said: "Give me the aid of soldiers with swords and staves and I will turn over to you the plunderer of the Prophets and the overthrower of the Law."

And they gave him the aid of soldiers, still thinking that Judas would bring them the thief who had robbed the temple and shamed the priestess of the sanctuary.

9. *The Cock that Entered Paradise*

Jesus was in the house of Simon the Leper and a roasted cock had been prepared to put before him. The cock was served by Akrosina, Simon's wife, just at the time Judas slipped away from the other disciples to betray Jesus. And as Judas left the house, Jesus said to the roasted cock:

"Rise up and follow the traitor!"

The cock rose up from the platter and hurried out after Judas. Some time later the cock returned. He reported that Judas conspired to betray Jesus, and told of the price Judas had received for the betrayal.

And Jesus said: "Because you have done this for me, you shall enter paradise."

And immediately the cock was taken up into heaven.

10. *The Hymn of Preparation*

The Feast of the Passover neared and the disciples of Jesus asked: "Where do you wish us to prepare the Passover feast for you?"

And Jesus said: "Let two of you go up to Jerusalem and enter the city. And, behold, you will meet there a man carrying a pitcher of water. Follow him. Wherever he enters, go and say to the owner of the house: 'Our master wishes to know whether the chamber is ready where he and his disciples will celebrate the Passover feast.' And he will show you a large upper chamber all set and ready for us."

The two disciples went up to the city and joined the great crowds streaming into Jerusalem for the festivities. They met a man carrying a pitcher of water and they followed him to the house where he delivered it. There they found the master of the house had already prepared a large upper chamber with all that was needed for the Passover feast. He had divined that guests were on their way whom he was to entertain with great honor, though he did not know who his guests would be.

The disciples who had come as the messengers of Jesus, returned to bring him and the other apostles to the chamber and the festive table that awaited them.

At the appointed hour they began the Passover ritual. And when they reached the Rite of the Fourth Cup, Jesus lifted his hands and said to his disciples:

"Behold, the time has come for us to drink the Fourth Cup of the Passover."

And departing from the prescribed song, Jesus lifted his voice and said: "Let us sing a hymn to our Father in Heaven, and with song on our lips go forward to whatever lies before us."

The disciples formed a ring around Jesus, their hands upon each other's shoulders.

"Glory to you, our Father who is in Heaven," chanted Jesus.

And the disciples going about in a ring, responded: "Amen!"

"Now, whereas we give thanks, I say: I would be saved and I would save."

"Amen!"

"I would be loosed and I would loose."

"Amen!"

"I would be pierced and I would pierce!"

"Amen!"

"I would hear and I would be heard."

"Amen!"

"I would be understood and I will understand."

"Amen!"

"I would flee and I would stay."

"Amen!"

"I have no place and I have many places."

"Amen!"

"I have no temple and I have many temples."

"Amen!"

"I am a door to you who knock."

"Amen!"

"I am a lamp to you who perceive me."

"Amen!"

"I am the way to you who are the wayfarer."

"Amen!"

At the end of the hymn Jesus left the disciples and went out alone into the darkness of the night and there he prayed for a long time. It was almost dawn when he returned and the disciples were fast asleep. Jesus awakened them, and said:

"Arise, for I am about to be delivered up by them who conspire against me."

And behold, Judas appeared leading a multitude of Roman soldiers with drawn swords. The betrayer walked directly to Jesus and kissed him, saying: "Hail, Rabbi!"

And at this which was a signal for them, the soldiers surrounded Jesus, bound his hands, and led him away.

Jesus was brought to the house of Caiaphas the high priest, where an assembly waited for the man who had robbed the temple. Judas pointed to the man whose hands were bound and said to the astonished priests: "This is he who is the plunderer of the Prophets and the overthrower of the Law."

CHAPTER TWENTY

The Sentence

1. *Jesus Accused*

At dawn the accusers of Jesus gathered before Pilate, and said: "A man walks about in this city whose father was Joseph the Carpenter and whose mother is Mary of Nazareth. Though he is a Jew, he tries to overthrow the Scriptures and to do away with the Sabbath."

Pilate asked: "How does he try to do away with the Sabbath?"

"He cures the sick on that day; and that is forbidden by the Fourth Commandment."

"If he makes people well," said Pilate, "he does no evil."

"But he cures them with the power of magic and sorcery, and with the aid of demons," said his accusers. "And that is forbidden."

"To cure people of their ills," said Pilate, "is not a diabolic work, but a grace from God."

The accusers then pleaded: "We beseech your highness to summon this man and question him so that you may convince yourself of the truth of what we say of him, who calls himself King of the Jews and the son of God."

"Tell me, how can I, who am only a procurator, question and try one who is a king?" asked Pilate.

"We do not say that he *is* a king," they replied. "He claims to be a king and for that reason you should try him."

Pilate took off his cloak and handed it to Rachaab, his messenger, and said: "Go, and show this cloak to Jesus, and say to him: 'Pilate the procurator asks you to appear before him.' And let Jesus be brought before me with all respect."

2. *The Adoration of the Runner*

Rachaab went out into the city and found Jesus. He called him to the praetorium and spread out upon the ground both his own and Pilate's cloaks: "Come, my lord, and walk upon these, because the procurator wishes to see you."

The accusers saw what the runner had done and they complained to Pilate: "Why have you seen fit to call Jesus by runner, as befits a grandee and a nobleman, instead of calling him by a crier, as befits a man accused? Now, see your runner spreading your cloak before him as before a king, saying, 'My lord, the procurator wishes to see you.'"

Pilate turned to his runner and asked: "Why have you done this and why have you spread out your cloak and mine upon the ground for him to walk upon?"

And Rachaab replied: "My lord procurator, when you sent me to Jerusalem to see the Jew Alexander, I saw this man entering the gate of the city upon an ass and the Children of Israel ran before him with branches in their hands, shouting: 'Blessed is he who comes in the name of the Lord!' And they spread the branches and their cloaks before him."

"The Jews spoke in Hebrew," shouted the accusers. "How could you, a Gentile and Greek, know what they said?"

And the runner replied: "I asked a Hebrew what they were shouting and he translated it for me."

Pilate turned to the accusers: "What were they shouting in Hebrew?"

"They were saying: *Baruch Habba beshem Adonoi!*"

"And what does that mean?" asked Pilate.

"It means: Blessed is he who comes in the name of the Lord!"

"Then in what way has the runner done wrong?" asked Pilate.

And the accusers were silent.

"Go now," said Pilate to Rachaab, "and bring Jesus in; and bring him in whatever way you will."

The runner went out once again and he spread the cloaks before Jesus, saying: "Come, my lord, and walk upon these cloaks, for the procurator wishes to see you."

3. *The Standards Bow Down*

The doors of the praetorium were opened for Jesus to enter. And all those present noticed in surprise that the standards held in the hands of the standard-bearers on each side of Pilate, were lowered as before a king.

The accusers of Jesus cried out: "What is the meaning of this? Why do the standard-bearers lower their standards before this man?"

Pilate asked the soldiers: "Why have you done this?"

And the soldiers replied: "We did not do this. The standards bowed down of their own accord."

When Pilate saw how unbelieving the priests and the accusers were, he said to them: "Select of your own, twelve young men, strong and powerful, and let them hold the standards upright, and let us see whether these soldiers are telling the truth."

The accusers selected twelve strong men of their own; they were placed before the procurator's tribunal, six on each side; and each bore a standard.

Then Pilate said to the runner: "Take Jesus out of the praetorium and bring him back in whatever way that pleases you." And then he said to his soldiers: "If you have lied to me, I swear by the health of Caesar that I will cut off your heads."

The procurator gave the signal for Jesus to be brought in again. And again the standards bowed down.

On seeing this, Pilate was seized with fear, and wished to leave the tribunal at once. But the accusers were not pleased by what they had seen and they said to Pilate: "Did we not tell you that this man is a magician?"

4. *Procla's Dream*

As Pilate swayed between fear and indecision, and wondered whether he should try Jesus or let him go, a messenger arrived with a message from his wife.

Pilate read the message and turned to the accusers: "You know that my wife, Procla, leans toward your faith?"

"Yes, we know."

And Pilate said: "I have just received a message from her, saying 'Have nothing to do with this just man. For he has appeared to me in a dream and I have suffered many things on account of him this night.'"

"Did we not tell you that this man is a magician?" said the accusers in triumph. "Now he has tried by the power of the prince of demons to bewitch your wife in her dreams."

5. *The Inquiry*

"You have heard what your accusers have testified concerning you," said Pilate to Jesus. "What have you to say to them?"

"Every man has the power over his own tongue to speak either good or evil, as he wishes," said Jesus.

"If this man were not a magician and a blasphemer, we would not have brought him to you for trial," said the accusers.

"Then why do you not take him and judge him according to your law?" asked Pilate.

"It is not lawful to us to put a man to death," they answered.

"If you are reluctant to put him to death, why should I?" asked Pilate.

"Because he claims to be the King of the Jews and therefore preaches rebellion against Caesar."

Pilate turned to Jesus and asked: "Is it true that you claim to be the King of the Jews?"

"My kingdom is not of this world," said Jesus.

Pilate then said to the accusers: "I find no fault with this man. For although you accuse him, I do not find him deserving of death, not even because he heals on the Sabbath."

"Tell us," said the priests, "if anyone blasphemes Caesar, is he deserving of death?"

"He deserves to die," said Pilate.

"If he who dishonors Caesar deserves to die, how much more deserves to die the man who dishonors God!"

"But what proof have you that this man dishonors God?" asked Pilate. "And if you differ with me and find his words blasphemous, take him and judge him according to your law."

The procurator looked about him at the crowd of Jews in the chamber who had gathered for the trial, and he saw many of them weeping.

"It seems to me," said Pilate, "that it is not the wish of the Jews that this man should die."

Encouraged by these words, one learned man came forward and said: "I beseech your highness to let me speak."

"Say on," said Pilate.

"I, Nicodemus, a Jew, the son of a Jew, and a rabbi in Israel, being present in the synagogue, said to the priests and the elders: 'What you have to say against this man is that he performs miracles such as no man has yet done. Leave him alone and devise no evil against him. For if his miracles are of God, they will stand; and if they are of magic, they will come to nothing. Assuredly Moses, who was sent to Egypt by God, did many strange miracles before Pharaoh. And in Egypt there dwelt many magicians, and the famed brothers Jannes and Mambres performed before the king. But the miracles of Moses prevailed; whereas the works of Jannes and Mambres came to naught, and they who believed in them perished.' Therefore I entreat you, my lord, not to allow this man to be put to death; for he is not deserving of it."

Then another Jew arose and said: "I beg of you, my lord Pilate, hear me also."

"Say what you wish," said Pilate.

"For thirty-eight years I lay helpless on my bed in great agony. And then one day some young men carried me, bed and all, to this man Jesus, and he pitied me and said: 'Leave your couch and walk!' And immediately I was made whole and well again."

"Ask him on what day that was," shouted the accusers.

"On the Sabbath," said the man.

"Just what we told your highness. He performs these cures on the Sabbath with the aid of demons."

And a certain woman, Veronica by name, cried out: "Hear me, O governor and procurator! For twelve years I was ill and could find no cure, until I touched the fringe of his garment and was made well again."

"A woman's evidence, according to our law, cannot be received in court," the accusers protested.

Then many men in the crowd began to murmur:

"I was born blind and Jesus pitied me and put clay on my eyes and I received my sight. And that was not on a Sabbath," said one.

"I was hunchbacked, and Jesus pitied me and took my hand, and I was immediately straightened. And that was not on a Sabbath," said another.

"I saw Jesus at a marriage feast at Cana in Galilee where wine failed the hosts, and Jesus, to spare them shame, turned the water into wine," said still another.

A nobleman arose and said: "My son lay dying in Capernaum when I besought Jesus to help me, and he said to me, 'Go home, your son will live.' And my son was healed in that same hour."

And a Pharisee arose and said: "I saw a great multitude come to Jesus out of Galilee and Judea, and from the seashore, and from the distant places on the Jordan; and many of them were sick with diverse diseases, and he healed them all."

And many more men and women rose to testify for Jesus and said: "We are not proselytes but Jews, the children of Jews, and we speak the truth of this man."

On hearing all this testimony, Pilate was inclined to release Jesus. But the accusers said to him: "If you release Jesus, you are no friend of Caesar's. For this man calls himself the son of God, and if you free him, he will become king and take away Caesar's kingdom. For this is the man to whom the Magi brought gifts at his birth. This is he whom Herod's father wished to put to death. And it was for that reason that Joseph the Carpenter and Mary his wife fled into Egypt."

When Pilate heard this, he ordered the crowd to be silent. "Is this really he whom Herod sought that he might put him to death?" he asked.

And they answered: "Yes, it is he."

"Then Herod shall judge him," said Pilate.

And he sent Jesus to Herod.

Herod rejoiced when Jesus was brought before him. He put on his white garments and seated himself in the judgment seat ready to pass judgment and condemn Jesus. But Jesus gave no answer to Herod's questions, and Herod was obliged to return him to Pilate.

6. *Pilate's Verdict*

(In the Gospel of Nicodemus the sentencing of Jesus by Pontius Pilate is told in one brief paragraph:

> Thy nation has charged thee with being a king. On this account I sentence thee, first to be scourged, according to the enactment of venerable kings, and then to be fastened to the cross in the garden where thou wast seized. And let Dysmas (Demas) and Gestas, the two malefactors, be crucified with thee.

But in the Council Concerning Jesus Fabricius presents, presumably word for word, the lengthy death sentence passed by Pilate. It begins:

> In the seventeenth year of Claudius Tiberius, Roman Emperor and invincible monarch of the whole world; in the 202nd Olympiad, or Greek reckoning of time by periods of five years, and in the 24th Iliad; in the 3996th year after the creation of the world according to the common reckoning; in the 73rd year of the Roman Empire, and in the 794th after the founding of the city of Rome; in the 440th year after the return from the Babylonian captivity; and the 487th after the establishment of the holy dominion; . . . in the midst of March, have I, Pontius Pilate, President of the Roman Empire, in the city of Jerusalem, in the palace of the arch-resident, after notice taken of the penal matter, convicted, condemned, and sentenced to death; and I also do hereby again convict, condemn, and sentence to death Jesus of Nazareth, who by the people is called the Christ and Messiah and the anointed one of Nazareth; that he, as a malefactor, be affixed, raised up, stretched out, set up, and hanged upon a cross.

The document recapitulates in detail the accusation of sedition against Jesus; the appointment of the centurion to carry out the sentence; the scourging "according to Roman custom"; the route to be followed in taking the condemned from the judgment hall to the "place of the skull"; and the inscription to be put on the cross, in Hebrew, Greek and Latin, reading: "Jesus of Nazareth, King of the Jews" as a warning to all rebels. The document concludes with a specific warning against any interference with the centurion and his men in the execution of the sentence on a rebel "against the Roman Empire" and against both the Roman and Jewish laws.

Though the exact dates when this document was drawn up are given at the beginning, it is witnessed and signed by a number of Pharisees, notaries, and priests, bearing sixteenth-century Italian names.)

CHAPTER TWENTY-ONE

The Sorrowful Journey

1. *The Roman Scourging*

Pilate pronounced sentence on Jesus; and the centurion Cornelius Vrancinus took the prisoner straightaway and bound him to a marble pillar in the judgment hall. And two mighty soldiers, with scourges made of heavy leather, tipped with brass, carried out the scourging, according to the Roman custom.

(Some say that 828 blows were prescribed, three for each bone of the body; and others give the number as 5475 strokes, each stroke resulting in a wound.)

After the scourging, the soldiers placed a purple mantle on the shoulders of Jesus, a crown of thorns upon his head, and a reed in his hand. Then they seated him in the judgment seat and derided him, saying: "Judge righteously, O King of the Jews!" And when they tired of their mockery, they led Jesus out of the praetorium between the two robbers, Demas and Gestas, who were to be crucified at the same time.

They placed the heavy crosses on the backs of the three condemned men, and started them from the judgment hall at the palace of the procurator, to Golgotha, the Hill of the Skulls.

2. *The Wood of the Cross*

The cross that Jesus bore from the praetorium to Calvary, and on which he was crucified, was fifteen feet high and its transverse beam was eight feet across. Three pieces of wood composed the cross: the upright beam; the crossbeam; and the tablet above on which was placed the inscription as Pilate had commanded. (And there are those who say that there was a fourth piece, upon which Jesus rested his feet.)

The upright beam was of cedar; the crossbeam was of cypress; and the tablet upon it was of the wood of the palm.

But these were no ordinary beams and pieces of wood.

The upright beam, it is told, was taken from the pool of Bethesda and came from a branch of the Tree of Life. And this is how it happened:

When Adam felt death approaching, he called his beloved son Seth to his side and said to him: "My son, go to the gates of paradise, and ask for the oil of the tree of mercy, which once was promised me, so that I might be healed."

Seth, his obedient son, immediately started out for the gates of paradise, following a green and fragrant path that still bore traces of the footprints left by his parents, Adam and Eve, when they fled from paradise. (For their feet, it is recorded, scorched the earth when they were driven out of paradise and no grass ever grew there again.)

Seth walked for a long time on that path, until he saw a great light and flames that reached to the clouds. Then he knew that he was near the walls of the Garden of Eden.

Seth approached the gates, and before him appeared the angel Michael, who asked: "What do you seek, Seth? Is it the oil of mercy which heals the sick?"

Seth admitted that he sought the oil of mercy.

"Do not ask for it," the angel Michael advised him. "For it has been decreed that this oil may not be used for another five thousand and five hundred years."

Seth, thinking of his father, began to weep. And the angel tried to console him.

"Weep not, Seth. But instead look three times upon paradise."

Seth looked through the open gates: the first time he saw the Garden of Eden filled with brightness, fragrance and happiness. Through the center of the garden flowed four streams in the shade of a tree of wondrous beauty. And on this tree grew five thousand different kinds of fruits.

The second time he looked Seth saw the tree despoiled of fruit and denuded of leaves, with a hideous serpent coiled about its trunk.

The third time Seth saw the tree rising to heaven, covered with leaves and fruit. The serpent had vanished, and on the crest of the tree sat a child of ineffable beauty.

The angel Michael explained that the first tree Seth saw was the condition of man before the Fall; the second tree was the condition of man fallen into sin; and the third tree was the beginning of the salvation of mankind.

Then he gave Seth a branch of the Tree of Life, and said: "Plant it; and when it begins to bear fruit, you shall have the healing oil you seek."

Seth took the branch from the angel and left. But when he reached home his father was dead. Seth planted the branch on Adam's grave, which is in the center of the earth and on the summit of Golgotha. The branch flourished and grew into a beautiful tree.

When Solomon noticed the tree and saw how beautiful it was, he ordered it cut down and used in building the temple of Jerusalem. The workmen faithfully tried to do as they were told, but no matter how carefully they measured the wood, and no matter where they placed it, it would not fit. It was either too short or too long; too narrow or too wide; too thick or too thin. Finally the angry workmen placed it across the brook Kedron, where it served as a bridge.

One day the Queen of Sheba, who was visiting Solomon, came to this bridge across the Kedron, and in a vision saw Jesus suspended upon the beam. She told Solomon of her vision and predicted that the one crucified on that beam would, by his death, cause the destruction of the Jewish kingdom. Solomon ordered the beam weighted with stones and thrown into the Lake Bethesda. (And that is why the waters of that lake have always had healing powers.) When Jesus was sentenced to be crucified, the beam from the Tree of Life floated to the surface and was used for the cross.

(Another story tells that the angel Michael gave Seth only three seeds from the fruit of the Tree of Life. Seth placed the seeds in his father's mouth before burial. And out of these three seeds grew three trees: a palm, a cypress and a cedar. They grew so closely together that they merged into one tree, exhaling a wonderful aroma, and all the sick who touched the tree were cured. And out of this three-trees-in-one were ultimately made all the parts of the cross that Jesus bore.)

There are many versions of this legend, but in all the variations, Solomon causes the beam to be buried or thrown into the pool of Bethesda; and they all point to the conclusion that "This tree was destined to destroy sin in the world."

3. *From the Judgment Hall to Golgotha*

From Pilate's palace to the Hill of Skulls the distance was one thousand three hundred and twenty-one paces (3333 feet). After Jesus had gone 26 paces, they placed the cross upon him. At the end of 80 paces, he stumbled and fell for the first time. He arose and after 61⅙ paces more he met his mother, Mary, and John, whom Jesus loved above all his disciples. Further on, 71⅗ paces, the Roman soldiers took the cross off his back and placed it on Simon of Cyrene, who was a disciple of Jesus. Veronica of Paneas joined the crowd 191⅕ paces further, following Jesus closely. At a distance of 336⅘ paces further on, Jesus fell a second time, and his followers wept bitterly. They had now reached a rough and stony road leading north toward the Hill of the Skulls, and Jesus walked 348⅘ paces to a place where two roads met. There he saw for the last time the weeping women, full of compassion, for they were not allowed to come any nearer to the place of execution. From there it was 161⅖ paces to the foot of Mount Calvary, where Jesus fell again, for the third time. They ascended 18 paces up the hill. There Jesus was given wine mixed with gall. And after another 12 paces, the soldiers nailed Jesus to the cross, and carried him 14 paces to where the cross was raised on Calvary.

4. *My Son!*

John was in the judgment hall when Pilate convicted and sentenced Jesus to death. As soon as the sentence was pronounced, John hastened to find Mary.

"What is it that has happened?" asked Mary anxiously.

"Know that the enemies of Jesus among the priests and the scribes have laid hold of him and brought him before Pilate, and he condemned Jesus to be crucified."

And Mary said in anguish: "Where is he now?"

"They are taking him away to Golgotha."

Mary cried out when she heard these lacerating words: "My son! My son! What evil have you done that they take you away to crucify you?"

She rose up as one blinded, and was led by John along the road, weeping bitterly.

Along the way they were joined by Martha, sister of Lazarus, and Mary Magdalene, and Salome the midwife, and many others who had heard of the sentence and had come hurrying to the Antoniana road. They reached the milling crowd, preceding and following Jesus. And Mary, the mother, cried out:

"Where is my son, John? Where is my son?"

"Do you not see him? He wears a crown of thorns and his hands are bound."

When Mary gazed upon her son, whom she at first had not recognized, and saw how he was scourged and bleeding, and moving slowly under the burden of the heavy cross, she fell to the ground and lay there for a long time. The women about her wept bitterly, and they revived the grief-stricken mother.

Mary opened her eyes and cried: "My son, my son! What have they done to you! Where has the beauty of your form gone? How can I endure to see you suffer such things?"

She beat her breast and lamented: "Where are they gone, the good deeds you have done to your brothers in Judea? What evil have you done that they should treat you so?"

5. Veronica's Veil

Veronica of Paneas, who had come to testify for Jesus before Pilate, followed the multitude, bowed down with grief. And as she walked she sorrowed: "My lord, my lord, whom Pilate has condemned out of envy! How shall we live without you?"

About halfway to Calvary she saw Jesus stumble and fall under the burden of the cross. She ran to his side and gently wiped the sweat and blood from his face with her veil.

And, behold, the impression of his countenance remained there on the veil of Veronica.

6. *The Wandering Cartaphilus*

There was a porter in Pilate's service named Cartaphilus, a knave, who tried to ingratiate himself with his master. And when Jesus came out of the judgment hall, scourged and bleeding, he struck the prisoner on the back, shouting:

"Go faster, Jesus! Go faster! Why do you loiter?"

Jesus looked at the man and said: "I am going. But you shall wait until I return."

And ever since that moment the man Cartaphilus wanders from place to place. He has no home; he has no family; he has no friends. He has no one to care whether he is well or ill; whether he lives or dies. After remaining in one place long enough for a neighbor to answer his greetings, Cartaphilus moves on. At the end of each century his body assumes again the appearance of a man of thirty — the age of Cartaphilus when he struck Jesus.

And thus he is doomed to live in loneliness and despair until Judgment Day.

7. *Ahasuerus the Shoemaker*

Among those who testified against Jesus before Pilate, there was a certain Jewish shoemaker named Ahasuerus. And after Jesus had been sentenced, the shoemaker ran home to gather his family so that they could watch the condemned man led to Calvary.

Ahasuerus stationed himself along the road, with his youngest son in his arms. And when Jesus came by, weary and faint, and stopped to rest, the shoemaker shouted, hoping to gain favor by his zeal: "Move on! Move on! Do not tarry!"

Jesus looked at the shoemaker and said: "I shall stand and rest, but you shall know no rest until Judgment Day."

And as Jesus spoke, Ahasuerus set down the child and followed him. He did not stop at the Hill of the Skulls, but wandered on and on.

And ever since then he has wandered the world over, unable to stand still or rest, and he is doomed so to wander until the Day of Judgment.

CHAPTER TWENTY-TWO

Crucifixion and Burial

1. Where the Cross Was Placed

Pilate's centurions stripped Jesus of his garments, and covered him with a linen cloth, replacing the crown of thorns on his head. For, according to Roman law, the personal belongings of an executed man became the property of the executioners. But when they came to divide the garments among them, they found that his cloak was seamless throughout. (For this was the cloak Mary had woven for Jesus when they were in Egypt, and it had grown in size as Jesus had grown, and in all the years it had remained as new.)

"Let us rend this cloak and divide it equally," said one soldier.

"No. Let us not rend it, but cast lots for it and see to whom it shall belong," suggested another.

And they cast lots for the garment.

Then they nailed Jesus to the cross. Some say that three nails were used, one for each hand and one for both feet. Some say that four nails were used. And some say that five nails were used and their names were:

SATOR
AREPO
TENET
OPERA
ROTAS

Over his head they nailed a tablet, as commanded by Pilate, with the inscription, in Hebrew, Greek and Latin:

JESUS OF NAZARETH
KING OF THE JEWS

Then they raised the cross and placed it on the spot marked with a stone bearing the inscription: the Cranium. For that was the exact spot where Adam had been buried; and the cross rested just above Adam's cranium.

2. *They Know Not What They Do*

The soldiers mocked Jesus on the cross, saying "You have cured the leper, made the blind see and the deaf hear. Now let us see you cure yourself."

They offered him vinegar mixed with gall, saying: "Drink, King of the Jews, and save yourself!"

Jesus held his peace and throughout gave no sign of having pain.

But his mother standing nearby wept in agony. And Jesus saw her from the cross and said to her:

"Mother, behold your son!"

Mary said through her tears: "How you suffer unjustly, my son! How you have been delivered to this bitter death! Where are your disciples, who boasted that they would die for you? Where are those you healed and helped? Why has no one come forward to help you?"

And looking at the cross, she cried out again: "O cross, bend down that I may embrace and kiss my son! Bend down, O cross, that I 'may throw my arms around my son and bid him farewell like a mother!"

The soldiers and the accusers of Jesus who heard Mary's lament came forward and tried to put a distance between her and the cross. And Jesus cried out in a loud voice:

"O Father in Heaven, let not this sin stand against them, for they know not what they do!"

3. *Demas the Repentant*

On the same day that Jesus was crucified two robbers were also crucified, and their crosses placed one on each side of Jesus. On the left hung Gestas, the impenitent robber; and on the right rose Demas, upon whom fell the shadow of Jesus.

Gestas said to Jesus bitterly: "See how many evil deeds I have done in my days, yet you, who call yourself the son of God, cannot help yourself now any more than I."

Demas rebuked his companion in thievery and murder, and said: "O wretched and miserable Gestas! Have you no fear of God even to the end? We are punished for the evil we committed, but Jesus is punished for the good he has done."

Gestas replied: "If he really is the Christ, then let me see him leave his cross, that I may believe in him."

"I can see he is the Christ without his leaving the cross," said Demas. "And I can see him adored by myriads and myriads of angels. For he is not of this world."

"And I," said Gestas, "can only see him suffer like ourselves, perishing along with us, not like a man, but like a wild beast."

And Demas addressed the executioners, saying: "What wrong has this man done that he should die with us?"

"Hold your tongue," the soldiers retorted. And they would not break Demas' legs to hasten death and shorten his torment.

Demas then pleaded with Jesus: "Forgive me the sins which I have committed. Make not the stars nor the moon to testify against me, for in the night I committed my wicked deeds. Nor urge the sun to tell the evils of my heart. I feel death already upon me. And though I have nothing to offer for remission of my sins, as my spirit departs, I beg of you to order my sins to be washed away, and remember me, the sinner, in your kingdom, O Jesus!"

Jesus said softly: "I say unto you, Demas, that before this day is over, you shall be with me in paradise."

"Amen! Amen!" said Demas.

4. *The Letter to Heaven*

The aprocryphal Narrative of Joseph of Arimathea presents the following epistle, as given by Jesus to the repentant robber.

And Jesus gave to the repentant robber an epistle:

I, Jesus Christ the Son of God, who have come down from the heights of the heavens, who have come forth out of the bosom of the invisible Father without being separated from Him, and who have come down into the world to be made of flesh, and to be nailed to a cross, in order that I might save Adam, whom I fashioned:

To my archangelic powers, the gatekeepers of paradise, to the officers of my Father:

I will and order that he who has been crucified along with me should go in, should receive remission of sins through me; and that he, having put on our incorruptible body, should go into paradise, and dwell there where no one has ever been able to dwell.

5. Darkness at Noon

On the sixth hour of the day, as noon was approaching, Jesus on the cross cried out:

"My God, my God, why have you forsaken me?"

Then Jesus looked at his mother, and at John Zebedee, whom he loved tenderly, and at the others of his kindred who had come from Galilee, and at the followers who adored him, and they heard him whisper:

"Pardon my death to all my enemies, and may it please God my Father to hold them excused, and that he may be willing not to do justice or take vengeance upon them, because they neither knew nor realized what they did."

Then he cried out: "I thirst."

The soldiers mixed a drink of gall and vinegar and gave it to him. He drank it, and said in a firm voice:

"My heavenly Father, I trust my soul into your hands!"

And he gave up the ghost.

In that instant the sun darkened, the stars fell from heaven, and the moon appeared red as blood. Men lit their lamps as at midnight, and walked about astonished. The entire earth, from pole to pole, quaked; rocks crumbled; and the tombs of the dead opened.

The twelve virgins ministering in the temple in Jerusalem were astounded by the darkness and the quaking of the earth, and they ran into the Holy of Holies for sanctuary. But there they saw an angel come down from heaven, his visage full of anger, and a long sword in his right hand. The angel, seeing that the virgins cowered in fear that he had come to slay them, said:

"Fear not, for no evil will befall you."

Then he stretched out the gleaming sword in his hand and slashed the veil of the temple, rending it in two, and dividing it from top to bottom. As the veil of the temple was rent, a deep voice came from out the horns of the altar, saying:

"Woe unto you, Jerusalem, who kill your prophets and stone them that are sent to you!"

Then the virgins, that they might be spared from God's anger, hastened to join Mary and those who were with her and with John Zebedee at Calvary. And there they found the multitude of the people lamenting, beating their breasts, and wailing:

"Woe unto us for our sins! The judgment has drawn nigh! The fate of Jerusalem is sealed!"

And over all Judea there was bewilderment and confusion. And over all the world there was surprise and astonishment. As far as Athens the people and their philosophers could not explain the reason for the upheaval in the elements of nature. In their perplexity they set up an altar and upon it inscribed: "To the Unknown God."

6. The Baptism of Demas

The day was drawing to an end and the sun was about to set, when Pilate sent his centurion Longinus to find out whether the three men crucified on Golgotha that day were still alive.

The centurion found the two robbers, Gestas and Demas, still breathing, and he broke their legs to hasten their end. Jesus was dead. And Longinus, who had taken part in the flogging in the judgment hall, and who spat upon him there, now pierced his side with a lance. And out of the wound poured forth a stream of blood and water.

The blood and the water flowed upon Demas, so that he was baptized before he died. And some drops of blood fell on the centurion, who had been troubled with sore eyes all his life. But as the blood of Jesus fell upon him, Longinus was healed, and his full sight restored.

7. The Fate of Judas

Judas began to tremble in fear and remorse when he heard Pilate pronounce sentence upon the Rabbi of Nazareth whose disciple he had been. In his despair he went to the men who had paid him the thirty pieces of gold, and he pleaded with them:

"I have sinned in betraying innocent blood. I know well that I have done evil. Take back the money which you have given me for the betrayal of Jesus."

"What is that to us?" they asked. "We have paid you for what you have done and our bargain is closed."

Judas opened his purse and emptied it at their feet. Then he fled from their midst to his home.

There he found his wife sitting upon a stool, turning a cock upon a spit over the glowing coals. And Judas said to her in a forlorn voice:

"Get me a rope, my wife, for I intend to hang myself for what I have done."

She tried to calm him, but he would not be calmed and said:

"I have unjustly betrayed my master, Jesus; and they have brought him before Pilate, who condemned him to die on the cross. But Jesus will rise again on the third day!"

And his wife said: "Calm yourself, for it is as likely that Jesus will rise again as it is for that cock roasting on the coals to crow again."

The words had barely left her lips, when the cock roasting on the coals flapped his wings and crowed three times.

Judas, astounded and tormented, made a halter out of a rope, ran out of the house, and hanged himself upon a sycamore. And that tree can be seen to this day on the west side of Mount Zion.

There are many variations of this story, all ending with Judas, in remorse, committing suicide. There are other stories in which he meets with a horrible death not of his own choosing. The latter legend, too, has many variations, mostly in surpassing each other in the miseries inflicted upon Judas.

In the following Mohammedan legend, Judas neither commits suicide nor is killed in an accident.

The moment Pilate pronounced judgment on the Prophet of Nazareth, Jesus ascended to heaven. But Judas was miraculously transformed so that he appeared like Jesus, and the soldiers, into whose hands Judas had betrayed his master, laid hands upon the betrayer and carried him off to be scourged and crucified.

Jesus in heaven knew how his mother would suffer at Calvary in the belief that it was her son who languished on the cross, and he came down to comfort her and to tell her what was really taking place.

And Judas suffered unspeakable agonies until he gave up the ghost.

8. *The Burial*

There lived in Jerusalem a God-fearing man, rich and well-born, whose name was Joseph of Arimathea. He came to testify for Jesus before Pilate; and after the sentence he followed him to Golgotha, and stood beside Mary and John until Jesus gave up the ghost on the cross.

Then Joseph went to Nicodemus and said: "I know, Rabbi, that you loved Jesus when living. Come with me to ask Pilate to allow us to take down his body from the cross for burial, for it is a great sin to leave him there unburied."

And Nicodemus replied: "I am afraid of Pilate's wrath and the evil that may befall me. But you are Pilate's friend. Go to him alone and beg for his permission. And if he grants it, I shall help you with the burial."

Joseph went to Pilate and entreated him: "My lord, let no hatred fall upon a dead man; and allow me to take the body of Jesus for burial."

"Why should he be so honored who was condemned as a sorcerer and a plotter against the kingdom of Caesar?" asked Pilate.

"My lord, all the evil that a man has done should perish with him at his death. Therefore I entreat you not to refuse my request."

And Pilate finally relented.

Joseph of Arimathea hurried to Nicodemus, and they gathered myrrh and aloes and white linen. Then they went to Calvary where Mary the Mother and Mary Magdalene and John and all the others waited to prepare the body for burial.

When Joseph and Nicodemus climbed up to take down the body of Jesus from the cross, they saw that the body on the cross to the right, that of Demas, had disappeared; and the body on the cross to the left, that of Gestas, had turned into the form of a dragon.

Joseph, with the aid of Nicodemus, came down from the ladder and they tenderly extended the body upon a white linen cloth that they had placed upon the ground. When they did this, the earth shook so violently that the hearts of all men were filled with fear.

Mary the Mother placed her son's head in her lap and kissed the face and covered it with tears; and she sorrowed for a long time as if she were about to die.

Joseph of Arimathea said to her: "O sorrowful mother, suffer us to place the body of your son, our master, in the shroud and carry him to the sepulcher."

And Mary replied, greatly troubled: "Haste not in taking away from me the sight of my son, or bury me with him."

John then came to her side and said: "See what hour it is. The night is beginning to overcome the day. Suffer the body of Jesus to be shrouded and buried before dark."

They shrouded the body and carried him to the sepulcher, Mary supporting the head, Mary Magdalene, the feet, and the others carrying the body; and all wept sorely.

The body was placed in the sepulcher, and the hearts of the mourners seemed to break as they listened to the piteous lamentations of the mother.

Joseph finally said to Mary and the others: "Let us return to Jerusalem, for there is nothing we can do here."

Yet no one stirred.

And as it was growing very dark, John said to Mary: "We cannot remain here. Let us return to Mount Zion to the house where our master supped last night."

And while the mourners returned to Jerusalem, the enemies of

Jesus, having learned that Pilate had permitted the burial, ran to the procurator and pleaded:

"Because Jesus said that after three days he will rise again, his disciples may try to steal his body by night; and then lead the people astray by such deceit. Therefore order the tomb sealed and guarded."

Pilate complied with their request. The tomb was sealed; and five hundred soldiers were placed about the sepulcher to guard it.

9. *The Tomb in Srinagar*

In the village of Quadian, in the district of Gurdaspur, in the far-away Punjab, there lived a man, not so very long ago, whose name was Mirza Ghulam Ahmad. He was a Muslim by birth, but at the age of fifty he declared himself to be the promised Messiah at the Second Coming, as well as the Mahdi, the last of the Imams and the promised spiritual leader of the Muslims. He had learned of his true identity, he claimed, by incontrovertible divine revelation; and he proceeded to explain his claim in three volumes, and by the authority of "the spirit and power" of Jesus.

By 1908, when Ahmad died at the age of sixty-nine, he had firmly established a mystical-religious movement, called Ahmadiya. This movement, or sect, exists in the Punjab to this day, small in number but fervent in belief. At first Ahmad's followers called themselves Quadiani or Kadiani; but now they are known as "Ahmadiya Muslims."

The teachings of Ahmadiya are not our concern here. The interested reader will find them discussed in studies of India's religions. But Ahmad makes one claim that is of great interest in lore, namely, that Jesus did not die on the cross.

This is the story as given by Mirza Ghulam Ahmad:

When the disciples took Jesus down from the cross, he was in a swoon and unconscious from the loss of blood. His wounds were treated with "Marham-i-Isa," a marvelous ointment of which (in the words of Ahmad) "over a thousand books on medicine contain a description." After three days Jesus revived from his swoon; and after forty days he was fully recovered.

Jesus then decided to seek and gather under his ministry the Ten

Tribes of Israel who inhabited Afghanistan and Kashmir. Ahmad even fortifies this claim by quoting the Gospels.

Jesus spent many years among the "lost sheep of Israel" and was known to them as the Shahazda nabi, the Prince and Prophet, Yus-Asaf, or Jesus the Gatherer. At the age of one hundred and twenty, Yus-Asaf died and was buried by the Kashmiris with the honors due a prince and a prophet.

By divine revelation, Ahmad identified the tomb of Jesus on Khan Yar Street in Srinagar, the capital of Kashmir.

The tomb was visited in the summer of 1913 by a member of the Royal Asiatic Society, H. A. Walter. "After considerable difficulty in learning the exact location, I visited the tomb, resembling hundreds of other tombs of Mohammedan saints, with rags tied to the inner gate by those (both Muslim and Hindus) who had left money with the keeper to pay for the intercession of the occupant of the tomb." Mr. Walter cites a Kashmiri publication which claims that documents "of unquestionable authenticity and veracity" exist, giving the testimony of eyewitnesses who read the inscription on the tomb in the days when it was clear, dating back nearly nineteen centuries. "The uncontrovertible testimony afforded by the tomb itself," the publication goes on to say, "backed as it is by the unanimous oral testimony of hundreds of thousands of men, and by written evidence in ancient documents, becomes, in our opinion, too strong to be resisted by the most determined of sceptics."

But Mr. Walter reports that his every effort to find documentary proof was in vain.

The tomb, however, is considered sacred and is kept reverently by the Muslims, who guard this burial place of Issa Sahib, the Shahazda nabi Yus-Asaf.

As legend and as lore, the tomb on Khan Yar Street in Srinagar, far beyond the Himalayas, is significant. For it indicates how deep in the folk mind, practically the world over, is the concern with every aspect and every event in the life of Jesus of Nazareth.

10. *The Names of Jesus*

Jesus revealed his names to his disciples one day, so that his followers would know how to glorify him and be purified of all sin.

He said to them: "Receive again and keep my word, together with my names. Know and perceive how you shall be saved from your sins, for my word is strong and powerful, as well as my names."

And he added: "These are my names and their meanings: *Abyater,* he who chastises; *Adanael,* he who pardons; *Afera-Afera-Afera,* he who gives and takes; *Afrael,* the guardian; *Afrona,* who is not given to anger; *Akonou,* the patient; *Amanouel,* his light is never extinguished; *Aqdaber,* the most high; *Demanahel,* who obscures all; *Elohe,* the venerable; *Geyon,* the rich; *Heda,* the healer; *Iyael,* feared by all; *Kenya,* the wise; *Lah'am,* Lord of lords; *Madyos,* the just; *Maryon,* who holds all in his hand; *Nolaoui,* the essence; *Oegzio,* the helper; *Ofekyour,* the constant; *Qatanaouk,* the creator of all; *Seqa,* the judge; *Sourahe,* the great. But of all these the greatest of my names is *Karaeb Elyon,* the Most High, and there is none which surpasses it."

Many more names are given in different sources. For the invocation of these names to be effective, according to some, they must be repeated three times, as in the names: "Rifon, Rifon, Rifon; Noros, Noros, Noros; Kiros, Kiros, Kiros; Linos, Linos, Linos."

In these listings of mystical names and their powers one recognizes the old belief in the powers of the Ineffable Name, Jehovah, and, in the folk mind, the repetition of such a name by the number of the Trinity, to make it that much more effective.

CHAPTER TWENTY-THREE

The Ascension

1. *The Descent to Hades*

A great light, as of a shining sun, suddenly lit up the nether regions on the midnight following the Crucifixion, as Jesus started the descent into hell to break the bonds and to destroy the bars of Hades. And all the patriarchs and the prophets and John, called the Baptist, rejoiced and said:

"We see a light. It is the light that the land of Zebulon and the land of Nephtalim, and all the people that sat in darkness may see!"

Satan, the unconvinced, on seeing the light and hearing these words, came to Hades in great excitement and said: "O all-devouring and insatiable Hades! There was a Jew named Jesus who boasted of being the son of God. But I know he was a man because before he was crucified I heard him say, 'My soul is exceeding sorrowful even unto death.' And now that he is dead, let us hasten to secure him. For he did me great damage when he was alive."

"What damage has he done you, Satan?" asked Hades.

"Those that I made blind, he made to see; those that I made lame, he made to walk; those that I made deaf, he made to hear; those that I made ill, he made well. And he healed them all with a word of his mouth."

Hades was troubled and said: "How could he be a man afraid of death, as you say, who is so powerful as to do such things by a single word?"

Satan, the heir of darkness, scraped and cowered: "O insatiable one! Are you afraid of this adversary of mine and our common enemy? I grew the wood for his cross, prepared the nails to pierce him with, mixed the gall with vinegar for him to drink, and sharpened the lance to pierce him. I feared him not. Now make you ready to lay fast your hold on him when he comes down here into your domain."

While Satan and Hades were thus speaking, a great voice as of thunder called out: "Lift up the gates for the King of Glory!"

Hades, frightened by this command, turned to his officers, shouting: "Shut the gates of brass! Secure the iron bars and bolts! Let no one leave or enter! For if Jesus comes down here, woe will seize us!"

But none of the officers moved. For they were surrounded by the pre-eminent of the world since the day of Creation.

One, who looked like an emperor, David by name, said: "When I was upon the earth, I made revelations to the people about the tender mercies of the Lord."

And another, who looked like a prophet, Jeremiah by name, said: "When I was upon the earth, I prophesied that the son of God shall come to dwell among men."

And still another, Isaiah by name, spoke up and said: "When I was upon the earth, I asked: 'Where, O death, is your sting?' And now I ask, 'Where, O Hades, is your victory?'"

All those who had fallen asleep since the beginning of the world, and were lying in the shadow of death, assembled around the patriarchs and the prophets to listen to their words. And the voice of thunder again commanded: "Open the gates, that the King of Glory may come in!"

At that moment the brazen gates of death crumbled and the great chains burst asunder; and, behold, Jesus entered in the form of a man, carrying a chain in his hands. Hades and Death and Satan and their legions of demons and impious officers trembled when they saw him, and whispered:

"Who are you, slain on the cross, yet come to free all men from death?"

Jesus seized Satan and bound him securely and cast him down into Tartarus, saying: "Throughout the ages you have committed many evils; today I deliver you to the everlasting fires."

Hades turned to revile Satan, saying: "O prince of perdition, Beelzebub, derision of the angels! In your unbelief you have offended heaven. O father of all the impious wretches and renegades, holder of the keys to the lower regions! You have acquired great possessions born of transgression; and now you have lost them all by the tree of the cross!"

Jesus then planted the cross in the midst of Hades, and said: "This cross shall stay in Hades from here to eternity!"

Then he stretched out his hands and gathered the forefathers, the patriarchs, the prophets, the saints and the martyrs, and they set out together for the gates of paradise.

2. Joseph's Release

The high priests Annas and Caiaphas sent for Joseph of Arimathea, and demanded: "Why have you asked for and buried the body of Jesus?"

And Joseph replied: "Because I knew that Jesus was a good man in all respects."

The high priests were angered by his words and ordered him imprisoned.

"The time does not allow us to deal with you now, because it is getting late and tomorrow is the Sabbath," said Annas and Caiaphas. "But early in the morning of the first day of the week we shall deal with you and you shall receive the sentence of death for what you have done."

Joseph was imprisoned in a cell which had no windows; and they sealed the door, securing it with many locks and fastenings; and they stationed guards without.

Alone in his dark cell, Joseph prayed all through the night and all through the day. And at midnight following the Sabbath he was still praying when he noticed the prison rise up into the air, and a great light, like that of lightning, surrounded him. In fear and trembling, Joseph fell to the ground and covered his face.

And he felt the embrace of someone lifting him, and he heard a voice saying: "Fear not, Joseph. Open your eyes and see who is with you."

Joseph kept his eyes closed and repeated quickly the Ten Commandments to banish the apparition, fearing that a phantom had entered his cell. The visitor in the prison repeated the Ten Commandments after Joseph.

"Are you, perhaps, Elijah the Prophet?" asked Joseph.

"No, I am not Elijah," came the answer.

"Then who are you?"

"I am Jesus, whose body you have taken down from the cross and shrouded in clean linen and laid in a new tomb."

Joseph opened his eyes. And he saw Jesus; and beside him stood another surrounded by the fragrance of heaven.

"Who is he?" asked Joseph.

"The robber Demas whom I sent to paradise. He has returned to be with me until I ascend to heaven."

Then Jesus read to Joseph a letter that the robber Demas had brought from paradise. And as he finished, Jesus was transfigured, and looked not as formerly before he was crucified, but altogether as if he were made of light.

Jesus carried Joseph away to Galilee, and there remained with him for three days.

Early on the morning of the first day of the week, Annas and Caiaphas sent for Joseph to be brought for the sentencing by the Sanhedrin. The guards were standing outside the door of the prison cell; the seal on the door was unbroken; the locks were still locked; and all the fastenings were securely fastened. But when the cell was opened, Joseph was not there.

And they were dismayed.

3. Phinees, Adas, and Haggai

Phinees was a priest; Adas was a teacher; and Haggai was a soldier. And these three came down from Galilee to Jerusalem, and said to the heads of the synagogue:

"We saw Jesus who was crucified, sitting with his eleven disciples on Mount Mophek. And we heard him say to them: 'Go out through the world and proclaim that he who believes and is baptized shall be saved; and he who believes not, he shall be condemned.' And while Jesus was speaking to his disciples, we saw him taken up into heaven. And there were five hundred others who saw that."

"By the living God," said the priests, "confess whether you really have heard and have seen this, or whether they are lies which you have told."

"By the living God, we do not lie, but tell the truth!" all three responded.

And the priests asked: "Have you come to Jerusalem to give us this account or to offer prayer before God?"

"We have come to offer prayer," the three replied.

"If you have come to pray, then why do you waste time in idle talk?"

Phinees the priest, Adas the teacher, and Haggai the soldier then said: "If what we have related is sinful, behold, we are before you to do with us as seems good in your eyes."

The priests brought out the Covenant of the Law and made the three swear that they would speak to no one of the account they had related. And after the visitors had prayed, they were given food and drink, and money besides, and escorted back to Galilee.

But word of the reports by Phinees, Adas, and Haggai had gone out on the wings of rumor, and a great crowd gathered near the temple.

Annas and Caiaphas said to the multitude: "Why are you so moved? Do you not know and have you not heard that the disciples of Jesus have given the guards of the tomb a sum of money to allow them to steal the body, and have instructed them to say that an angel of the Lord rolled away the stone from the entrance of the tomb?"

"But if his body was stolen and he is dead," said the people, "how is it that Jesus has been seen with his disciples in Galilee?"

And to that Annas and Caiaphas had no answer.

But Rabbi Nicodemus arose and said: "Three men have come to us and declared under oath that they saw and heard Jesus and his disciples on Mount Mophek in Galilee, and that they saw Jesus taken up into heaven. Yet no one asked them in what way Jesus was taken up. For in our holy scriptures we are told of Elisha and Elijah crossing the Jordan, and Elisha returning alone to Jericho; and when they asked him 'Where is your master, Elijah?' he replied that he had been taken up to heaven in a fiery chariot. Then they went out to seek Elijah for three days; and when they did not find him, the people knew that Elijah had been taken up. Therefore, let us also send out messengers into Galilee and to Mount Mophek to seek Jesus there, and in every district of Israel, that we may learn the truth."

And so it was done. And Jesus, indeed, they did not find; but they found Joseph of Arimathea who had been miraculously freed from his prison. He came to Jerusalem and told of all that had happened to him since the day of the crucifixion.

Many who had doubted before, now fell upon their knees and fasted until the ninth hour. And they sent messengers to Galilee to ask forgiveness of Phinees, Adas, and Haggai, and invited them to come to Jerusalem to testify before the Sanhedrin on the manner in which Jesus went up to heaven.

The three men returned and each, separated from the others, related: "While Jesus was teaching his disciples on Mount Mophek, we saw a shining cloud overshadow them. And when the cloud lifted, his disciples lay upon their faces on the ground, praying; but Jesus had been taken up by the cloud into heaven."

And their accounts were the same in every respect.

4. What Happened to the Cross?

The following are taken from the lore on the cross, which is so great that a whole volume could not contain it all.

The Cross in the Tomb: One day Joseph of Arimathea came to Rabbi Nicodemus and said: "Let us go and see whether the cross on which Jesus was crucified still stands."

They went to Golgotha under cover of night and found the cross still there. And they also found the crosses of the robbers, Gestas and Demas.

"What shall we do?" asked Nicodemus. "For if we try to take them into the city we shall be discovered."

And Joseph said: "Let us place them in the tomb where we buried Jesus. It is empty and no other body has been in it. No one will seek for them there, for the tomb is mine."

They took the three crosses into the tomb, which was nearby, and they rolled the stone to the entrance, and returned home when it was still dark.

The Healing Cross: The cross on which Jesus was crucified, the crown of thorns, the spear which pierced his side, and the robes he wore were taken away by the enemies of Jesus, under cover of darkness. These, along with the two crosses of the robbers, were buried in the ground thirty cubits deep.

Some years later, a hole was dug in the earth and the diggers reached a buried crossbeam deep in the ground. Whoever touched it was at once healed of all disease. The rumor of this went out, and in a short while all the lame and the blind and the deaf and the sick came to the spot. And 10,502 persons in Jerusalem were cured by touching the beam.

When the Hegemon heard of this, he ordered that the hole be filled with stones up to ten times the height of a man. And after that none could be cured.

But a man named Jonadab stole a nail from the cross and took it home. And they who were sick would come to him and pay him to allow them to touch the nail; and the touch cured them. And many people were cured by the nail in Jonadab's possession.

5. *The Stranger on the Road*

Two men walked along the dusty road from Jerusalem to Emmaus, seven miles away. The name of one was Zachus and the name of the other was Cleophas. They walked in silence for their hearts were heavy. And as they trudged wearily along they were joined by a stranger going their way.

"You seem sad and discouraged," said the stranger to Zachus and Cleophas. "Has some great grief befallen you?"

Cleophas turned his head sideways and asked: "Are you a stranger in Judea? Have you not heard what has happened in this land?"

"What has happened?" asked the stranger.

"Have you not heard of the Prophet of Galilee, mighty both in word and deed, who came to drive the Romans from Jerusalem and become the King of the Jews?"

"Tell me about this man," said the stranger.

"His name was Jesus," said Cleophas with a sigh. "He was born in Bethlehem. And his home was in Nazareth in Galilee. He loved the people so much that he loved them more than himself. And he had the power to heal the sick and to comfort the sorrowing. The priests and the Pharisees envied his power and denounced him before Pilate. And, through perjury, they found Jesus guilty of a score of crimes. Last Friday he was taken to Golgotha and was crucified in the Roman manner."

Cleophas fell silent, and Zachus continued: "He died and was buried in a rich man's tomb, out in the garden of Siloam. That was three days ago. But this morning, when his friends went to the tomb, they found it empty. And now the news has gone out abroad that Jesus has risen from the dead. But it is also said that his friends have taken him away so that it may seem so."

"I have heard of this man," said the stranger. "But I cannot understand why, after all that the prophets prophesied about him long ago, the people knew him not when he came."

"It is claimed that the prophecies were meant for still another," said Zachus.

As they were talking, they reached Emmaus, and the house where Zachus and Cleophas lived. The day had waned and night was upon them. Cleophas and Zachus invited the stranger to break bread with them and stay the night.

They sat down at the table, and as the meal was served, the stranger broke the bread and blessed it in the name of Jesus the Christ. Zachus looked at Cleophas and Cleophas looked at Zachus in astonishment. Then they turned to their guest. But the stranger had disappeared.

The two men left their food untouched and hurried back to Jerusalem to relate that they had seen Jesus, who had risen from the dead; and that he had sat down with them to the evening meal and broke the bread of life for them.

6. At Ravanna's Feast

Prince Ravanna of India prepared a great feast in his palace in Orissa, in honor of the wise men of the East. Among the guests invited were Meng-ste of China, Vidayapati and Lamaas of India, Kaspar of Persia, Ashbian of Assyria, Matheno of Egypt, and other men of thought from every part of the world.

The sages sat at the feasting tables when the door opened and a stranger entered unannounced.

"All hail!" said the stranger, raising his hands in benediction.

The sages turned their heads to the stranger and a light, unlike the light of the sun, filled the room. They saw a halo shining about the stranger's head, and they all rose and bowed to him, saying: "All hail!"

"Behold, I am risen from the dead," said the stranger. "Look at my hands and my feet and my side."

And the sages saw where the nails had pierced the hands and feet, and where the lance had pierced the heart. And they knew it was the Hebrew prophet Jesus who had come to join them.

Jesus sat down near the table, and said: "The Roman soldiers pierced my hands and feet with nails. And then one pierced my heart. They put me in a tomb, and I wrestled with the conqueror of men. But I conquered death and stamped upon him and arose; and I painted on the walls of time a rainbow for all the sons of men. For what I did, all men shall do. This gospel of the resurrection of the dead is not confined to Jew or Greek. It is the heritage of every man in every age and in every place. For I have risen to demonstrate the power of life over death."

And when the sages showed surprise, Jesus arose and shook hands with each in turn, saying: "Behold, I am not a phantom or a vision. I am flesh and blood and brawn!"

Then they sat and talked together for a long time.

At last Jesus arose and he said: "I now must go my destined way. But you shall all return to your homes throughout the world and preach the gospel of the Power of Truth, and the Resurrection of the Dead."

Then Jesus disappeared.

And the sages went from place to place, proclaiming throughout the world: "Thus spoke Jesus: 'What I have done, all men can do; and what I am, all men will be.' Peace! Peace on earth; good will to men!"

7. *The News in Capernaum*

The Apostles were at home in Galilee: Peter and James, John and Andrew, Philip and Nathaniel. And they were joined by Jonah and Zebedee. They went out together in their boats to fish on the Sea of Gennaseret. All night long they dragged their nets; and in the morning they returned homeward without any fish. But as they neared the landing, a man on the shore called to them:

"How many fish have you caught?"

"None," Peter shouted back.

"Then cast your nets upon the right side of your boat, for a school of fish is passing there now."

They cast their nets upon the right side of the boat, and soon the nets were filled with so many fish they could hold no more. Yet the nets did not break.

John was the first to turn away from the nets to the man upon the shore, and he exclaimed: "Look! It is Jesus who stands before us!"

Peter dived overboard and swam ashore. And the others quickly raised the nets, secured the boats, and came ashore to join Peter.

"My children," said Jesus, "let us break bread together."

They found some live embers upon the sand; Peter brought and dressed the fish, and others brought loaves of bread they had had with them. And they all sat down together to the meal.

"Peter, do you love the Lord your God with all your heart; and do you love your neighbor as you love yourself?" asked Jesus.

And Peter said: "Yes, I love the Lord my God with all my heart; and I love my neighbor as I love myself."

"Then feed my sheep," said Jesus.

And Peter understood.

Then Jesus asked the same question of James; and James replied: "Yes, my Lord, I love the Holy Breath with all my heart; and I love my neighbor as I love myself."

"Then protect my sheep," said Jesus.

And James understood.

Jesus asked the same question of John; and John replied: "Yes, my

Lord, I love Christ with all my heart; and I love my neighbor as I love myself."

And Jesus said: "Then feed my lambs."

And John understood.

Meanwhile the news had spread throughout Capernaum that Jesus had risen from the dead and was at that very moment breaking bread with his disciples on the shore. And a multitude gathered unbelieving. But when they came to the seashore they saw Jesus with their own eyes; they exclaimed: "Now we know that Jesus has truly risen from the dead; for we have seen him with our own eyes and face to face."

8. *Christ Is Risen!*

Early at dawn on the fourth day of the month of Heziran, which is the first day of the week and the end of Pentecost, in the year three hundred and thirty-nine of the kingdom of the Greeks, the disciples of Jesus assembled on Mount Zaithe.

And Jesus was with them, though he was not visible to them. He placed his hands upon the heads of the eleven disciples and gave to them the gift of the priesthood. Then a shining cloud came down to receive Jesus. And the disciples saw him go up into heaven.

The disciples lifted their voices and praised God who had permitted them to live to the time of the Resurrection and to see the Ascension.

PART VII

The Acts of the Apostles

Of the twenty-seven books of the New Testament, four are devoted to the Gospels, and the rest to the Acts, Epistles and Revelations of the apostles. Since the Gospels of Matthew, Luke and Mark are Synoptic, or, more correctly, derived from the same earlier Gospels which no longer exist, the apostolic deeds and martyrdoms assume an even more prominent part in the New Testament than appears at first. And the lore fully reflects this concern with the deeds of the men who went out to spread the Gospel.

The legends about the apostles differ sharply in style and approach from the rest of the New Testament lore. Most of them are written in the form of early romances, with the apostles as the central characters; the discourses in them tend to be long; their basic theme is almost invariably eschatological — preaching the end of this world and preparation for the World to Come; and most of them are zealous in their ascetic teachings, particularly in their warnings against sex, even within the bonds of marriage.

Were this book to follow the pattern of either the New Testament or the lore, at least two thirds of the legends would be given to the Acts of the Apostles.

CHAPTER TWENTY-FOUR

The Adventures of John the Fisherman

1. *The Storm at Sea*

The Apostles met and divided into twelve parts the countries of the earth to which they were to disperse and teach the Gospel. Then they cast lots to determine where each was to go.

To John, son of Zebedee, fell the lot to go to Asia; and Prochorus, one of the Seventy-two Disciples, was sent along to help the gentle John in his work.

After taking leave of the other apostles and disciples, these two, John and Prochorus, went from Jerusalem to Joppa and there boarded a cargo vessel that had come from Egypt and was on its way to the shores of the Marmarwan Sea.

In the tenth hour of that day, John said to Prochorus: "My son, I can foretell that a great trial will befall us on this journey. Therefore, should we be separated by a storm I shall proceed to the city of Ephesus, if I survive, and there I shall reside for two months. If by that time you have not found me, return to Jerusalem and do whatever James, the brother of Jesus, tells you to do."

No sooner had Prochorus promised John to follow his command, than a great storm arose that lasted from the tenth hour of the day to the third hour of the night, the fury of the wind and the power of the water increasing with every passing minute. The sea roared with a deafening noise, and the vessel was tossed up into the air on waves the height of mountains, and dropped into troughs between, as dark and deep as valleys. There was confusion on the vessel from the start, and nothing on board remained in its place. The voices of men were like drops of oil in roaring flames; and the running riggings and the standing riggings were soon scattered like straws in a gale. Then one great wave arose mightier than all the others, and with the sound of thunder flung the vessel down like a heap of loosened boards, tearing the vessel asunder. And each man clung to a different plank or board.

Then the storm subsided and receded, and in the sixth hour of the next day the gentle waves cast forty-six of the shipwrecked men onto the sands of the shores of Seleucia. So faint were the survivors from fear and hunger that they lay prostrate on their faces for three hours before anyone could speak. Then their spirits were revived, and they turned on Prochorus, one of the survivors, and asked: "Where is your companion, John, whom we heard predict disaster?"

"That man is a wizard," said the sailors. "It was he who caused our misfortune. Deliver him to us, or we shall deliver you to the governor of the city that he may slay you."

Prochorus protested against their calling the apostle a sorcerer; nor could he produce John for them. And the sailors dragged him into the city and caused him to be imprisoned. Three days later he was brought before the hostile magistrates who asked with great unpleasantness: "What is your name? Where do you come from? What is your religion? What is your profession?"

"My name is Prochorus, and I come from Jerusalem. I am a Hebrew who became a Nazarene. I was shipwrecked like all the others; but what became of my companion I do not know."

And the magistrates said: "You lie. You bewitched the boat with the intent to rob it of its treasures. But your companion contrived to escape. We can see there is much blood in your neck. Though you have been delivered from the storm at sea, you shall perish on dry land for your sorcery."

Before the magistrates could pronounce by what manner of death Prochorus was to die, the king's privy councilor, named Seleucus, arrived from Antioch to collect tribute money from the magistrates. And when he heard the disciple's story, he believed in him and ordered Prochorus freed.

Prochorus wandered along the seashore for forty days, eating little and resting little, constantly searching for John. On the fortieth day Prochorus sat on a rock near the sea, fatigued and low in spirits, when he suddenly saw a drowning man carried toward the shore on a rolling wave. He gathered his waning strength and waded out to the man's rescue. And when he brought him safely to shore, Prochorus saw that the man was the apostle, John. They embraced and they wept with exceeding joy. And the disciple told the apostle of all that had happened since they were separated in the storm; and the apostle told the disciple all he had experienced during the forty days and forty nights in the depths of the sea.

And as soon as they were refreshed with food and water, they started out for Ephesus, their destination.

2. *Domna Acquires Two Slaves*

At the outskirts of Ephesus there was a bathhouse which belonged to the chief of the city, Dioscorides. At the time the bathhouse was built, a living girl, a virgin, was placed under the foundation stone to ensure good fortune for the enterprise; and from that day forth Satan had the place under his power.

On the steps of this bathhouse John and Prochorus sat down to rest from their long journey. And the apostle said to his disciple: "My son, promise me not to let anyone know who we are nor why we came here, until the time arrives for us to reveal ourselves. And suffer all humiliations that come our way, for God wills it so."

"I promise," said Prochorus.

As they were talking, there appeared before them a giant woman, powerful and terrible to behold, not because of her visage, which was fair, but because of the fear her strength inspired. Her name was Domna, and it was said of her that when her nation went to war, Domna went into battle with stones in her bare hands and frightened the enemy away. Domna was the keeper of the bathhouse, and boasted about how she beat her workers and never gave them any rest.

Domna had espied the two foreigners in their strange and travel-worn clothes on the bathhouse steps, and she at once conspired to frighten them into becoming her workers. The strangers were willing to work for her, they said, John as a stoker of the fires and Prochorus as a bathman; for which she offered to pay them three pounds of bread each day.

After several days Domna came to them in a rage when she learned that John had failed to stoke the fires.

"O wicked servant," she shouted. "If you were unfit for this work, why did you accept my bread? I can see that when it comes to eating you are full of energy; but when it comes to working you are idle and weak as a child."

John said nothing in reply to her wicked talk; nor did he protest when she struck him.

"You are my slave," said Domna, "and you must obey me."

"Yes," said John, "we are your slaves, I, your stoker, and Prochorus, your bathman."

And Domna said to herself: "These two men are simpletons; I shall make them my slaves forever."

The next day Domna went to a friend among the officers of the court and said: "I have two slaves whom my father bequeathed to me. Some time ago they ran away. But now they have returned, and I would like to have a deed of servitude."

"If they admit they are your slaves and you can get three witnesses to testify to that, we shall give you the deed."

Domna brought the apostle and the disciple to the court, where they were registered in servitude to the bathhouse keeper, and Domna was given her deed. And after that Domna treated John and Prochorus with even greater cruelty.

3. *John's Revelation*

When the spirits of the disciple were very low, he would come to John and beseech him to tell of his days with Jesus. For Prochorus knew that Jesus had loved John above all his followers.

"I saw him always differently," said John, "for his face and his figure seemed different to me than to his brother James, or Father Peter. And stranger still, I never saw him with his eyes closed. Other disciples saw him when he slept. But when I looked at him, his eyes were always open. And when I leaned my head upon his breast, sometimes it was as hard as a rock, and sometimes I could feel no material body beneath the garment. And when we walked along the shore, my feet left their imprints, but there appeared no imprints where Jesus walked."

"Tell me, tell me, tell me more," Prochorus pleaded, his spirits already revived by the apostle's words.

"After the Lord Jesus was taken up to heaven," John related, "I found myself one day on Mount Tabor, where I began to pray; and there I prayed for seven days. At the end of that time the skies opened and the air became fragrant and the light was brighter than the sun. And I saw a book, the thickness of seven mountains and sealed with seven seals. And I pleaded: 'Reveal to me, O Lord, what is written in that book!' And I heard a voice saying: 'In this book is written what shall come to pass in the days when I come again to establish my kingdom on earth. In it are written the signs that will precede my coming; in it are given the descriptions of the antichrist who will come to rule the earth for a while; in it are told all the calamities that will befall man and beast at the time of the Resurrection; and in it are described the state of mankind after the Resurrection.'

"Then I pleaded again, and I asked: 'O Lord, when, O when, will these things come to pass?' And the same voice answered me: 'When you trample underfoot the garment of modesty; and when two shall be one, and that which is without as that which is within; and the male and female shall be neither male nor female.'"

And Prochorus was made happy by these talks and he endured Domna's wickedness with greater patience.

4. *Miracle in the Bathhouse*

One day the son of Dioscorides came to his father's bathhouse, and Satan laid hold of him and killed him. Domna began to wail and to scream: "Woe is me! What will my master do when he hears that his beloved son died in the place of my keeping?"

John came out of the furnaceroom when he heard the wailing. And Domna, seeing him, rushed at the apostle with clenched fists, declaring that he was a sorcerer and had contrived the boy's death. John did not rebuke her, but went in where the boy lay dead, made the sign of the cross over his face, and commanded him to rise. And the boy Satan had slain, arose and was well again.

John led the boy out to Domna and said: "Here is your master's son, for I have made him well again."

The giant woman became confused, and was struck with terror

for the wicked things she had done to the holy man. She fell on her knees and pleaded: "I beg of you, forgive me! Tell me who you really are. Can it be that you are a god or a son of a god that you can bring the dead back to life again?"

"I am neither a god nor the son of a god," said John. "But I can help you find the Son of God and become one of his people, if you truly repent and believe in him."

When Dioscorides learned all that had happened to his son, he invited John and his disciple to the palace. And all the people of the city heard the apostle preach and they were converted.

5. John Before Domitian

The fame of the teachings of John, son of Zebedee, went out from Ephesus to Rome. And the report reached Domitian, called Caesar and King of the World, that John, the Hebrew Nazarene, had foretold in Ephesus the downfall of the Roman Empire, and that another and more powerful king would come to rule the world.

Domitian was troubled by this report, and he sent a centurion with one hundred soldiers to seize John and bring him to Rome.

The centurion and the soldiers went to far-off Ephesus. As they walked through a street of the city, they saw in the doorway of a house a little man of common appearance, dressed like a stoker of a furnace, and they asked him: "Can you tell us where John, the son of Zebedee, lives?"

"I am he," said the little man.

"Jest not with us," said the centurion, "for we have come to take John before King Domitian."

"I am ready," said John.

"But it is a long journey. How long will it take you to prepare?"

"I am always prepared," said John. "And all I own I have with me."

"What of food? For we shall be many days on the way," said the centurion.

John went into the house and soon returned with a few dates in a clean linen cloth, ready for the journey to Rome.

At the end of the first day they stopped at an inn, and the centurion ordered a great supper for himself and his men. He invited

John to join them. But John, who had fasted all day, said: "I am more sleepy than hungry." And he went to bed without food.

The next day, and the next, the same thing happened. But on the seventh day, it being the Sabbath of the Lord, John said: "Today I shall join you at the meal."

He washed his hands and face, brushed his dusty clothes, and spread out before him his clean linen cloth. From the few dates on the cloth he took one, and he ate it in the sight of all.

This continued for the rest of the long journey.

When they arrived in Rome, the centurion brought the apostle to the king, and said: "Worshipful King, here is John, whom you commanded me to bring to you. But I do not think that he is a man, for he has tasted no bread since the day we apprehended him in Ephesus."

The king was amazed at what he heard and asked the apostle: "Are you the John who predicted that my kingdom would speedily be uprooted?"

And John answered: "You shall reign for as many years as are allotted you. But out of heaven shall come a king to rule the world, and his name is Jesus the Christ."

"What proof have you of this?" asked the king.

"Give me a large cup of the deadliest poison, and I will give you the proof you ask," said John.

A goblet filled with poison was brought to John, and the apostle drank it as if it were fresh water from a fountain.

"He is a sorcerer," said the king's advisers, "and the poison he drank was not harmful."

"Send for a man in your prison whom you have condemned to die," said John.

And when such a man was brought, John handed him the goblet and ordered him to drink the dregs. The criminal drank the poison and fell to the ground, dead.

After the court physicians proclaimed the prisoner dead beyond recall, John said: "Though this man was doomed to die for his crimes, it is not meet that I should be the cause of his death in order to convince you." The apostle took the hand of the dead man on the ground and commanded him in the name of Jesus Christ to rise. And the man arose.

Domitian dismissed his court and took John aside and said to him: "I have issued a decree that all men who predict the downfall of the Roman Empire shall perish without trial. I cannot disregard my own edict. Therefore, I will banish you to the Island of Patmos, so as not to seem to go against my own decree. But on that island you may preach and teach to your heart's content."

John went to Patmos and there he preached to the people of the island until Emperor Nerva, Domitian's successor, recalled him to Ephesus, the capital of the Roman province in Asia.

6. *John and the Robber*

On his way from Patmos to Ephesus, John the Apostle came to one city bringing with him a very young boy, an orphan he had baptized, strong in body and comely in appearance. He took the boy to the bishop of the newly-formed church and said to him: "I wish to leave this youth in your care to be brought up in the ways of righteousness. He is a good boy and I want you to take care of him."

The old bishop accepted the responsibility. And when John left, he brought the youth to the home of a trusted presbyter, where he was received with great kindness. The bishop undertook the boy's education himself, and kept him under strict guardianship.

But as the boy grew into manhood, and the bishop became older, the boy was allowed great freedom; and his guardians did not know that their ward had fallen into the company of idle and dissolute young boys his own age. They enticed him into costly entertainments, then taught him how to obtain the price by theft and robbery in the dark of night.

Each time the wicked companions performed an evil deed, they dared the bishop's ward to equal it; and he went out and did an even greater evil. And like a hard-mouthed and powerful young stallion, the youth took the bit into his own teeth and rushed forward to exceed every daring deed.

It was not long before he was so deep in evil-doing that he despaired of all salvation. He left the bishop and the church and organized a band of robbers who terrorized the highways with fierce and bloody and cruel exploits.

Some time later, the apostle John returned to that city and asked the bishop: "How is the boy I left in your care and placed under your guardianship?"

"Alas," the old bishop answered amid tears, "the youth you left with me is dead."

"How did he die?" asked John.

"I mean he is dead to the Lord," the old bishop replied. "For he turned wicked and has become the leader of a band of outlaws who hide in the mountains and terrorize the people like vicious tigers."

John rent his clothes in mourning, and lamented: "The fault is not with the youth for his wild yearnings; but with those who were to guard and direct his soul. Bring me a horse and I shall go and find him."

John rode into the mountains and before long he was stopped and surrounded by a band of robbers. The apostle neither tried to escape nor entreated them to free him, but said: "Take me to your leader!"

The leader, on horseback and fully armed, was waiting for his followers to bring their victim. But when he recognized the apostle, he turned his horse and galloped away. And John galloped after him. As the apostle finally caught up with the leader of the bandits and rode alongside him, he pleaded: "Why do you flee from me, my son? I am unarmed and cannot hurt you. Pity me, my son, and stop, for I am too old to ride like this much longer. Stop, and let me talk to you. Come back with me and repent your ways. I assure you that you will be forgiven. If need be, I am ready to give my life for yours, that you may gain salvation."

On hearing these words from the holy man, the robber stopped his horse, dismounted, and, without saying a word, began to weep bitterly. John came down to him, embraced him, and assured the youth that he knew his waywardness was not caused by any wickedness, but by the neglect of his guardians.

"Come back with me to the church," said John, "for I wish to baptize you a second time."

On returning to the church, John fasted many days and prayed; and the youth fasted and prayed with him.

After this the repentant robber was for many years an example in that church of true repentance; and all who sought regeneration came to him. And he never tired retelling the story of how he was saved by John the Apostle.

7. Epistle from Ignatius

One day John the Apostle received an epistle from Ignatius the Syrian, Bishop of Antioch, who was also called Theophorus. Ignatius sent many epistles to many people and churches; but in this letter he made a special request. It read:

His friend Ignatius to John the holy presbyter:

If you will give me leave, I desire to go up to Jerusalem, and see the faithful saints who are there, especially Mary the mothe whom they report to be an object of admiration and of affection to all. For who would not rejoice to behold and to address her who bore the true God from her womb, provided he is a friend of our faith and religion? And in like manner [I desire to see] the venerable James, who is surnamed the Just, whom they relate to be very like Christ Jesus in appearance, in life, and in method of conduct, as if he were a twin-brother of the same womb. They say that, if I see him, I see also Jesus Himself, as to all the features and aspects of His body. Moreover, [I desire to see] the other saints, both male and female. Alas! why do I tarry? Why am I kept back? Kind teacher, bid me hasten [to fulfill my wish], and fare you well. Amen.

There are some words missing in the original manuscript of this letter, and the translators have supplied, in brackets, what they surmised were the missing words or phrases.

8. The Sandals at the Fountain

John the Evangelist preached in Patmos for many years, and he performed many miracles. And when he grew old, he called together his followers one day, led them to the graveyard, and asked the young men to dig a deep grave. And when the trench was finished, John undressed and threw his clothes into the grave. Standing in his loincloth only, he prayed. And his followers prayed with him. And when he had finished he took leave of them all, and asked them to go to their homes.

On the morrow, when they came to the grave, they found a sparkling fountain where the grave had been, and the apostle's sandals lay nearby.

CHAPTER TWENTY-FIVE

The Adventures of Thomas Didymus

1. *Thomas Sold as a Slave*

When the apostles drew lots on where each of them should preach the Gospel, India fell to Judas Thomas, whom Jesus called Didymus. But Thomas refused to go there, arguing that he was a Galilean Hebrew and did not know how to proclaim the truth among the idolators of India. Even when Jesus came to him in a dream to reassure him, Thomas still would not obey, saying: "I shall go where you wish me to go; but to India I shall not go. For the men there are hard men who will not receive the hearing of the Gospel."

Meanwhile all the other apostles prepared to leave, each to the country he had drawn by lot. Peter, who was on his way to the city of Rome, went along some distance with poor Matthias, who was on his way to the city of the Cannibals. And Thomas Didymus went along with them.

On their way they came to a town and sat down in the market place, conversing among themselves. Soon they fell into conversation with a stranger, a rich nobleman, who proved himself also wise and learned.

And as they were talking, along came another stranger who stopped before them, asking: "Whence are you from, O brethren? And what do you here?"

"We are from Jerusalem on our way to distant lands," said Peter. "Whence are you and what do you here?"

"I am from India," said the stranger. "My name is Abbanes, and I am here to buy a slave, a carpenter, for our King Gundaphoros."

The nobleman then spoke up and said: "I have three slaves. One of them is a master carpenter, and I wish to sell him."

"Where can I see him?" asked Abbanes.

"He is right there," said the nobleman, and pointed at Thomas.

Abbanes looked at the handsome Thomas, and saw that he had the appearance of a learned and fine young man. "What is his price?"

"His price is three pounds of gold," said the nobleman. "And his name is Judas Thomas; but I call him Didymus, which means 'the twin.' "

When Peter and Matthias and Thomas heard this they bowed their heads and kept their peace.

"I have bought him from you," said Abbanes.

He delivered the unminted gold, and the nobleman wrote out the deed of sale in his own hand, reading: "I, Jesus, the son of Joseph the Carpenter, declare that I have sold my slave, Judas by name, to you Abbanes, representing Gundaphoros, King of the Indians."

And Thomas girded his loins after the manner of a slave, took leave of Peter and Matthias, and followed after Abbanes.

2. *Thomas and the Flute-girl*

At dawn the following morning, Abbanes led Thomas to the shore where the vessel lay anchored that was to take them to India. The king's steward had many belongings to load on board. But Thomas had only three pounds of gold to carry; for Jesus had given him the money before he left, saying: "Take your price along with your grace on your journey." Thomas therefore helped Abbanes load his possessions onto the ship.

The vessel sailed and, with fair wind, soon reached the royal city, Andropolis, on the way to India. While the ship was loading and unloading, Abbanes and Thomas went ashore, and they heard the pleasing sounds of flutes, water organs and trumpets resounding throughout the streets of the city.

"What festival is this?" they asked.

"Our princess, the king's only child, is given today in marriage," the people told them. "The king has invited to the marriage feast the poor as well as the rich, the bondsman as well as the free-man, the stranger as well as the native; and whoever fails to come to the feasting tables shall be answerable to the king."

Abbanes said to Thomas: "Let us join the festivities so that we may not offend the king, especially since we are strangers."

They rested at an inn for a while and then they went to the banqueting halls and were seated among the guests. Abbanes, being a king's steward, was seated among the lords; and Thomas was seated among the other guests.

But when the food and wine were served, Thomas would touch neither food nor drink. The guests seated near him looked with suspicion at the stranger in their midst. And when the ointments and perfume were brought for the guests, Thomas neither anointed his face nor perfumed his beard. But from the garlands that were brought them he took a wreath of myrtle for his head and a reed to hold in his hand. And the guests at his table regarded him with hostility.

Then a flute-girl came by playing her flute, and she stopped for a long while behind the handsome Thomas. For she was Hebrew by race and recognized in him one of her own people. She played and she played, and she hoped that the stranger would turn to look at her. But Thomas's eyes were fixed on the ground. A cup-bearer, serving the guests, noticed the apostle's strange manner and, as he came by, he struck Thomas on the head.

Thomas looked up at the cupbearer and said: "In the World to Come, may God forgive you for your wickedness; but in this world the dogs will soon drag through the gutters the hand that struck me."

None of the guests understood him, for he spoke in Hebrew; but the flute-girl understood him, and she gasped at his words. Thomas then looked up at her with kindly eyes and sang:

"Maiden, O daughter of light, whose father is truth and whose mother is wisdom; O maiden, whose garments are like spring flowers, with a fragrance greater than myrrh or the scent of balsam; thirty and two are they who sing her praises, and their tongue is like a curtain which is drawn for them who go in; the number of the groomsmen are seven, and her bridesmaids are seven, and they surround her like a mighty wall; and twelve is the number of them who do her bidding, whose eyes are on the bridegroom through whom they are enlightened; and they shall all partake in the wedding of everlasting joy, and they shall drink the wine that brings them no thirst nor any desire of the flesh. O daughter of light, whose neck is like the stairway to heaven and whose hands are like the gates of the city!"

The guests listened to his song, and they understood not the words nor their import. But the flute-girl wept, for she understood him. And she came and sat at the table opposite Thomas the Apostle and gazed upon him as long as the festivities lasted.

When the feast was over, the cupbearer who had struck Thomas went down to the fountain to draw water, and a lion hiding in the shadows killed him, and left him lying there. And the black dogs of the city came and dragged the carcass through the gutters.

The flute-girl, on hearing what had happened to the cupbearer, broke her flute and wept, saying: "Surely this stranger at the feast is an apostle of God. For I heard him foretell what would happen to the cupbearer."

Some of those about her believed her; and they carried the message to the king. And the king came himself to the apostle to invite him to the bridal chamber that he might pray for the princess, his only child.

Thomas stood before the bride and the groom in their chamber, and he prayed for guidance. And, inspired by Jesus, he said to the young people: "Children, if you wish to become as holy and pure temples, free of affliction and troubles whose end is destruction, refrain from intercourse. In that way you will not be involved in the cares of children for whose sake parents become grasping and avaricious, coveting the property of widows, and in the end subject themselves to the most grievous punishment. For children are in every way unprofitable; they may be born lame or deaf or dumb or half-witted or possessed by demons and be a care to their parents all the days of their lives. Even if they are well and whole, they may grow up to engage in abominable works, tempted by adultery, theft, or even murder. But if you keep yourselves pure, you shall be free from cares in the bridal chamber of immortality."

The bride and groom remained in prayer all night long, and vowed to follow the apostle's advice, and to dedicate themselves to the God of the stranger.

In the morning the king and queen came to see the princess and her husband. And the bride and groom told of their vow.

The king rent his garments in grief and ordered his servants to find the sorcerer who had brought such affliction into his house. The faithful servants went in search of Thomas and returned with the tidings that he and Abbanes had already sailed away.

At the inn where Thomas had stayed, the flute-girl wept when she heard that he had gone, and she, too, vowed to remain a virgin and to spend her days in prayer; and to wait until she would hear from the holy man who had gone to save sinners in the cities of India.

The Apocryphal Acts abound in vehement ascetic teachings; particularly in the matter of continence. Thomas's address to the newlyweds in this story is a mild example of the Encratite teachings, as they are called. Strange as these attacks on the institution of marriage may seem to us, they were quite prevalent during the first two or three centuries of Christianity when these ideas thrived, as many apocryphal works of those times testify.

3. *Plans for a Palace*

After many days at sea, Abbanes and Thomas finally arrived in India, and Abbanes presented the apostle to King Gundaphoros.

"Here is the carpenter you sent me to seek."

"Are you a good builder?" the king asked Thomas.

"I am a mason, and I am a carpenter, and I am a doctor," said Thomas. "As for the art of carpentry, I can mend measures, scales, weights and ploughs; as for masonry, I build temples, fortresses, high towers and palaces suitable for kings."

The king was pleased and said: "Will you build me a palace and a tower such as I have designed?"

"First I must see the place where the palace is to be built," said Thomas.

The king took him at once to a large wooded space outside the city. "Show me how you would mark out the palace for me," said the king.

Thomas took a reed and began to measure out the dimensions on the ground. He pointed out where he would place the doors to catch the light, toward the rising sun; and where he would place the windows to catch the breeze, toward the setting sun. And the backhouse he marked toward the south, so that the moving air would carry the odors away from the palace; and the water tank he placed toward the north.

All this pleased the king and he said: "How soon will you start to build my palace?"

"Between Dius and Xanthicus," said Thomas.

"But that is in the wintertime," the king protested, "and most builders build during the summer."

"In that way I am unlike most builders," said the apostle.

"If it must be that way — " said the king, and shrugged his shoulders. Then he turned to Abbanes and commanded: "Take this builder to my treasurer Lucius and tell him to give this man out of the royal treasury all the money needed to build my palace and fortress. And tell him also to treat this man not as a slave, but as the king's craftsman."

4. Thomas Makes a Convert

Lucius, the king's treasurer, had a wife and her name was Arsanuni, and she was as beautiful as her name implied. When her husband went off on a long journey, leaving Thomas in his house to plan the royal palace, the apostle went to Arsanuni and read to her the Gospel of the Lord Jesus and the prophecies of the Hebrew prophets.

Then Thomas said to her: "O Arsanuni, I can see by your eyes that you are unhappy. That is because you worship idols of gold and silver. These idols are your vanity but not your consolation. They have ears and hear not; they have eyes and see not; they have mouths and speak not. But our Father who is in heaven, whatever he wills, his will is done; and whomsoever he loves, him he favors."

And as Thomas said these words, all the idols in the house fell to the ground and crumbled.

Arsanuni sank to her knees in awe and asked: "O good servant who has come into my house! Are you a slave, are you a man, or are you a god?"

Thomas stretched out his hand and lifted her up and said: "There is no room for fear in the heart that believes in the living God."

He baptized Arsanuni in the name of the Father, the Son, and the Holy Ghost; then they prayed together, she for the new faith she had found through Thomas; and he for the first convert he had made in India.

Sometime later Lucius returned home. He bathed and anointed himself in his private chamber, and he called to his wife with longing eyes and a thirsting voice. But she came to him weeping, and said: "O my lord! God has rooted out of my heart this wicked inclination!"

"What words are these you say?" Lucius asked incredulously.

"Besides," said Arsanuni, "today is the Sabbath of the Lord."

"This is the work of the Hebrew slave who has bewitched you! For this he shall be made to suffer!"

Lucius commanded his servants to take Thomas and strip him and flay the skin off his body. And he commanded his wife to watch the flaying from the window for having listened to the words of the wicked wizard.

Arsanuni, watching the torture of the apostle, became so full of unendurable grief that she fell down to the ground, dead. Then Lucius, maddened by his loss, commanded his servants to bring salt and vinegar and pour them on Thomas's wounds.

Thomas prayed: "O Lord! My heart and my body and my spirit are weary! And great is my loneliness, for I have neither kin nor friend in this distant land! I did not want to come to this city, but, O Lord, you commanded me to come for the salvation of its people. Now see what has befallen me!"

And Jesus appeared to him and said: "O my beloved Thomas! Let your heart be as strong as your faith, since your pain is for the sake of mankind!"

And Thomas arose from the ground as if he had not been touched by pain, and he went to Arsanuni where she lay dead, and placed upon her some of his flayed-off skin; and in a strong voice he said: "In the name of the living God, arise!"

Arsanuni opened her eyes and looked at the apostle. Then she arose and bowed her head.

Lucius, her husband, and Arsanuni's parents, and all the servants in the house, and the great multitude that had gathered to witness the flaying, when they saw the great miracle that had taken place before their eyes, together called out to Thomas: "Truly there is no God but the God whom you serve!"

Lucius fell to his knees and begged the apostle to forgive him the wickedness he had committed in his ignorance; and Thomas told him that God does not punish those who truly repent.

And all the people of that city were converted to the faith preached by Thomas Didymus.

5. *The Palace of King Gundaphoros*

King Gundaphoros sent a messenger to Thomas asking how far the palace he was building had progressed.

And Thomas sent back the message: "The building is built, but the roof remains to be done."

The king sent the builder more uncoined gold and silver, urging him to finish the task without delay.

But after some time the king received a disturbing report. He was told that the Hebrew builder spent his days in fasting and prayer, and gave all he received from the king to the poor and the needy. He was kind. He was gentle. He was considerate of the widow and the orphan. He healed the sick and consoled the bereaved. But of the palace he had promised to build — of that there was not any sign.

The king immediately summoned Judas Thomas before him.

"Where is the palace and where is the fortress which you promised to build and for which I sent you gold and silver from my treasury?" the king demanded.

"Your highness," said Thomas, "the palace and the fortress are now complete."

"Are you jesting?" asked the king.

"I am telling the truth," said the apostle.

"Then show them to me," the king demanded.

"That I cannot do until the day you die."

"Why not?"

"Because," said Thomas, "the palace and the fortress I have built for you are in heaven. And when you die you shall inhabit them."

The king grew red and the king grew purple with rage. First he ordered Abbanes, his steward, put in irons for having bought such a deceitful slave; and then he sat down to consider by what death to kill Thomas so as to cause him the greatest suffering.

The king was still considering with which tortures to punish Thomas, when a messenger arrived to tell him that his brother, Gad, was dying, and that he called for the king. Gundaphoros hastened to his brother's side, but he arrived too late. For Gad had died the day before the king could reach him.

That night Gundaphoros dreamt that his brother came to him and said: "My beloved brother, you should know that when I died and went to heaven, I saw there a palace of great beauty, but I was not allowed to enter because I was told it belonged to you. And when I asked when my brother had acquired this wonderful palace with such great towers, I was told that it was built for him by a holy man named Thomas, whom you know as your Hebrew slave."

When the king awoke he at once sent to the prison for the apostle. He asked forgiveness of Thomas, and pleaded to be baptized.

And from that day forth King Gundaphoros devoted himself to gathering the people to be converted by the apostle Judas Thomas whom Jesus called Didymus.

6. *The Man Who Killed His Beloved*

A certain young man in India, whom Thomas had converted, came to the church of the apostle one day to pray, and as he raised the Eucharist to his mouth, his hands suddenly withered.

The apostle called the young man aside and said: "My son, your affliction has convicted you. Confess, therefore, what you have done."

The young man wept and said: "I have committed an evil deed, yet had I intended to do good. I was in love with a certain young woman and she was in love with me. And when you converted us both, we vowed to live in chaste and brotherly love in accord with your teaching. But she threatened to break her vow, and rather than see her in the arms of another man, I took a sword and killed her. Then I came here to ask forgiveness for my crime."

Thomas brought a basin of water and blessed it. And when the young man washed his hands in it, they became whole and well again.

Then Thomas said to the young man: "Lead me to where your beloved lies dead."

The young man led him to an inn outside of the city, and there they found the dead girl lying on the ground in the garden. They took her into the inn and placed her on a couch, and Thomas said: "The hands that killed her shall bring her back to life again; therefore, my son, say what I tell you to say, and do what I tell you to do."

And whatever Thomas told him to say, the young man said after him, tenderly; and whatever he was told to do, he did affectionately.

The young woman opened her eyes. She looked at her lover and she looked at the apostle, and at once began to relate what had happened to her as soon as she was dead:

A black creature, hateful in appearance and filthy in his garb, received her soul, the young woman related. And he took her down to a chasm of hateful odor and unbearable heat, where souls were lashed to whirling wheels of fire. From there, the young woman continued, she was taken to another chasm, and still another, each more horrible than the preceding, and in each she saw the souls of those who committed adultery, obscenity, seduction and whoredom.

When she finished her long account, the young woman wept and said to the apostle: "Now I am before you, O holy man! And I beg of you to keep me from those horrible places I saw below. And I vow that I shall remain chaste all the days of my life."

And when it became known throughout the land what had happened to the young woman, thousands flocked to the apostle and accepted his teachings.

7. *The Girdle from Heaven*

One day Thomas appeared in the Valley of Jeosophat and there, to his surprise, he found assembled John and his brother James, Peter and Paul, Andrew, Philip, Luke and Bartholomew, Matthew and Matthias the Just, Simon the Canaanite, Jude and his brother Nicodemus, Maximianus and other disciples.

"Why are all of you here?" asked Thomas.

"We were brought here," said Peter, "to attend Mary's burial."

And the disciples related how an earthquake shook the earth one day, and the heavens were full of thunder. And great clouds came down and transported the apostles and their disciples from all the corners of the earth to the spot where Mary dwelt with the three virgins, Sephora, Abigea and Zael who ministered to her needs.

"Why have you come here?" Mary asked the apostles.

"We were brought here," said Peter, "but we know not why."

Then Mary told them that the angel Gabriel had visited her, and announced that on the morrow she would die, and she asked the apostles to remain with her all night in prayer. She arrayed herself like a queen, turned her face eastward and prayed in Hebrew.

The next day, the twenty-first day of Tobi, Jesus, surrounded by a host of angels, came down to receive Mary's soul. The apostles fetched linen, and spices, and perfumes, and prepared the body for burial. On her body they placed three palms from paradise, and three branches of the olive tree from which the dove had brought the sign to Noah. And they carried Mary from Mount Sion to her tomb in the Valley of Jeosophat.

"How long ago was the burial?" asked Thomas.

"Eight days ago," said John.

"The Lord did not suffer you to be present," added Peter, "because you were always unbelieving."

Thomas bowed his head and smote his breast, saying: "I ask all of you to forgive me for my obduracy and unbelief."

And they prayed for him.

Then Thomas asked: "Where is the tomb in which you buried Mary?"

They pointed to the sepulcher in the valley. But Thomas shook his head and said: "Her body is not in there."

Peter reprimanded him: "You did not believe in the Resurrection until you touched his body, Thomas! And now you doubt us!"

But Thomas insisted: "Her body is not in that tomb."

As if in anger, the apostles rolled away the stone from the tomb where they had placed Mary's body. But the tomb was empty.

Thomas then related to them how he had been transported on a cloud from India to the top of the Mount of Olives, and had witnessed Mary's Assumption.

"As I knelt in prayer while the angels carried her body up to heaven," Thomas concluded, "the angels threw this down to me." And he showed them the tasselled girdle with which they themselves had girt Mary's shroud eight days earlier.

All the apostles and their disciples bowed before Thomas. They asked his pardon; and they asked his blessing, for he had been found worthy to witness the Assumption of Mary.

The same clouds which had brought the apostles together now appeared again and carried them back, each to his own assigned place.

And Thomas was carried back to India.

8. *The Martyrdom of Judas Thomas*

And it came to pass that after the Apostle Thomas had performed many miraculous deeds and converted great multitudes in India, he traveled to the city of Zabodka in Macedonia, to preach there. But the idolatrous priests of that city were angered by his words and works and caused the magistrates to put the apostle in prison.

Then the slanderers went to King Matthaus of Macedonia and said to him: "We have a man in our prison who is a dangerous sorcerer; and if we do not destroy him he will surely cause us much trouble. For though he has been placed in irons, he commands the prison doors to open, and they open. And he receives many visitors. Last night even your wife, Queen Tertanai, and your daughter, Princess Margita, came to visit him."

"You lie," said the king. "Neither my wife nor my daughter would do such a thing."

"Ask them," said the brazen slanderers, "and ask the prisoner."

The king sat down on his judgment seat and commanded the apostle be brought before him, and that the prisoner should be stripped of all save an apron around his waist. And when Thomas was before him, the king asked: "Are you a slave or are you a free-man?"

"I am a slave of the Lord," said Thomas.

"What is the name of your master?"

"His name cannot be heard or uttered, but we, his disciples, call him Jesus the Christ."

"You are naught but a villainous sorcerer and mischief-maker whose wickedness is known throughout India. I shall have you slain and you shall soon be forgotten, you and the Jesus you preach."

The king ordered fifteen swordsmen to take the prisoner out of the city to the top of a mountain and there execute him.

When the place of his martyrdom was reached, Thomas begged that his hands be freed and that he might be permitted to pray before he died, and his wish was granted.

The apostle fell on his knees and stretched out his hands toward heaven:

"O Lord, my Guide and my Savior! I have now fulfilled the commandment which you gave me, and I have delivered your message in this land. My steps were wide in the path of your gospel of peace. I have ridden upon the plough and never once looked backwards, lest the furrow might be crooked. I have kept the first watch, and the second and the third, that I might see your face! I have embraced poverty and privation and despised all things of the flesh; and I have not once turned backwards. Now I am weary. Let not the serpent stand in my way, nor let the adders rise up against me. But receive me, O Lord! Amen!"

Then Thomas rose to his feet and went to the swordsmen and said: "Now finish your king's command."

Two soldiers came at him from each side and pierced him with their spears in four deadly thrusts. And the Apostle Thomas fell down to the ground and yielded up his ghost. The soldiers wrapped him in a clean shroud and sumptuous raiment and buried him in the graveyard of the kings.

That night Thomas appeared to King Matthaus in a dream, and said to him: "You did not believe in me when I was alive. Will you believe in me now that I am dead? When you rise tomorrow, come to my grave and open it, and see what you shall see."

The next day the king opened the grave in which Thomas had been buried; but the grave was empty.

The king gathered up a handful of dust from the spot where the apostle had lain in death and he poured it into a bag. Then he returned to the palace and hung the bag about the neck of his son who had been possessed by a demon since childhood. The prince immediately became well.

King Matthaus confessed his sins and accepted the apostle's faith and he caused it to be preached throughout his kingdom.

And so the mission of the Apostle Judas Thomas, whom Jesus called Didymus, was fulfilled in his death as in his life.

CHAPTER TWENTY-SIX

The Adventures of Andrew and Matthias

1. *Matthias in the Land of the Cannibals*

To Matthias, who replaced Judas Iscariot among the apostles, fell the lot of preaching in the distant country of the Cannibals. Without a moment's hesitation or delay, Matthias prepared for the journey to the land where men ate no bread and drank no wine, but fed on the meat of men and drank the blood of strangers in their gates. When a stranger reached the gates of their principal city, he was blinded and drugged with a magic potion so that his heart was altered and his mind deranged. Then he was fattened in a prison for thirty days before being slaughtered and consumed.

Matthias reached the gates of the city of the Cannibals. And at once the men-eaters laid hold of him, blinded him, and placed him in a prison where there were many others awaiting their horrible fate. But the magic potion they had forced on Matthias neither altered his heart nor confused his mind, for all the while he had prayed for protection. And when left alone in the prison, Matthias opened his eyes, and he could see. So he sat down in his prison cell and began to sing.

Each day the executioners would arrive to take out those who had been properly fattened and whose time was up. And when they came to visit Matthias, he closed his eyes and pretended blindness and confusion until they left. After they were gone, he prayed again and sang, and never lost hope.

2. *Andrew and the Pilot*

Twenty-seven days after Matthias was imprisoned in the city of the Cannibals, the apostle Andrew in far-off Lydda had a dream.

And in this dream Jesus came to him and commanded him to rescue Matthias from the men-eaters. Though only three days remained before Matthias was to be executed, and the journey from Lydda to the land of the Cannibals was long and difficult, Andrew prepared to obey the command, believing that he who created the wind could carry him to his destination in time.

Andrew awakened his disciples and informed them of the journey before them. And at once they started out for the sea. As they neared the shore they saw a small boat with three men in it.

"Where are you going in this boat?" asked Andrew.

"We are going to the country of the Cannibals," the pilot of the boat replied.

"We, too, seek to go there," said Andrew.

"How is it that you go there?" asked the pilot. "It is a place every man avoids unless he has a mission there."

"We have a mission there," said Andrew.

"Then I will take you there," said the pilot.

And Andrew said: "But before we board your boat I must explain that we have no passage-money to pay you. Nor do we have food for the long journey."

"How do you expect to make this journey, if you have no money for your passage nor food to eat?" asked the pilot in surprise.

"Listen, brother, do not think that I am trying to cheat you out of your fare," said Andrew. "But we are the disciples of Jesus Christ, and he commanded us to carry no money, nor bread, nor shoes, nor two coats when we go on a journey to preach the Gospel or to do his will."

"If such is the commandment of your Master," said the pilot, "I would rather have you as my passengers than those who can give me gold and silver. Come aboard that we may be on our way."

As soon as they came on board, the pilot commanded one of the sailors to bring three loaves of bread for the passengers.

Andrew turned to his disciples and said: "My children, come and eat of the bread given us in great kindness by the pilot of this boat."

But his disciples were not able to answer him, for, though they had not yet left the shore, they were already in distress because of the sea.

Andrew turned to the pilot and said: "Brother, may the Lord repay you with heavenly bread from his kingdom for your kindness to his disciples!" Then he ate of the bread.

The sailors released the boat, the pilot took his place beside the rudder, and the boat moved away from the shore.

As they sailed on, Andrew called out to his disciples who were without experience of the sea, saying: "Fear not, children, for the Lord will not forsake us. Remember the time we were in the boat with Jesus and a great storm arose so that the waves rose above our sails and threatened to swallow us, and Jesus rebuked the winds, and there was calm in the sea? Now, therefore, fear not but pray and go to sleep."

And the disciples fell fast asleep; but the pilot and the apostle were awake.

After some time of silence, Andrew said: "For sixteen years I have sailed the sea, but never have I seen such skill in steering as yours."

"Since you are the disciples of the man you call Jesus, the sea has recognized you and become calm," said the pilot. "Tell me more about him whom you call Jesus."

As they sailed through the starlit night on a calm sea, Andrew recounted to the skillful pilot how Jesus had made the blind see, the lame walk, the deaf hear; how he had cleansed the lepers and turned water into wine; how he had fed the hungry and comforted the sorrowing who believed in him.

"He did all this before those who believed in him," said the pilot. "Could he do it before the high priests and the idolators who did not believe in him?"

"Yes," said Andrew with a sigh. "He did it before the high priests and the idolators, but they still did not believe in him."

Then he related in great detail one particular instance, when Jesus and his twelve disciples went into the temple of the Gentiles and there, before the very eyes of the high priests, performed many miraculous things, after commanding a sculptured sphinx to be his messenger; and still the high priests' hearts had hardened against Jesus.

"Can you remember other happenings like this?" asked the pilot when Andrew had finished and grew silent.

"O man, you certainly have the spirit of inquisitiveness!" said Andrew, and recalled still another event.

Each time Andrew completed an account the pilot urged him on, saying: "What else can you recall? Say on, say on, for I prudently listen to profitable words."

Finally, after many hours of wonderful accounts, Andrew, too, fell into a deep sleep.

Morning came and Andrew opened his eyes. To his surprise he found himself lying on his cloak on dry ground, with the sleeping disciples beside him. Andrew called out to them: "Wake up! Wake up, my children, wake up! See what has happened to us! For we are at the gates of the city of the Cannibals!"

"Who brought us here?" asked the amazed disciples.

And Andrew replied sadly: "We were brought here by the Pilot, and we knew him not!"

They prayed, asking to be forgiven for having spoken to him as to a man and to a sailor; and then they started out for the prison where Matthias was confined.

3. *The Empty Prison*

Andrew and his disciples entered the city of the Cannibals unnoticed and went directly to the prison gates guarded by seven giant wardens. Andrew prayed and made the sign of the cross. At once the wardens fell to the ground dead, and the huge prison gates opened of their own accord.

The disciples entered the prison, following the sound of a sweet voice singing, and soon they came to the cell where Matthias sat on the ground singing a psalm. Matthias rose when he saw Andrew, and they saluted each other with a kiss.

"Only three days more and you would have been fare for the men-eaters," said Andrew.

"I feared not," said Matthias, "for my faith was constant. And, behold, here you are to free me."

They looked about them and saw naked men and women, blinded and deranged, feeding on grass like cattle fattened for slaughter. Andrew and Matthias prayed; and as they prayed, they laid their hands upon the heads of the prisoners. And straightaway they regained their sight and their reason. They covered their nakedness as best they could and waited for Andrew to tell them what to do.

"Go out of the city," Andrew said to them. "Fear not, for not a dog will bark at you. Walk until you come to a great fig tree, laden with fruit. Wait there for me. Eat of the fruit of the tree each according to his appetite, for the more fruit you pick, the more will appear to nourish you."

And there were two hundred and seventy men and seven times seven women whom Andrew released from prison.

After they left, Andrew commanded a bright cloud to take Matthias and the other disciples to the distant mountain where Peter was teaching.

And Andrew remained alone in the city of the Cannibals.

4. *The Conversion of the Men-eaters*

Every morning the executioners of the city of the Cannibals went to the prison to bring out the men condemned to be slaughtered that day. The victims were taken to the troughs and the ovens in the city square, and there they were prepared before the rulers of the city, and the entire populace that came to the feast.

But on the day Andrew the Apostle arrived in their city, the executioners came running to the rulers and to the waiting crowds, reporting with alarm that they had found the gates of the prison open, the prisoners gone, and the seven giant guards near the entrance, dead.

The rulers of the city held a council among themselves, then said to the executioners: "Bring the dead guards and prepare them, that we may not go hungry today."

"But what of tomorrow and the next day?" asked the people.

"We shall send the young men in boats to distant lands," said the rulers, "and they shall lure strangers to our city with golden promises. Then our prisons will be full again."

"But that will take a long time, and meanwhile we shall die of hunger," the people complained.

"Meanwhile," said the men-eating rulers to their men-eating sub-jects, "we shall assemble the aged in our midst; and lots shall be drawn each day for the seven to be slain."

Andrew, who had hidden himself behind a brazen pillar in the city square where he could not be seen, but could see all that was going on, saw the seven dead prison wardens brought to the square and the executioners begin to prepare them for the feast. The evil sight brought tears to the apostle's eyes and he prayed: "O Lord, Jesus Christ, who sent me to this place to reason with the barbarian, cause the hands of these human butchers to be without power."

At once the knives fell from the executioners' hands, and their arms turned into stone.

The rulers of the city shouted in distress: "The same magician who emptied our prison has now bewitched our executioners! Go, therefore, and gather the old men without delay, seeing that we are going to be hungry."

Andrew saw them bring two hundred old men into the square. The rulers of the city cast lots amongst them, and the lot fell on seven men. One of the seven began to plead: "Pray, let me go! I have a son and a daughter that you may slay in my stead, if you will let me go!"

And the rulers of the city said: "If you will produce your son and daughter to take your place, we will grant your plea."

The old man left and soon returned with his son and his daughter. They were little children, and they wept and begged not to be slain for they were still so small. But the cruel rulers and their wicked old father would not listen to their pleas and they were dragged to the execution troughs.

On seeing this Andrew wept again, and again he prayed for the executioners' hands to be stayed. The knives in the killers' hands melted like wax in a fire. And all the people in the square were dismayed.

Then came Satan, disguised as an old man, and he shouted: "I know where this evil comes from. There is a stranger in our midst whose name is Andrew. It was he who came from a distant land to open our prison gates and free our prisoners. It was he who caused the hands of the executioners to turn into stone. Search for this man in our city, and when you find him, destroy him. Otherwise he will destroy all of us."

Andrew came out from the place where he had been hiding, and said in a loud voice: "Behold, I am Andrew whom you seek!"

The multitude of men-eaters rushed at him, and laid hold of him, and asked the rulers of the city what to do with him.

"Behead him," said one, "and let us devour him."

"No," said another, "beheading will not be enough punishment for what he has done. Let us burn him."

"No," said a third, "if we burn him, he will not be fit to eat."

And so they argued for a long time. Finally they agreed to put a rope about Andrew's neck and drag him through the streets and lanes of the city until he was dead. Thus they would be avenged by the sight of his torture, and when he was dead they could still eat him.

They put a rope around the apostle's neck and dragged him through the streets until his blood flowed like water. But at the end of the day he was still alive. They bound him and left him in prison overnight. The next day and the next they repeated this torture. And yet Andrew was alive after three days.

On the third night in prison, Andrew prayed for deliverance. And he arose from his prayer feeling strong and well. He looked about him and saw in the middle of the prison a huge pillar, and upon it an alabaster statue. Andrew managed to free his hands. He folded and unfolded his arms seven times; then he made the sign of the cross at the pillar. Immediately a torrent of water began to stream out of the statue; a torrent so great that it soon filled the prison and rose like a flood in the streets of the city. The water kept rising and rising until it inundated all the dwellings. And when the people tried to flee from the city, they found it surrounded by a ring of fire. They could neither flee nor could they stay. For by the time they returned to the city the water had risen up to their necks.

They begged Andrew to stop the flow of the water and to forgive their great wickedness; and they promised to believe in the Gospel he preached.

Andrew, who knew that their affliction was great and their repentance sincere, commanded the pillar to cease the flow of water.

And when the water subsided, he gathered the people in the city square, and there he baptized them and forgave them all their sins. Only the old man who had given up his children to be slain Andrew did not forgive, but condemned him to the abyss below.

Andrew preached to the people, and he drew plans for a church to be raised in the city square. So eager were the people to please him, that the church was erected in a very short time.

Then Andrew announced that he must leave and return to his disciples. The news was received with great sorrow. The elders put ashes on their heads, and the children wept when they learned that their holy man wished to leave them.

Andrew remained with them for seven days to console them. Then he instructed them in the true gospel so that they would remember it forever, and he departed from the city of St. Andrew, which was once the city of the Cannibals.

CHAPTER TWENTY-SEVEN

The Adventures of Philip

1. *Worshipers of the Golden Idol*

Philip the Apostle, and the seventh of the Seventy Disciples, drew by lot the territory of Africa in which to spread the Gospel.

"I would fain you went with me," said Philip to Father Peter.

"So has the Lord commanded, my son," Peter replied.

After they had journeyed together for some time, they met a man possessed by a demon, and Peter cured him with the sign of the cross.

And the restored man said: "From this day on, wherever you go, I shall go; whatever you wish me to do, that I shall do; and whatever you tell me to believe, that I will believe."

And the three journeyed on. Soon they came to the gate of a great city, with a very high tower upon it.

"Tower, bend down!" commanded Peter in the name of Jesus.

And the tower lowered itself to the ground. Peter placed the new convert upon the top of the tower and commanded it to rise again. The tower rose, and from its great height, the man from whom the unclean spirit had been driven, called out in a voice that could be heard in the farthest streets of the city:

"O men, inhabitants of this idolatrous city! Gather at the gate to receive the disciples of the Lord Jesus, for they have come here to bless you and to lead you from your sinful ways to the road of redemption!"

The citizens did not obey. And thunder and lightning assailed the city, so deafening and so blinding, that all the inhabitants of the city fled for safety to nearby caves.

Then the man on the tower shouted in a voice that would cower the lionhearted: "There is no hiding place for you!"

The thunder and lightning pursued the people wherever they

fled, and many died. Only then were the people ready to listen. They gathered around the two apostles, beseeching them to stop the storm. The apostles prayed for the lightning and thunder to cease, and the fearful storm was over at once.

The people were ready to worship the man on the tower as a god. But he told them his story and commanded them to listen to Peter and Philip.

Philip spoke to them and asked: "Who is the god you worship?"

"We worship the statue of a man made of pure gold," the people replied.

"Bring him to me," said Philip.

The idol was brought to the gates, but the high priests of the temples of the city warned the people: "These strangers are sorcerers. They have come to destroy our god so that we may become defenseless in time of war. They preach of a god who was born of a woman and who died on a cross. Whoever heard of a god made of gold and silver ever dying?"

Philip prayed again. And a ring of fire descended from heaven, and encircled the high priests. The heat of the fire was so fierce that the priests cried out in great pain.

"Why do you weep and howl?" asked Philip. "Have you not said that your god can help you in time of war? If he can spare you in battle, let him spare you now."

Peter then lifted the idol high above his head and said: "See what happens to an idol fashioned by the hands of man!"

He was about to fling the idol into the ring of fire surrounding the priests, when the idol cried out: "O disciples of Jesus! Why do you want to punish me instead of those sinful men? Was it my fault that they melted me and moulded me and placed me in a temple? They asked the people to bring sacrifices of meat and wine for me. I can neither eat nor drink, but the priests deceived the people and devoured all that was brought for me. They are your culprits, not I."

When the priests heard themselves condemned before the multitude by their own idol, they admitted their guilt and promised to leave off their evil ways.

Philip said to them: "If you believe in the Lord Jesus you will be forgiven."

The priests cried out together: "We believe in the Lord Jesus the Christ!"

At once the ring of fire turned into a lake of sweet water.

And upon this spot the people built a church, where Peter and Philip taught for six days. They appointed a bishop, presbyters and deacons to administer the newly-founded church. And then Peter returned to fulfill his mission in Rome; and Philip went on to Africa.

2. *Philip in the City of the Serpents*

In the city of the Serpents there dwelt a very good man, whose name was Stachys. When the apostles Philip and Bartholomew, and Philip's sister, Mariamne, came to preach in this city where the inhabitants worshiped the images of the viper and the serpent, Stachys invited them to his great house and permitted them to preach in his home to all who were willing to listen to the Gospel.

At this time, Nicanora, the wife of the proconsul of the city, lay in her bed afflicted with many ailments, especially those of the eye that make the vision dim. A servant brought her the news of the Hebrews in the home of Stachys, who preached salvation and cured the sick.

"Perhaps they can cure me," said Nicanora. And she ordered the slaves to place her on a silver litter and secretly carry her to the apostles.

At the gate of Stachys' house, Nicanora met Mariamne, Philip's sister, who said to her: "*Alemakan, ikasame, marmare, nachaman, mastranan, achamen.*"

"So be it!" cried out Nicanora.

"Then you understood what I said?" asked Mariamne.

"Of course," said Nicanora. "You said, in Hebrew: 'Daughter of the father, you are my mistress, who had been given as a pledge to the serpent; but Jesus the Redeemer has come to deliver you through us, to break your bonds, and cut them, and remove them from you from their root, because you are my sister, one mother brought us forth as twins. You have forsaken my father, you have forsaken the path leading you to the dwelling place of your mother, being in error; you have left the temple of that deception, and of the temporary glory, and have come to us, fleeing from your enemy, because he is the dwelling-place of death. Behold, now your Redeemer has come to redeem you; Christ the Sun of righteousness has risen upon you, to enlighten you.' That is what you said."

"How did you learn Hebrew?" asked Mariamne.

"I am a Hebrew and a daughter of the Hebrews, and I delight in the language of my fathers, which is never heard in the city of the Serpents."

Mariamne brought the proconsul's wife to her brother Philip and to Bartholomew. They prayed for her to be cured, and she was instantly well; then they prayed again and thanked the Lord for his mercies.

Before they could finish their "Amen," a man, raging like an unbroken horse, rushed into their midst, laid hold of Nicanora, and shouted: "O shameless wife! When I come to your bed, you complain of your ills and the inflammation of your eyes. But you were well enough, and could see well enough, to come to these magicians. How shall I punish you for this?"

Nicanora replied in a soft voice: "O tyrant, forsake your wickedness and your brutality, if you wish me beside you. Promise to live in chastity and self-restraint, as I have vowed to live the rest of my life."

The tyrant seized his wife by the hair of her head and dragged her along out of the house. Then he turned and ordered his men to lay hold of Mariamne, the apostles and their host, Stachys, and throw them all into prison. The proconsul ordered his men to whip them with rawhide thongs, and drag them through the streets, with feet tied, as far as the gates of the temple of the Serpents.

"As for that woman, Mariamne," said the wicked proconsul, "strip her of her clothes so that all the people in the streets may see her in her nakedness."

"What shall we do with them when we reach the temple?" asked the men.

"Nail them up on the gates of the temple," said the tyrant. "And hang that impudent Philip up by his heels."

When his orders were carried out and Mariamne was stripped of her clothes, a bright cloud descended from heaven and covered her as with a cloak; and all who had looked upon her were blinded.

When Philip saw what they tried to do to his sister, he called out: "I, whom Jesus named the son of Thunder, shall avenge this evil and destroy the wicked serpent worshipers with fire, for I shall pray that Hades open its mouth and swallow them all."

Philip prayed in Hebrew, and Hades opened its mouth and swallowed up the ungodly people of the city.

Then Jesus appeared to Philip, saying: "O Philip, why have you inflicted such destruction upon this city? Have I not taught you not to repay evil with evil? Have I not been beaten, scourged, crucified and made to drink vinegar mixed with gall upon the cross, and yet, have I not said: 'Forgive them, for they know not what they do!'? How often have I told you about him who gives away his own lamp to another, and himself sits in darkness? Or he who gives up his dwelling-place to another, and himself dwells on the dunghill?"

"Why are you angry with me, Lord?" asked Philip. "Is it because I cursed my enemies?"

"You have disobeyed my commandment not to repay evil with evil. Because of this you shall complete your martyrdom now and die. And after forty days I shall send the archangel Michael to bring you into paradise," said Jesus.

Then Jesus marked the air with a cross, and all the people who had been swallowed up into the dark abyss came up again on the ladder of the luminous cross. And a great multitude gathered around Philip who was still hanging, head down, upon the gate of the temple. They came near and wanted to take him down, but he stayed them, telling them that he must die for his transgression.

"Before you leave us, O holy man, tell us what above all we must know to keep on the path of righteousness!"

"Blessed is the man who endures temptation," said Philip. "For when he is tried, he shall receive the crown of life which the Lord has promised to them that love him."

And having said this, the Apostle Philip gave up the ghost.

Bartholomew and Mariamne took down his body while the multitude wept and mourned.

Three days later a great vine appeared where the blood of the apostle had dropped. And the people of the city built a great church upon that spot, and appointed Stachys as the bishop.

A quite different version of the martyrdom and death of the Apostle Philip is given in The Mythological Acts of the Apostles. *In this version Philip does no wrong and, though tortured cruelly, he continues to preach the Gospel. When finally the idolatrous priests and evil men throw the apostle into a great fire, an angel snatches "his pure body out of the fire before them at noon-tide" and takes it to Jerusalem and hides it in a tree.*

CHAPTER TWENTY-EIGHT

The Adventures of Peter and Paul

1. *It Is Easier for a Camel*

One day the apostles Peter, Andrew, and Matthias, accompanied by their disciples Alexander and Rufus, were on their way to the city of the Barbarians.

As they neared the city, Andrew asked: "Father Peter, shall we undergo in this city the afflictions I suffered in the city of the men-eaters, where they dragged me through the streets for three days until every street and lane was stained with my blood?"

"I do not know," said Peter. "But we shall approach the first man we see and ask him for bread. If he gives it to us, it is a good omen; if he refuses, we shall know that great suffering awaits us."

The first man they saw was an aging farmer, sowing his fields.

"Hail, farmer!" Peter greeted him.

"Hail to you, merchants!" the farmer replied.

"We are not merchants," said Peter, "and we are hungry. Have you any bread to give us?"

"If you will look after my plough, the oxen and the land," said the old farmer, "I will go to the city and get you something to eat."

The farmer left his work in the care of the apostles and their disciples and went into the city. While he was gone, Peter girded up his cloak and undergarment, and the others followed his example. And together they began to sow the field. As they sowed, they blessed the seed to come up and repay the old farmer tenfold for his kindness and hospitality.

When the farmer returned with food, he found the seed he had just sown, full grown, the ears heavy with corn. The farmer fell upon his knees and pleaded: "Tell me my lords, are you gods come down from heaven?"

"Stand up, man!" said Andrew. "We are not gods, but only servants. And we have come to teach your people the Gospel of Jesus, so that they may gain everlasting life."

"Is it hard to gain everlasting life?" asked the farmer.

"No," said Andrew, "it is not hard. Love God with all your heart and all your soul; do not commit murder, or adultery, or ever swear falsely. And do not do to others what you do not want them to do unto you. And you will earn life everlasting."

It soon became known in the city that Apostles of Christ had come to heal the sick and to forgive the sins of the repentant, and before long a great multitude gathered to greet them.

There was in that city a certain rich man, named Onesiphorus. He saw the miracles performed by the apostles, and he asked: "If I were to believe in your god, would I also be able to perform miracles such as these?"

"No," said Andrew.

"Why not?" asked the rich man.

"First, you would have to give up all your possessions," said Andrew.

"And if I did, would I be able to perform miracles?"

"No," said Andrew.

"Why not?" the rich man wanted to know.

"You would also have to give up your wife and your children, as we have done," said Andrew.

The rich man flew into a rage, and said: "You are nothing but a sorcerer to urge me to desert my family and to give away all my possessions." And he struck Andrew with his scarf. Then he turned to Peter and asked: "Do you also advise me to desert my wife and my children and give away my possessions?"

And Peter replied: "All I can say to you is this: 'It is easier for a camel to go through the eye of a needle than for a rich man to go through the gates of heaven.'"

"Ha!" said Onesiphorus. "You are an even greater sorcerer than he! For who has ever heard of a camel going through the eye of a needle? If you can show us such a miracle, I, and all the people in our city, will believe in your god. But if you fail, you shall be grievously punished."

Peter said: "Bring me a camel and bring me a needle."

There was one merchant in that city who had been converted by the Apostle Philip, and he began to search for a very small camel and a very large needle. But Peter said to him: "My son, nothing is impossible with God. Bring me rather a very big camel and a very small needle."

And when these were brought to him, he stuck the needle into the ground, and called out in a loud voice: "In the name of Jesus Christ, I order you, O camel, to jump through the eye of this needle!"

The assembled multitude saw the eye of the needle open up like a gate and the camel went through it with ease.

But Onesiphorus said craftily: "You are indeed a great sorcerer who can do this with a needle and a camel of your own choosing. But show us whether you can do this with my needle and my camel."

He then called his servants and whispered his instructions to them. And they soon returned with a camel upon which sat an impure woman. (For it is well known that the power of sorcery fails in the presence of an impure woman.) Peter understood what was in the rich man's mind. He set the needle in the ground, and said in a loud voice: "In the name of our Lord Jesus the Christ, I order you, O camel, to go through the eye of this needle!"

The eye of the needle opened wide like a great gate, and the camel, with the woman upon it, passed through it easily. And Peter commanded the camel to do it again; and the camel did it again.

Then Onesiphorus cried out and said: "Truly great is your god, and I shall believe in the Lord Jesus Christ. Furthermore, I have corn fields and vineyards; I have three times three times three pounds of unminted gold and fifty pounds of silver. And I have slaves great in number. All these I shall give to the poor, so that I, too, may be able to perform at least one miracle like you, Father Peter."

Onesiphorus rose and commanded the camel to go through the eye of the needle. The camel stuck its head through as far as the neck, but could go no further.

"That is because you have not yet been baptized," said Peter.

Onesiphorus went to his home with the apostles to receive baptism. A thousand souls followed, and they were all baptized with Onesiphorus by the Apostle Peter.

The Mythological Acts of the Apostles *attributes these events to Thaddeus, and the story is given with many embellishments. And it is further related that the magistrates of the city of the Barbarians (into whose hearts Satan had entered) tried to prevent the apostles from coming into their midst. They dared not slay them, but, said they to each other, "We have heard of them that they hate fornication. Let us take a woman, a harlot, and strip her, and place her at the gate of the city. And if they wish to enter the city, they will see her, and they will go away, and will not return to destroy us." But the archangel Michael lifted up the woman by her hair high into the air, and the apostles entered the city, and walked through the streets preaching the Gospel undisturbed.*

2. *The Cure for Luhith*

One day, when Baramus, the Emperor of Rome, sat on his throne, with his chamberlains standing upon his right and upon his left, a cloud descended before the throne bearing two men. The frightened chamberlains rushed upon the strangers to beat them, but the Emperor stayed them, saying: "Do not strike them for they have the appearance of angels."

Then he said to the strangers: "How stupid of you to appear before me unbidden! If my own daughter did such a thing she would be beheaded. Who are you? Where do you come from? And what do you want here?"

"I am Peter of Saida in Galilee," answered one of the men, "and this is my brother, Paul of Tarsus. We are servants of the King of Kings, whose name is Jesus the Christ. And we have come to cleanse Rome of its wickedness and to turn the people to the true faith."

"You shall have to prove the truth of your words," said the Emperor. "And as a test I shall bring before you my only daughter. Her right eye was blinded by a bird, and you shall show me whether you can restore her eyesight."

And Peter said: "Bring your daughter Luhith before us and we shall try to heal her."

"How did you know her name?" asked the astonished Emperor.

Peter said: "I know her name. And I know the name of your grandfather, who is no longer alive. He was called Dorotheus. Give up your idolatrous ways and believe in our God, and you shall learn more astonishing things than these."

The emperor gave the command for his daughter to be brought before the apostles. And when she arrived, Peter asked Baramus: "What was the sin you committed, for which your daughter was punished like this?"

The Emperor, ashamed to confess his sin before his wife and the chamberlains, flew into a rage, and said: "How dare you ask a king such questions?"

"If you will not tell us," said Peter, "then the bird that blinded your daughter will tell us."

Peter and Paul summoned the bird and demanded that it tell them exactly what had happened. And the bird told the following story:

"It was on the Emperor's birthday, when he gave a great feast, and himself drank until he was drunken. He saw an exceedingly beautiful maiden and sought to sleep with her, but she did not consent to it. When he insisted and she resisted him, he had her shut up in the stable with the cattle and ordered that she should be given neither bread to eat nor water to drink. And he decreed that whosoever should try to give her food or water would be beheaded. For twelve days this maiden remained in the royal stable. But Luhith, the Emperor's daughter, grieved for the girl whom her father in his folly had condemned to die of hunger and thirst. She secretly came to the stable window and tried to get bread and water to the prisoner. And I, the bird, was nearby. A demon possessed me, and I plucked out her right eye.

"When I did the evil deed I became blinded in the right eye myself. I flew into the desert and fasted thirteen days. And now I have come to tell you what the Emperor did and to confess my own sin."

The Emperor wept at the bird's story, and was full of shame before his wife and the chamberlains. And the Empress implored the apostles to heal her daughter.

Peter laid his hands upon Luhith's unseeing eye and prayed; and when he removed his hand her eye was fully restored.

"What can I do to repay you for what you have done for me?" asked the Emperor.

"You can allow us to preach in your city and testify before the people what the power of faith in our God can do," said Peter and Paul.

3. *Satan and the Apostles*

Wherever the apostles went, Satan and his hosts preceded them, trying in every way to frustrate their work.

And when Satan saw what Peter and Paul had accomplished in Rome, and the many converts they had made, he was sore distressed.

The Prince of Darkness changed his form and he changed his color. He altered his visage to appear as a Hindoo. He put on the garments of a king and placed a crown on his head. Then he summoned a demon to act as his steed; and four others he disguised as Roman princes carrying staves in their hands. And seated on his fiery Mongolian horse, with the crown on his head and four princes walking before him, Satan arrived at the gates of the palace of the Emperor of Rome.

To the gatekeepers he said arrogantly: "Tell the Emperor Baramus that a brother king, of India, is at the door!"

The Emperor welcomed the King of India and made a place for him on the throne. He ordered a great feast to be prepared for the ruler who had come to Rome from such a distant land.

After the reception ceremonies were over, and the two rulers were alone, the Emperor asked his royal guest: "What brings you here?"

The King of India did not reply, and began to weep like a child that has lost its mother.

"Why do you cry, O my brother! And why are you so sad?" asked Baramus.

"It is a long story," sobbed Satan, clad in the raiment of a king.

"Tell it to me, nevertheless," said Baramus.

"As you see," said the royal guest, "I am full of grief. For I was a king like you, and I ruled over Scindia and India. I had great armies in every country from Er-Rum to Nubia; my governors ruled from

Egypt to Syria; the Berbers, the Arabs, and the Hilalians were my subjects; and there was not a nation on earth that did not pay homage to me. My word was law everywhere."

"Then what happened?" asked Baramus anxiously.

"One day two men appeared on a cloud and came down before me in my throne room. And the name of one was Peter, and the name of the other was Paul. They said they had come to establish a new kingdom on earth by the authority of one they called Jesus. This Jesus, so they said, could turn water into wine; feed five thousand people on just five loaves; make the blind see and the lame walk; and he could even make the dead come back to life again."

Baramus had grown pale as a hooded ghost. "What happened then?" he asked.

"Then my troubles began. First my chamberlains fell under the spell of the two sorcerers. Next my own wife and children believed in them. Then my chiefs and governors began to listen to them with rapt attention, but would not listen to me. Maidens rejected their suitors and refused to get married. Wives turned away from their husbands. My soldiers hurled their weapons into my face and followed these men. And all that remains to me of my great kingdom now are these four princes whom I brought with me."

There were tears in Baramus' eyes, for he sympathized with his royal guest as only one king can sympathize with another. "Why then did you come to me?" he finally asked.

"I came to warn you, O my brother! For if these two sorcerers should come to Rome and you let them preach unmolested, your fate will be as mine."

Emperor Baramus rose from his throne, his face ashen gray and his feet unsteady, and he thanked the King of India for having come to warn him of the danger to his rule. "There are two such strangers as you described in my kingdom, and they call themselves Peter and Paul."

"Where are they now?" asked Satan.

"They have gone to Philippi."

"Then waste no time and have them brought before you with chains on their necks and bonds on their feet," shouted Satan.

Emperor Baramus dispatched a captain with a thousand armed soldiers to Philippi; and they were ordered to bring Peter and Paul back to Rome. The captain and his soldiers returned in due time, but Peter and Paul were not with them.

"Where are the sorcerers whom I ordered you to fetch?" demanded the Emperor.

The captain and his men threw down their arms and cried out: "They are not sorcerers but holy men who came to teach us the gospel of Everlasting Life."

The Emperor placed the captain and his men under arrest and they were put into prison until it was decided by what death they should die. And four thousand horsemen were dispatched to Philippi to apprehend Peter and Paul.

The horsemen had just left Rome, when Baramus saw a cloud drifting right up to his throne, and seated upon the cloud were the two apostles, Peter and Paul.

"We found out that you wanted to see us," they said. "And here we are."

"Have those men put in chains," Satan advised. "And tomorrow have them burned in the city square as a lesson to your people not to listen to foreign wizards and sorcerers."

Baramus followed Satan's advice. But on the morrow, when the Emperor came out to witness the torture of the apostles, he suddenly found himself lifted from his royal litter high up into the air; and there he remained suspended.

"Help!" shouted the Emperor. "Let me down!" he cried. "Take me back down to earth and I shall do anything you want!" he pleaded.

"First," said Peter, "you must order the release of the captain and his thousand men who refused to take part in your wickedness."

"How can I give such an order when I am suspended in mid-air?" asked the Emperor.

"Send your daughter Luhith to release the men," said Peter.

And Luhith was sent to release the men from prison. When they came out they saw their disgraced Emperor suspended ingloriously in the air.

"Now," said Peter, "repent."

"How shall I do that?" asked the unhappy Baramus.

"Repent your boasting of power and your friendship with the

devil; and promise never again to put your hand against those who believe in Jesus the Christ!"

"Give me an inkhorn and papyrus," said the repentant Emperor, "and I will give you my promise in writing."

They brought the Emperor writing materials and he wrote down in his own hand: "I, Baramus, Emperor of Rome, believe that there is no god either in heaven or on earth, other than Jesus the Christ, King of Peter and Paul."

Satan witnessed what was going on with deep displeasure; and he quickly changed his disguise from that of the King of India to a fierce black bull. He rushed at Paul, ready to gore him.

Paul, in terror, called out: "Save me, Father Peter! Save me from this devil in frightening shape!" And he threw his arms around Peter.

"Fear not, my brother," said Peter, who had much experience in such matters. "By the power of Jesus, you take hold of one of his horns, and I shall take hold of the other, and we shall drag this bull around at will."

And so they did. Satan began to whine and plead: "Let me go and I shall not trouble you again."

"Will you swear that you will not oppose us again?" asked Peter.

"I swear," said Satan.

But as soon as they let him go, Satan began to laugh, saying: "Whoever heard of the devil telling the truth or of keeping his word?"

And he disappeared.

The great multitude that had gathered to see Peter and Paul executed, remained to listen to their Gospel and to follow in their ways.

4. *Thecla of Iconium*

There was a young maiden named Thecla (her mother's name was Theoclia), who lived with her parents in the city of Iconium. Thecla was eighteen years old; and every day she was told that she was the prettiest girl in the province of Lyconium. Besides her beauty, a gentle disposition, and loving parents, Thecla had a suitor,

Thamyris, of whom her parents approved. And Thamyris, after the manner of all suitors, called her many endearing names, which she liked to hear. Above all she liked to hear him talk of the day, very soon, when they would be wed.

One afternoon, as Thecla sat near a certain window of her room, facing the house of their neighbor, Onesiphorus, she heard a voice, though she could not see the face, and it was the voice of a stranger speaking to Onesiphorus. The things the stranger said at first struck terror in her heart; then they pleased her; and at last she was fascinated and drank in the words thirstily as if they were water from a fresh spring to one in the desert.

And what she heard the man say was this:

"Blessed are the pure of heart, for they shall see God;

"Blessed are they who keep their flesh undefiled, for they shall be the temple of heaven;

"Blessed are they who have wives, as if they had them not, for they shall be made into angels;

"Blessed are the bodies and souls of virgins, for they shall not lose the reward of their continued virginity."

And the man spoke of charity, and faith, and the power of prayer.

Thecla's mother, Theoclia, called her. But the young girl was so rapt in listening to the stranger that she did not hear her mother call. Nor would she move from her place for three days. The mother was greatly alarmed and sent for Thamyris.

The suitor came in haste and saluted Thecla before entering her room so as not to startle her. Then he embraced her and kissed her and said: "Thecla, my dear one, why do you sit here in melancholy, and like one astonished? Turn your face to me that I may see it."

Thecla withdrew from his arms without looking at him, and would not answer him, as she had not answered her mother.

And Theoclia said to the young man: "It is that stranger in our neighbor's house. His name, I am told, is Paul. He arrived in Iconium three days ago and he has been preaching against our gods and that our women should live in chastity."

Thamyris went out and found two men, Demas and Hermogenes, who had attached themselves to Paul. They were hypocrites who pretended they loved the apostle, yet were ready to betray him for a sum. And when Thamyris offered them that sum, they looked about them furtively, then whispered in the suitor's ears: "This man Paul is one who teaches the new and forbidden religion of the Christians. If you tell the governor of his teachings the governor will be obliged, by the order of Caesar, to put him to death. Then you can have your Thecla."

The next day Thamyris caused Paul's arrest and the apostle was brought before the governor.

"I don't know where this man comes from," said Thamyris. "Nor do I know his profession. But he has come to Iconium to pervert our city and to teach that matrimony is unlawful and wedded bliss is unclean."

The governor looked at the accused, a short, bowlegged man, thick-set and hollow-eyed, his nose long and crooked, but his face full of grace. And he asked: "What have you to say for yourself?"

"My name is Paul of Tarsus and I am a Hebrew teacher by profession. I have come here in the name of God, who is a God of vengeance and who stands in need of nothing but the salvation of his creatures. And I am here to teach them to sin no more."

When the governor heard these strange words, he ordered the guards to bind Paul and place him in prison overnight while he considered how to punish the stranger. And his command was carried out.

That night, in secrecy, Thecla appeared at the prison gate. For the price of her earrings, the turnkey opened the prison door to let her in. And for the price of her silver looking glass the jailer allowed her to enter Paul's cell. There she saw the apostle for the first time.

She sat down at his feet, and told him her story; and then she listened to his words of consolation. As he spoke, she kissed the chains that bound him.

Meanwhile, at Thecla's home they had missed her, and when they questioned the servants, it was soon learned that the girl had gone to visit Paul in prison. Thamyris roused the city. He gathered a mob to advance on the prison. And there they found Thecla in Paul's cell. They took the apostle and the young girl to the judgment hall, the men shouting in the streets: "He is a sorcerer! Let us kill him!"

The governor in his judgment seat asked Thecla: "Why do you not marry Thamyris according to the law of the Iconians?"

Thecla refused to reply, keeping her eyes fixed on Paul.

Theoclia then cried out: "She is bewitched! She is no daughter of mine!"

The governor decreed that the stranger Paul, being a Roman citizen, who could not be put to death, should be banished from Iconium; and that Thecla, as a warning to all the other women in the city, should be burned at the stake.

The men gathered wood and straw and stripped Thecla for the burning at the stake. And when the governor looked at her, he wept because of the greatness of her beauty that was soon to be destroyed.

Then the men set fire to the pyre. But though the flames were exceedingly great, they did not harm Thecla. She stood in the midst of the fire praying, and she said: "I thought I could not endure my lot but Paul has come to comfort me." For she looked up and thought she saw Paul before her.

Whereupon a cloud came down and drenched the fire; and an earthquake swallowed many of those who had tried to do her harm.

And still the trials of the young and beautiful Thecla were not at an end.

For when she left the stake unhurt, she went in search of Paul, knowing that he was banished. And she found him in a cave outside the city, with Onesiphorus and his family, and they were praying.

When Paul turned and saw Thecla safe in the cave, he cried out: "O God, who searchest the heart, you have answered my prayer!"

Then Paul sent Onesiphorus and his family back to Iconium and the apostle, accompanied by Thecla, proceeded to Antioch. There Thecla's troubles began again. For when they entered the city, a certain brazen magistrate, a Syrian named Alexander, saw her and desired her and seized her in the street and kissed her before a multitude of people.

"Do you think that because I am a stranger you can force yourself on me?" Thecla cried out. And she ripped his coat, tore the magistrate's crown from his head and trampled it underfoot; and in every other way made him ridiculous before the people.

Alexander, in shame and anger, rushed to the governor with

accusations against Thecla. And the governor decreed that she should be thrown into a den of wild beasts.

Thecla was taken to the amphitheater and cast into the den of a fierce lioness. But as Thecla entered, praying, the great multitude of spectators saw the lioness slowly approach the girl with a lowered head and a deep growl and, when it reached the girl, the animal stopped and licked her feet. Thecla began to scratch the lioness's whiskers, as one would scratch a kitten.

Alexander the Syrian ordered that other wild beasts should be let loose on Thecla. They released lions and wolves and bears and tigers and cougars and other beasts kept in Corinth to loose upon the Christians for the amusement of the Corinthians. But as these ferocious beasts entered the den, the lioness stationed herself before Thecla and would let none of them approach. Then the wild beasts surrounded the young girl and lay down at her feet.

The governor, from his shaded lodge in the amphitheater, shouted to Thecla in the den: "Who are you that the wild beasts will not harm you?"

"I am a servant of the living God and a believer in Jesus Christ!" she replied. "I am what you call a Christian!"

In fear and trembling the governor released her.

After many other harrowing experiences, Thecla spent years in solitude in a cave. Then she went out among the people, whom she served, and for whom she performed many miraculous cures. Though she lived to be a very old woman, Satan never tired of trying her virtue; and Satan was defeated at every turn.

At the age of ninety, seventy-two years after she had first heard the words preached by Paul, Thecla's soul went up to heaven, the first woman martyr and apostle of God, and she was buried two or three stadia from the tomb of the Apostle Paul.

5. *Paul Goes to Rome*

After his work was done in the Island of Gaudomeleta, the Apostle Paul started out for Rome, for he longed to join the Apostle Peter.

The fame of Paul's work had preceded him, and his enemies went to Emperor Nero, with heavy gifts of gold and silver, and they pleaded:

"We are afflicted enough with Peter in our midst; now we hear that Paul is on his way to join him. He is a troublemaker. Therefore send out an edict to all the ports that wherever Paul appears he should be killed and his head sent you as a confirmation."

Emperor Nero accepted the gifts and sent out the edict.

The Apostle Peter, in Rome, who learned of the edict, secretly sent two men with a letter to warn Paul not to come directly from Africa to Italy, but to travel from Gaudomeleta to Syracuse, and from Syracuse to Rhegium of Calabria, and from there to Mesina, and from Mesina to Didymus, and from that city to Pontiole. And then to proceed cautiously to Baias, and Gaitas, and Taracinas, and finally sail up the river to Tribus Tabernes. Then he would be only thirty-eight miles from Rome. The letter ended with:

"As God does not separate the two great lights which he has created; so does he not wish to separate us, neither Peter from Paul, nor Paul from Peter."

The warning reached Paul, and he traveled with caution until he reached Pontiole.

Meanwhile all the toparchs in the Roman Empire, having received Nero's edict, watched every incoming vessel in the ports. And one day they seized a captain in Pontiole who was short, bald-headed and bearded, bowlegged, whose eyebrows met over a rather long nose and who, in every other way, answered to the description that had been sent out of Paul. This man, who called himself Dioscorus, spoke boldly of his Christian beliefs. They therefore laid hands on him and beheaded him. And, in accord with the edict, they sent the head to Nero.

The Emperor called together Paul's enemies and announced: "Rejoice! For Paul your enemy is dead!" And he showed them the head.

The tidings were brought to Peter and his followers, who mourned with a bitter mourning for Paul, whom they now assumed to be dead.

Paul in Pontiole heard what had happened to Dioscorus, the kind captain who had brought him from Syracuse to Rhegium and who had accompanied the apostle to this city, and he was very grieved.

He prayed to God to punish the city in which such vile crimes could be committed without the populace rising up against the male-factors; and his prayers were answered. (The city of Pontiole and all those who condoned wrongdoing sank one fathom beneath the sea. And there it can be seen to this day, as a memorial for Dioscorus, who looked like Paul and who died in the apostle's stead.)

Paul proceeded on his journey, stopping in many places to estab-lish churches and to ordain presbyters and deacons; to listen to dis-putes among the believers and to adjust their differences.

In Appii Forum, not far from Vicusarape, where Paul stopped for one night, he saw a man sitting on a golden chair, surrounded by many slaves who amused their master with stories of crimes they had committed, each more hideous than the other.

"I have caused a son to murder his father," one man related.

"And I have caused a house to fall down and kill all the people in it, including the infants," boasted another.

"That is nothing at all," said still another. "For I managed that the Bishop Juvenalius, whom Peter ordained, should sleep with the Abbess Juliana."

Paul sent word at once to Bishop Juvenalius of the slander he had heard, and ordered him to inform Peter in Rome. The good bishop ran to Peter, fell at his feet weeping and lamenting, because of the slander contrived against him in Appii Forum.

"But how did you learn about it?" asked Peter.

"Paul sent word that he had heard it there," said the bishop, "and he ordered me to come and tell you about it."

"How can that be?" asked Peter. "Paul is dead and his head was brought to Nero!"

"He is alive," said the bishop. "Send your disciples there and you will find him."

Peter sent his trusted followers to find Paul; and they soon re-turned with the apostle. And seeing each other, Paul and Peter wept with joy.

Then Paul related to Peter all that had befallen him since last they parted; and Peter related to Paul his trials and triumphs in Rome.

"What is your greatest problem in this city?" asked Paul.

"It is Simon the Magian," said Peter with a sigh. "For he has caused me more suffering than any with his plots."

"I wish to meet this evil man," said Paul.

"You will," said Peter.

6. *The Encounter with Simon the Magian*

Word was carried on the wind that Paul had arrived in Rome and was staying with Peter. A large multitude gathered before Peter's door, clamoring for Paul to speak to them.

The multitude was divided between the Christian-Jews and the Christian-Gentiles. And there was a great uproar amongst them.

Said the Christian-Jews: "We are the real Christians, for we are of the seed of Abraham, Isaac and Jacob, and of the Prophets who spoke with God. We have been given the Commandments from Sinai; and we have been promised the Messiah from the beginning of time. And we have been circumcised in our Covenant with our Lord."

And the Christian-Gentiles argued: "We are the true and only Christians, for although we were idolaters who had not crossed the sea on dry land nor tasted of the manna from heaven, yet as soon as we heard the truth of the Savior, we believed in him."

Paul said to them: "Why do you contend among yourselves instead of loving each other, as a brother loves a brother, and gather your strength against those who persecute all Christians, whether they are Jews or Greeks?"

Then the Christian-Jews were angered and they said: "Are you, Paul, not yourself a Jew, and of the Jews? Are you not yourself, like Peter, circumcised in the Covenant of the Law? Do you wish now to destroy the Law and the Sabbath upon which God rested from all his works?"

And Peter replied to them: "Just as Eve was made from the side of Adam, so also was the church created out of the side of Jesus; so that all who believe in him may enter, Jew and Gentile alike, circumcised and uncircumcised, side by side as brothers."

While they were thus disputing, Simon the Magian went to the Emperor Nero to testify against the apostles and their disciples, both Jew and Greek. Simon, through sorcery, made a brazen snake crawl before him, and he caused the stones on which he walked to laugh with a loud laughter. At times Simon the Magian walked on the ground, and at times he floated through the air.

And as he appeared before the Emperor, Nero looked at Simon, but what he saw was a very young child, standing in front of him.

"Who is this child?" he asked his chamberlains.

"Which child?" they asked.

Nero turned his head, and there was no child before him but a very old man, shriveled and bent over with age. Nero turned to his chamberlains in surprise. When he turned his head again the old man was gone, and in his place stood a tall, stately youth. Each time Nero turned his head, Simon changed his form. Finally the Emperor asked in reverence: "Who are you, that you have such powers?"

"I, good Emperor, am the son of God," said the wicked Simon. "But there are in our midst two men, Paul and Peter by name, who deny my claims and plan your destruction."

"It is plain that Paul cannot be in Rome," said Nero, "for I have had him slain."

"Send to Peter's house," said Simon, "and you will find that Paul the Wizard is with Peter the Conjurer at this very moment contending with a multitude as to who can be considered a true Christian."

Nero sent his messengers to Peter's house with the order to apprehend both Paul and Peter. And so it was done.

"There are the men," said Simon to Nero, "who have come to pervert your people and to deny my heavenly power. But I shall now order my angels to come and avenge me."

"We do not fear your angels," said Peter.

"Are you really not afraid of Simon?" asked Nero in surprise. "For I have seen him perform great miracles."

"Not miracles," said Peter, "but acts of sorcery."

"Test his powers," said Nero.

"If he is really the son of God, as he claims, he would know the thoughts of all men. I shall tell you in secret what is in my mind, then let me hear this Simon tell you my thought." And Peter

THE ADVENTURES OF PETER AND PAUL

whispered in the Emperor's ear: "Order a loaf of barley bread for me!"

Simon protested that the thoughts of men are known to God but none other, not even to his son.

"But I can tell what you think," said Peter. And he whispered again in the Emperor's ear.

"I shall cause great dogs to come and devour you before the Emperor's eyes," Simon the Magian threatened.

And great, black dogs appeared and rushed at Peter. But Peter stretched out his hands with the barley loaf in them and he prayed and the dogs disappeared like passing shadows. And to Nero Peter said: "Did I not tell you: 'He talks of angels but thinks of dogs'?"

Nero suddenly turned to Paul: "Why are you so silent all this time? We have not heard one word from you."

"O Emperor, know this," said Paul, "if you continue to listen to this magician, it will bring great sorrow to your people and your empire will be diminished. For this man is ungodly, and he knows nothing of angels."

Simon retorted: "If I had a high tower, I would ascend it and call upon my angels to take me up to heaven within sight of all and put these men to shame."

"Tomorrow you shall have your chance to prove it," said the Emperor. "For I shall order such a tower built for you."

"Not tomorrow," Simon said. "For I wish to be beheaded first. And I shall arise from the dead after three days. And then, on the third day, I shall ascend to heaven."

The Emperor agreed, and ordered Simon beheaded in a dark place. And Simon, by his magic, brought a ram in the form of a man and who appeared exactly like the Magian; and the executioners beheaded the ram. The moment the animal was dead, they could see that it was not the Magian but a ram; but they dared not report what had happened for fear they would be slain for failing to do their Emperor's bidding.

On the third day Simon appeared before the Emperor and said: "Here I am, as I foretold. Though I was beheaded three days ago, I have risen from the dead to prove that I am truly the son of God. And now I am ready to climb the tower and be carried by the angels to heaven."

"Why cannot the angels come down here?" asked Peter.

"The angels cannot come down to earth because of sinners," said Simon. "But they will come to me on the tower."

"Then accomplish what you have promised," said Peter.

Simon slowly climbed to the top of the tower that had been erected in the public square. A great crowd gathered to watch him. Then they saw him on the top of the tower, crowned with laurels, stretching out his hands and beginning to fly as if carried by wings.

A cry went up from the multitude when they saw this, and Nero turned to the apostles and asked: "Now what say you of Simon?"

Peter looked up, made the sign of the cross, and said: "In the name of Jesus the Christ, I command you demons in the shape of angels to let go of Simon the Magian!"

And immediately Simon fell from the great height to the ground, and his body was severed in four parts.

Nero became enraged and ordered the apostles put in irons; and Simon's body he ordered held in great honor for three days, believing that he would rise again after that time.

"Because you have caused Simon's death," said Nero, "both of you shall be clubbed to death with iron clubs."

"It seems to me," said Agrippa the executioner, "that both men are not equally guilty, since it was Peter who caused Simon's death."

"In what manner then shall they die?" asked the Emperor.

"It is just that Paul's head should be cut off. But Peter should be raised to suffer on a cross, for he caused the death of Simon the Magian."

"You have judged most excellently," said Nero.

And both Paul and Peter were led away from the presence of the Emperor of Rome to be executed.

7. Perpetua's Reward

The Apostle Paul, condemned to die, was placed in irons and taken three miles out of the city of Rome to be beheaded. As the three soldiers and their prisoner left the city gates, about the distance of a bow-shot, they discovered a certain woman, named Perpetua, following them and weeping bitterly. The soldiers knew this woman, blind in one eye since her childhood, and they did not molest her.

As Perpetua came close to them on the road, Paul asked her for a handkerchief, and she gave it to him willingly.

"You foolish woman," the soldiers scoffed. "We are taking this man to be beheaded, and you shall never get your handkerchief back!"

"I care little for that," said Perpetua. "But I adjure you by the health of Caesar to bind his eyes with my handkerchief before you execute him."

The soldiers kept their promise and blindfolded Paul when they reached the place called Aquae Salniae, and there they executed the apostle near a pine tree. On their way back to the city they met Perpetua again, and they returned her handkerchief which had become stained with the apostle's blood.

Perpetua took the handkerchief in great grief and began to wipe away her tears. Suddenly she realized that the unseeing eye, blind since her childhood, was full of vision.

"You warned me that I might lose my handkerchief," said Perpetua to the soldiers, "but instead I have found my sight!"

CHAPTER TWENTY-NINE
The Sermon on the Mount

The Gospel According to St. John ends with the statement that "There are also many other things which Jesus did, the which if they could be written every one, I suppose that even the world itself could not contain the books that should be written." (John 21 : 25).

This seems to have been proved by the gatherers of the apocryphal literature, and more particularly the ante-Nicene church fathers. There are vast numbers of apocryphal gospels, acts, epistles, fragments, discourses, and encyclopedic early church histories. There are numerous accounts of the parents of Mary; the Virgin Mary and Joseph the Carpenter; the miracles of Infancy and Boyhood; the Ministry and the Sayings; the events of the apostolic age; and the additions made by newly discovered documents or reports of current miraculous events. All this literature is dedicated to the glorification of Jesus and the proof of his divinity.

And yet this literature in all its vastness does not add one iota to the stature of the preacher of the Sermon on the Mount. For in the entire range of world literature, both sacred and secular, there is not another singular expression to equal the Sermon either as ethics or as literature. It appeals at once to the heart as it does to the mind; and few are too young or too old to be stirred by the thoughts and hopes expressed in this brief sermon.

The Sermon on the Mount is given here as it appears in the Life and Morals of Jesus of Nazareth, *commonly known as the* Jefferson Bible, *one of the most unusual religious expressions by a President of the United States.*

And seeing the multitudes, he went up into a mountain: and when he was set, his disciples came unto him: And he opened his mouth, and taught them, saying,

Blessed are the poor in spirit: for theirs is the kingdom of heaven.

Blessed are they that mourn: for they shall be comforted.

Blessed are the meek: for they shall inherit the earth.

Blessed are they which do hunger and thirst after righteousness: for they shall be filled.

Blessed are the merciful: for they shall obtain mercy.

Blessed are the pure in heart: for they shall see God.

Blessed are the peacemakers: for they shall be called the children of God.

Blessed are they which are persecuted for righteousness' sake: for theirs is the kingdom of heaven.

Blessed are ye when men shall revile you, and persecute you, and shall say all manner of evil against you falsely, for my sake.

Rejoice, and be exceeding glad: for great is your reward in heaven: for so persecuted they the prophets which were before you.

But woe unto you that are rich! for ye have received your consolation.

Woe unto you that are full! for ye shall hunger. Woe unto you that laugh now! for ye shall mourn and weep.

Woe unto you when all men shall speak well of you! for so did their fathers to the false prophets.

Ye are the salt of the earth: but if the salt have lost his savour, wherewith shall it be salted? it is thenceforth good for nothing, but to be cast out, and to be trodden under foot of men.

Ye are the light of the world. A city that is set on a hill cannot be hid.

Neither do men light a candle, and put it under a bushel, but on a candlestick; and it giveth light unto all that are in the house.

Let your light so shine before men, that they may see your good works, and glorify your Father which is in heaven.

Think not that I am come to destroy the law, or the prophets: I am not come to destroy, but to fulfill.

For verily I say unto you, Till heaven and earth pass, one jot or one tittle shall in no wise pass from the law, till all be fulfilled.

Whosoever therefore shall break one of these least commandments, and shall teach men so, he shall be called the least in the kingdom of heaven: but whosoever shall do and teach them, the same shall be called great in the kingdom of heaven.

For I say unto you, That except your righteousness shall exceed the righteousness of the scribes and Pharisees, ye shall in no case enter into the kingdom of heaven.

Ye have heard that it was said by them of old time, Thou shall not kill: and whosoever shall kill shall be in danger of the judgment:

But I say unto you, That whosoever is angry with his brother without a cause shall be in danger of the judgment: and whosoever shall say to his brother, Raca, shall be in danger of the council: but whosoever shall say, Thou fool, shall be in danger of hell fire.

Therefore, if thou bring thy gift to the altar, and there rememberest that thy brother hath aught against thee,

Leave there thy gift before the altar, and go thy way; first be reconciled to thy brother, and then come and offer thy gift.

Agree with thine adversary quickly, whilst thou art in the way with him; lest at any time the adversary deliver thee to the judge, and the judge deliver thee to the officer, and thou be cast into prison.

Verily I say unto thee, Thou shalt by no means come out thence, till thou hast paid the uttermost farthing.

Ye have heard that it was said by them of old time, Thou shalt not commit adultery:

But I say unto you, That whosoever looketh on a woman to lust after her hath committed adultery with her already in his heart.

And if thy right eye offend thee, pluck it out, and cast it from thee: for it is profitable for thee that one of thy members should perish, and not that thy whole body should be cast into hell. And if thy right hand offend thee, cut it off, and cast it from thee: for it is profitable for thee that one of thy members should perish, and not that thy whole body should be cast into hell. It hath been said, Whosoever shall put away his wife, let him give her a writing of divorcement: But I say unto you, That whosoever shall put away his wife, saving for the cause of fornication, causeth her to commit adultery: and whosoever shall marry her that is divorced committeth adultery.

Again, ye have heard that it hath been said by them of old time, Thou shalt not forswear thyself, but shalt perform unto the Lord thine oaths:

But I say unto you, Swear not at all: neither by heaven; for it is God's throne: Nor by the earth; for it is his footstool: neither by Jerusalem; for it is the city of the great King. Neither shalt thou swear by thy head, because thou canst not make one hair white or black. But let your communication be, Yea, yea; Nay, nay: for whatsoever is more than these, cometh of evil.

Ye have heard that it hath been said, An eye for an eye, and a tooth for a tooth:

But I say unto you, that ye resist not evil: but whosoever shall smite thee on thy right cheek, turn to him the other also.

And if any man will sue thee at the law, and take away thy coat, let him have thy cloak also. And whosoever shall compel thee to go a mile, go with him twain.

Give to him that asketh thee, and from him that would borrow of thee turn not thou away.

Ye have heard that it hath been said, Thou shalt love thy neighbour, and hate thine enemy:

But I say unto you, Love your enemies, bless them that curse you, do good to them that hate you, and pray for them which despitefully use you, and persecute you;

That ye may be the children of your Father which is in heaven: for he maketh his sun to rise on the evil and on the good, and sendeth rain on the just and on the unjust.

For if ye love them which love you, what reward have ye? do not even the publicans the same? And if ye salute your brethren only, what do you more than others? do not even the publicans so?

And if ye lend to them of whom ye hope to receive, what thank have ye? for sinners also lend to sinners, to receive as much again.

But love ye your enemies, and do good, and lend, hoping for nothing again; and your reward shall be great, and ye shall be the children of the Highest: for he is kind unto the unthankful, and to the evil.

Be ye therefore merciful, as your Father also is merciful.

Take heed that ye do not your alms before men, to be seen of them: otherwise ye have no reward of your Father which is in heaven.

Therefore when thou doest thine alms, do not sound a trumpet before thee, as the hypocrites do in the synagogues and in the streets, that they may have glory of men. Verily I say unto you, They have their reward.

But when thou doest alms, let not thy left hand know what thy right hand doeth:

That thine alms may be in secret: and thy Father, which seeth in secret, himself shall reward thee openly.

And when thou prayest, thou shalt not be as the hypocrites are: for they love to pray standing in the synagogues and in the corners of the streets, that they may be seen of men. Verily I say unto you, They have their reward.

But thou, when thou prayest, enter into thy closet, and when thou hast shut thy door, pray to thy Father which is in secret; and thy Father, which seeth in secret, shall reward thee openly.

But when ye pray, use not vain repetitions as the heathen do: for they think that they shall be heard for their much speaking.

Be not ye therefore like unto them: for your Father knoweth what things ye have need of before ye ask him.

After this manner therefore pray ye: Our Father which art in heaven, Hallowed be thy name. Thy kingdom come. Thy will be done in earth, as it is in heaven.

Give us this day our daily bread:

And forgive us our debts, as we forgive our debtors.

And lead us not into temptation, but deliver us from evil: For thine is the kingdom, and the power, and the glory, forever. Amen.

For if ye forgive men their trespasses, your heavenly Father will also forgive you.

But if ye forgive not men their trespasses, neither will your Father forgive your trespasses.

Moreover, when ye fast, be not, as the hypocrites, of a sad countenance: for they disfigure their faces, that they may appear unto men to fast. Verily I say unto you, They have their reward.

But thou, when thou fastest, anoint thine head, and wash thy face;

That thou appear not unto men to fast, but unto thy Father which is in secret: and thy Father, which seeth in secret, shall reward thee openly.

Lay not up for yourselves treasures upon earth, where moth and rust doth corrupt, and where thieves break through and steal:

But lay up for yourselves treasures in heaven, where neither moth nor rust doth corrupt, and where thieves do not break through nor steal:

For where your treasure is, there will your heart be also.

The light of the body is the eye: if therefore thine eye be single, thy whole body shall be full of light.

But if thine eye be evil, thy whole body shall be full of darkness. If therefore the light that is in thee be darkness, how great is that darkness!

No man can serve two masters: for either he will hate the one, and love the other; or else he will hold to the one, and despise the other. Ye cannot serve God and mammon.

Therefore I say unto you, Take no thought for your life, what ye shall eat, or what ye shall drink; nor yet for your body, what ye shall put on. Is not the life more than the meat, and the body than raiment?

Behold the fowls of the air: for they sow not, neither do they reap, nor gather into barns; yet your heavenly Father feedeth them. Are ye not much better than they?

Which of you by taking thought can add one cubit unto his stature?

And why take ye thought for raiment? Consider the lilies of the field, how they grow; they toil not, neither do they spin:

And yet I say unto you, That even Solomon in all his glory was not arrayed like one of these.

Wherefore, if God so clothe the grass of the field, which today is, and tomorrow is cast into the oven, shall he not much more clothe you, O ye of little faith?

Therefore, take no thought, saying, What shall we eat? or, What shall we drink? or, Wherewithal shall we be clothed?

(For after all these things do the Gentiles seek:) for your heavenly Father knoweth that ye have need of all these things.

But seek ye first the kingdom of God, and his righteousness; and all these things shall be added unto you.

Take therefore no thought for the morrow: for the morrow shall take thought for the things of itself. Sufficient unto the day is the evil thereof.

Judge not, that ye be not judged.

For with what judgment ye judge, ye shall be judged; and with what measure ye mete, it shall be measured to you again.

Give, and it shall be given unto you; good measure, pressed down, and shaken together, and running over, shall men give into your bosom.

And why beholdest thou the mote that is in thy brother's eye, but considerest not the beam that is in thine own eye?

Or how wilt thou say to thy brother, Let me pull out the mote out of thine eye; and, behold, a beam is in thine own eye?

Thou hypocrite, first cast out the beam out of thine own eye; and then shalt thou see clearly to cast out the mote out of thy brother's eye.

Give not that which is holy unto the dogs, neither cast ye your pearls before swine, lest they trample them under their feet, and turn again and rend you.

Ask, and it shall be given you; seek, and ye shall find; knock, and it shall be opened unto you:

For everyone that asketh receiveth; and he that seeketh findeth; and to him that knocketh it shall be opened.

Or what man is there of you, whom if his son ask bread, will he give him a stone?

Or if he ask a fish, will he give him a serpent?

If ye then, being evil, know how to give good gifts unto your children, how much more shall your Father, which is in heaven, give good things to them that ask him?

Therefore all things whatsoever ye would that men should do to you, do ye even so to them: for this is the law and the prophets.

Enter ye in at the strait gate: for wide is the gate, and broad is the way, that leadeth to destruction, and many there be which go in thereat:

Because strait is the gate, and narrow is the way, which leadeth unto life, and few there be that find it.

Beware of false prophets, which come to you in sheep's clothing, but inwardly they are ravening wolves.

Ye shall know them by their fruits. Do men gather grapes of thorns, or figs of thistles?

Even so every good tree bringeth forth good fruit; but a corrupt tree bringeth forth evil fruit.

A good tree cannot bring forth evil fruit, neither can a corrupt tree bring forth good fruit.

Every tree that bringeth not forth good fruit is hewn down, and cast into the fire.

Wherefore by their fruits ye shall know them.

A good man out of the good treasure of the heart bringeth forth good things: and an evil man out of the evil treasure bringeth forth evil things.

But I say unto you, That every idle word that men shall speak, they shall give account thereof in the day of judgment.

For by thy words thou shalt be justified, and by thy words thou shalt be condemned.

Therefore whosoever heareth these sayings of mine, and doeth them, I will liken him unto a wise man, which built his house upon a rock: And the rain descended, and the floods came, and the winds blew, and beat upon that house; and it fell not; for it was founded upon a rock.

And every one that heareth these sayings of mine, and doeth them not, shall be likened unto a foolish man, which built his house upon the sand:

And the rain descended, and the floods came, and the winds blew, and beat upon that house; and it fell: and great was the fall of it.

Apostles and Disciples

The lore of the Old Testament teems with prophets; and the lore of the New Testament, with apostles.

By definition, any pioneering missionary of the Gospel is called an apostle; and anyone suffering hardships and martyrdom for spreading the teachings of Jesus earned the same appellation. By this definition, the number of the apostles is indeed very great. The term is applied to Jesus himself, as well as to the twelve chosen by him and who had witnessed his Ministry, Crucifixion and Resurrection. To these were added: Matthias, elected to take the place of Judas Iscariot; Paul, the "Apostle to the Gentiles"; Barnabas, Mark's nephew and Paul's friend; and Luke, the gentle physician and gifted writer.

The term is often also applied to the seventy disciples (or seventy-two disciples); and to such distinguished missionaries as Barsabbas, Junias, Timothy, Titus and all the other early missionaries mentioned in the Acts and the Epistles. In the lore, all the sons of Joseph the Carpenter are accounted apostles of special distinction, since they were brothers of Jesus. Later, the term was applied to men like Angar, Apostle of the North; Boniface, Apostle of Germany; Patrick, Apostle of Ireland; Gregory the Illuminator, Apostle of Armenia; Augustine, Apostle of the English; Denis, Apostle of the French; Cyril, Apostle of the Slavs; Neri, Apostle of Rome; John Eliot, Apostle of the Indians; and so on.

Traditionally, however, only the twelve appointed by Jesus and selected mainly from among his Galilean neighbors (five of them from the tiny village of Bethsaida) are called apostles. To these are added: Matthias and Paul. All the others of the very early apostolic period were included among the seventy disciples.

In addition to the apostles (known as the disciples and companions

*of Jesus) tradition has established a list of seventy disciples – and
some hagiologists claim the number to be seventy-two. The Greek
and the Roman accounting of the disciples differ in many respects.
Even their names are often confusing because many of the disciples
(like all the apostles) were Jews; and many assumed Greek or
Roman names that had no relation whatsoever to their given Hebrew
names, or assumed symbolical names, such as: Jesus Justus, Philologus, Tertius, Quartus, Carpus, Marinus and Trophimus. When an
apocryphal work mentions one of these by his Hebrew name, we
have no way of knowing to which particular disciple reference is
made.*

THE APOSTLES

*The following notes about the apostles are of necessity brief, and
given mainly in their relation to the lore. There are many excellent
books on this topic and anyone wishing to explore it further should
consult one of the several biographical dictionaries of the saints, or
the lives of the saints. For the lore on all or any of them,* The Golden
Legend *(See: Reading List) is a good starting point.*

1. SIMON, called Peter

*Simon, son of the Galilean Jonas and his wife Johanna, was
called by Jesus "Peter" and also "Cephas," so that, according
to the lore, he who later became the Prince of the Apostles
should have three names. Peter married Perpetua, daughter
of Aristobulus, and they had a son and a daughter. Petronilla,
the daughter, was a paralytic but very beautiful, and there
are many legends woven about her. Peter heard John the
Baptist preach, and was one of his followers for a time. Later
he became the most aggressive disciple of Jesus and, after
the Crucifixion, the most prominent leader of the new faith.
He was cast into prison in Jerusalem by Herod Agrippa, but
an angel freed him. And Peter traveled and preached throughout Asia Minor, helped by his faithful wife, Perpetua. For a
time Mark attached himself to Peter, from whom he gathered
firsthand material for the Gospel. Peter finally went to Rome*

where he became the first bishop of the Church of Rome. And there, by order of Nero, he was crucified head downwards, on June 29, 64 A.D.

2. ANDREW, the Fisherman

Originally a fisherman on the Sea of Galilee like his brother, Simon called Peter, Andrew too was a follower of John the Baptist; and the first to be called by Jesus. In the lore he is described as a large person, a little stooped and having a large nose and high eyebrows. His Hebrew name is not known; we know him by his Greek name only. Andrew preached in Scythia; and it is claimed that he was crucified in Patras on a cross in the shape of the Roman numeral X, called a decussate cross, and also known as St. Andrew's cross. The most vivid legends about Andrew's adventures during his missionary days appear in The Acts of Andrew and Paul. Among other marvelous deeds, Andrew cleaves the sea with a cup of fresh water.

3. JAMES, the Greater

The elder son of Zebedee and Salome (some sources give the mother's name as Bronte) was one of the four fishermen of Bethsaida, Andrew, Peter, John and James, who always head the list of the apostles. Because of his zeal James was singled out by Herod Agrippa and beheaded in 42 A.D. According to tradition none of the apostles left Jerusalem until after James's execution, but some church writers claim that James traveled extensively through Spain before his martyrdom; and he is considered the patron saint of that country.

4. JOHN, the Son of Thunder

John, the younger brother of James, is known by many names. He is called: John the Evangelist; John the Divine; John the Theologian; and in the Gospel he is called Boanerges, or Son of Thunder, because of his eloquence and fiery temper. There are many legends about the disciple "best loved" by Jesus. He was the only apostle who did not desert Jesus during his trial and Crucifixion, and for that reason John was appointed as Mary's guardian. John traveled to many lands. When he reached Rome, according to legend, he was thrown into a vessel of boiling oil, but came out unscathed. As a very old man he was banished to Patmos, where he had a number of visions, and these he set down in his Revelation. He is considered the author of The Gospel According to St. John and the Epistles of John. Legend has it that John never died. He fell asleep in Ephesus, and there he sleeps to this day; and will not wake until the Second Coming.

5. PHILIP, the Coachman

The fifth apostle to come from the village of Bethsaida, Philip was a coachman by trade; and that he was married we know only from the legend that he had four daughters who died with him in Hieropolis. (Some suggest that there is a confusion here with Philip, deacon of the Church of Jerusalem, who had four daughters.) In the lore Philip kills a fiery dragon, black, and over a hundred cubits long. Philip was often accompanied by his sister Mariamne, who was with him at his martyrdom. And though there are stories in the lore about Jesus being displeased with Philip's ire, there is the tradition that Philip was the disciple in whom Jesus confided.

6. BARTHOLOMEW, the Herdsman

Bartholomew came from Endor. He was the son of Sosthenes and Urania, of the Tribe of Issachar; though some say his father was Talmai, and his real name, Nathanael, "The Israelite without Guile." In a work variously known as

The Gospel According to Bartholomew, the Questions of St. Bartholomew, The Apocalypse of Bartholomew, and the Coptic Book of the Resurrection of Christ by Bartholomew the Apostle, we are given a detailed description of what Jesus saw and did in the domain of Hades during the Forty Days, as given in an answer to Bartholomew's questions. And in the apocryphal Apostolic History of Abdias there are remarkable legends about Bartholomew, his adventures and martyrdom in India.

7. THOMAS, "the Twin"

Thomas, or Judas Thomas, son of Diophanes and Rhoa, was a Galilean of the Tribe of Benjamin. Jesus named him Didymus, or "the Twin"; and in some apocryphal works he is also called Jude. There is a legend that when Jesus first appeared to the apostles after the Resurrection, Thomas would not believe his eyes until his hands had touched the wounds; and since then, so runs the legend, a man who will not take anything on faith is called "a doubting Thomas." Actually, the apocryphal story upon which this legend is based tells that Jesus, on that occasion, enjoined Peter to touch the wounds on his hands, Andrew to touch the wounds on his feet and Thomas to touch the lance wound in his side, so that their doubt would be dispelled. The remarkable adventures of Thomas are given in the Acts of Thomas.

8. MATTHEW, the Publican

Matthew the Galilean was also called Levi, for he came of the tribe by that name; though the Gospel of the Twelve Apostles gives his origin as of the Tribe of Naphtali. His birthplace is variously given as: Jerusalem, Nazareth, Capernaum and Berytus. He is credited with The Gospel According to Matthew, directed especially to his brethren the Jews. He is also credited with the apocryphal Book of the Infancy,

*called the Book of Pseudo-Matthew. His adventures in Ethi-
opia and his martyrdom there are given in the Apostolic
History of Abdias. The Arabs claim that Matthew spent the
latter years of his life among them and died of old age in
Naddabar. But the Greek tradition is that he was burned to
death. It is also claimed that he must have been killed with
a sword since the emblem of Matthew is the sword.*

9. JAMES, the Stonecutter

*There is considerable confusion about James, called "the
Less" either to distinguish him from James the Greater or
because he was short in stature. He is called the son of
Alphaeus; and he is called the son of Joseph. He is listed as
the ninth apostle and as the first of the disciples. James the
Less appears frequently in the lore and he is always treated
tenderly. At the Last Supper James vowed not to eat or drink
again until he saw Jesus risen from the dead. And after the
Resurrection Jesus came to James and commanded him to
eat again. James the Less is assumed to be the author of the
Epistle of St. James as well as the Protevangelium or the
Book of James, which is the most important of the Infancy
Gospels and the oldest of the apocryphal works extant.*

10. THADDEUS, the Obscure

*The apostle's full name was Judas Thaddeus Labbaeus. He
was not called Judas so as not to confuse him with Judas
Iscariot. Thaddeus was supposed to have been a son of
Joseph the Carpenter, and therefore a brother of James the
Less. His place among the apostles is disputed. And some do
not even place him among the seventy disciples. The Epistle
of Jude is ascribed to Judas Thaddeus. Otherwise very little
is known about him. In the lore he is noted for his mission to
Abgarus, King of Edessa, and he presumably became the
apostle to the Syrians.*

11. SIMON, the Zealot

This apostle too was the son of Alpheus and Mary, daughter of Cleophas, and therefore related to Jesus. Simon Zelotes (the Zealot) first appears in the lore as the boy who was bitten by a snake and restored by Jesus. Later he is represented as the bridegroom in the marriage feast of Cana. He belonged to a Jewish faction noted for its fierce advocacy of strict adherence to the Mosaic Law. Later he was just as fierce in preaching the Gospel. He is identified with Simeon who was crucified for preaching in Samaria.

12. MATTHIAS, Chief of the Tax Collectors

This apostle was chosen to take the place of Judas Iscariot. According to the Book of the Resurrection of Christ by the Apostle Bartholomew, Matthias was a wealthy man, but gave away all his possessions to follow Jesus. His missionary adventures in the city of the Cannibals and elsewhere are described in the Acts of Andrew and Matthias and in the Acts of Peter and Andrew. Little is known about his personal life or how he died. It is believed that he is called the "Chief of the Tax Collectors" because he is confused with Matthew the Publican.

13. PAUL, the Apostle to the Gentiles

In the lore, as in the New Testament, Paul occupies a more prominent place than any of the other apostles and disciples. He was born in Tarsus, a city in Asia Minor, where there was a large Jewish community. His father was a Pharisee, and so was Paul until his conversion. He studied in the school of Gamaliel in Jerusalem for the Rabbinate, while supporting himself as a tentmaker. And he was a zealous persecutor of the members of the new sect, the Nazarenes or Christians, and participated in the trial against Stephen, "the first Christian martyr." After Paul's conversion he devoted his life to establishing Christian communities throughout the world. There are many apocryphal epistles and apocalypses attributed to him. Paul's life has been the repeated subject of biographers and novelists. And when reference is made to "the apostle," the reference is always to Paul. A large volume would be necessary to contain the legends about his adventures.

THE SEVENTY DISCIPLES

About most of the disciples we know little, other than their names, where they officiated as bishops and, in some instances, where and how they died. And there is as little about them in the lore.

1. JAMES
Youngest son of Joseph the Carpenter and brother of Jesus; who became Bishop of Jerusalem (see: Apostles)

2. CLEOPHAS
A cousin of Jesus, who succeeded James as Bishop of Jerusalem. According to legend he was martyred in Emmaus

3. MATTHIAS
Of Bethlehem, appointed to take the place of Judas Iscariot; preached the Gospel in Ethiopia, and died a martyr (see: Apostles)

4. THADDAEUS
A disciple of Thomas, carried the epistle of Jesus to King Abgar of Edessa (see: Apostles)

5. ANANIAS
Who restored the sight of Saul of Tarsus and baptized him; Bishop of Damascus; probably stoned to death near Damascus in 40 A.D. by

order of Balas, field marshal to King Aretas

6. STEPHEN
A Greek Jew and known as "the First Christian Martyr," was one of the seven deacons of the Christian church in Jerusalem; he was tried and condemned to death by stoning; Saul of Tarsus, later the Apostle Paul, participated in the trial against Stephen

7. PHILIP
One of the seven deacons of Jerusalem and later Bishop of Trallium in Asia; sometimes confused with the Apostle Philip, because of his four daughters

8. PROCHORUS
One of the seven deacons of Jerusalem; afterwards Bishop of Nicodemia in Bithynia. He was thought to be a nephew of Stephen, "the First Martyr," and a companion of the Apostle John. He suffered martyrdom in Antioch

9. NICANOR
A Jew from Cyprus, was one of the seven deacons of Jerusalem; according to legend, he died when Stephen suffered martyrdom

10. TIMON
Another deacon of Jerusalem; later Bishop of Bostra in Arabia. He was martyred by the Hellenes

11. PARMENAS
Another deacon, afterwards Bishop of Sali; martyred at Philippi in Macedonia under Trajan

12. NICOLAUS
The seventh of the Deacons of Jerusalem; afterwards Bishop of Samaria

13. BARNABAS
Paul's friend and companion, was a Jew born in Cyprus, whose real name was Joseph or Joses. He was Mark's cousin, and joined Paul on a missionary journey to various cities in Asia Minor; later became Bishop of Milan. He was put to death for his faith in 61 A.D. at Cyprus. By some Barnabas is counted among the Apostles; and is called "the Prince of the Disciples of Our Lord." It is claimed that Barnabas was so majestic in appearance that when he came to Leptra the people thought he was Jupiter. According to one tradition, Barnabas was stoned to death and his body was found in 482 near Salamis with a copy of the Gospel of Matthew beside it

14. MARK
The Evangelist, was, together with Peter, founder of the Christian congregation at Alexandria. His Jewish name was John, but he changed his name to the Latin Marcus or Mark; and Peter refers to him as "my son Mark." It is believed that he was a native of Jerusalem, where his mother owned a great house which she dedicated to the use of the newly formed Christian community. Mark accompanied Paul and Barnabas on their return to Antioch and continued with them until they reached Cyprus. But Paul and Mark had differences, and Paul would not allow Mark to follow him on subsequent journeys. Mark and Barnabas, both separated from Paul, remained together in Rome. It is believed that Mark was in Rome when Paul was executed. Mark is traditionally associated with Alexandria, where he was supposed to have been the first Christian bishop. Mark is best known for The Gospel According to St. Mark, considered the earliest of the Fourfold Gospel. Just as the Gospel of Matthew was addressed primarily to the Jews, the Gospel of Mark was addressed primarily to the Romans. According to one tradition Mark wrote his Gospel in Latin at the request of the Roman Christians. He died in peace in Alexandria, 68 A.D.

15. LUKE
The Evangelist, was a native of Antioch who became a Jewish proselyte. He was a ship's doctor whose travels brought him in touch with Paul, whom he later accompanied on many journeys; it is believed that he witnessed Paul's arrest and saw him beaten with rods. "The Beloved Physician," as Luke is called, was never married. Legend has it that Luke had four faces: the face of a man, the face of a lion, the face of an ox, and the face of an eagle. He was noted for his humility. In addition to writing The Gospel Ac-

cording to St. Luke, which was addressed to the Greeks, he is also credited with being the author of the Acts of the Apostles. He was also a painter, and portraits of Jesus and of Mary, attributed to him, are presumably still in existence in Vallombrosa and in a Moscow cathedral. Luke died in Bithynia at the age of eighty-four. He is the patron of physicians, artists, butchers, and notaries

16. SILAS
Another companion of Paul. A Hellenistic Jew and Roman citizen; one of the Elders of the church of Jerusalem before he joined Paul in Antioch; later became Bishop of Corinth

17. SILVANUS
Who followed Paul on his missionary journeys, and became Bishop of Thessalonica; he is mentioned at the beginning of both Epistles to the Thessalonians. There are claims that Silvanus is the same person as Silas, Bishop of Corinth

18. CRESENS
Who helped Paul and later went to preach the Gospel in Galatia. He presumably founded the first church in Vienna, and was also the Bishop of Carchedon

19. EPAENATUS
Called the "beloved" of Paul; Bishop of Carthage, according to Greek tradition

20. ANDRONICUS
A kinsman of Paul, later Bishop of Pannonia or of Spain, who became a Christian before Paul. For in the last chapter of the Epistle to the Romans, Paul writes: "Salute Andronicus and Junia, my kinsmen and my fellow-prisoners, who

are of note among the apostles; who also were in Christ before me"

21. AMPLIAS, or AMPLIATUS, or AMPILUS
A follower of Paul; Bishop of Odyssus

22. URBANUS
Another of Paul's disciples; later Bishop of Macedonia

23. STACHYS
Another of Paul's disciples; later Bishop of Byzanthium. Legend has it that Stachys died in prison in Tarsus

24. BARNABAS
Bishop of Heraclia

25. PHYGELLUS
Bishop of Ephesus

26. DEMAS
A companion of Paul, who later deserted him; and Paul wrote to Timothy: "For Demas has forsaken me, having loved the world — "

27. HERMOGENUS
Co-prisoner with Paul; Bishop of Megara; later left the church and was considered a heretic

28. APPELLES
Bishop of Smyrna

29. ARISTOBULUS
Brother of Barnabas, and for a while a companion of Paul, who sent Aristobulus to Great Britain. In Wales, Aristobulus is known as Arwystli Hen

30. NARCISSUS
Made Bishop of Athens by the Apostle Philip

31. HERODION
Of Tarsus, a kinsman of Paul; became a Bishop of Novae Petrae, and was probably beheaded in Rome

32. AGABUS
The Prophet, the only one of the Apostles and Disciples to be called a prophet, who came from Jerusalem to Antioch to prophesy a great famine in the days of Claudius Caesar

33. RUFUS
Bishop of Thebes, presumably the Rufus who was the son of Simon of Cyrene, who carried the cross for Jesus part of the way to Golgotha

34. ASYNCRITUS
A disciple of Paul, who preached in Mesopotamia; later Bishop of Hyrcania

35. PHLEGON
Bishop of Marathon

36. HERMES
Bishop of Dalmatia

37. PATROBULUS, or PATROBUS
A disciple of Paul; later Bishop of Puteoli and Naples

38. HERMAS
Bishop of Philippi, to whom some church writers ascribe the authorship of the "Pastor"

39. LINUS
Bishop of Rome

40. CAIUS
Of Ephesus

41. PHILOLOGUS
Bishop of Sinope; ordained by St. Andrew

42. OLYMPAS, or OLYMPANUS
Peter's companion, who was beheaded in Rome under Nero

43. RHODION
Beheaded in Rome with Peter

44. LUCIUS
Bishop of Laodicea, in Syria

45. JASON
Bishop of Tarsus

46. SOSIPATER
Paul's relative and disciple; first Bishop of Iconium

47. TERTIUS
Paul's follower, and second Bishop of Iconium

48. ERASTUS
Disciple of Paul; Bishop of Paenas, in Palestine

49. QUARTUS
Bishop of Berytus

50. APOLLOS
First preached at Corinth; afterwards became Bishop of Caesarea

51. CEPHAS
Opposed Paul at Antioch; afterwards Bishop of Conia

52. SOSTHENES
Chief of the synagogue at Corinth; afterwards Bishop of Colophon; probably coauthor of Corinthians

53. TYCHICUS
A fellow prisoner of Paul in Rome; later became Bishop of Chalcedon. The claim is made by some that there were three saints by the name of Tychicus, and two are listed among the Disciples

54. TYCHICUS
The second by this name listed among the Seventy Disciples

55. EPAPHRODITUS
Bishop of Andriace in Syria. There is a claim that there were three Epaphroditi, each a bishop in a different area

56. CAESAR
Of Dyrrhachium. One source says cryptically: "He never existed"

57. MARINUS
Of Apollonia

58. JESUS JUSTUS or JOSES BAR-SABAS
Bishop of Eleutheropolis

59. ARTEMAS
Bishop of Lystra, in Asia Minor

60. CLEMENT
Of Sardica

61. ONESIPHORUS
Who followed Paul to Spain; later became Bishop of Colophon or of Coronea

62. CARPUS
Bishop of the church in Berytus, in Thrace

63. EVODIUS
Of Antioch, mentioned among those present when Jesus called upon Peter and Andrew to aban-

don *their boats and become "fishers of men"*

64. ARISTARCHUS
Of Apamea, in Syria; Bishop of Thessalonica; beheaded by Nero in Rome

65. MARK
Bishop of Niblus in Phoenicia, whom Luke called John

66. ZENAS
Of Diopolis

67. PHILEMON
To whom Paul wrote the Epistle to Philemon; Bishop of Gaza (or of Colussae). Philemon figures prominently in the Acts of Andrew and Paul. He and his wife, Appia, were buried up to their waists and stoned to death outside Colossae

68. ARISTARCHUS
Companion of Paul; later Bishop in Syria, or Palestine; beheaded in Rome under Nero

69. PUDENS
For whom the claim is made that he was Bishop at Antioch after Peter. His wife was a British lady, Claudia Rufina. Pudens was beheaded in Rome under Nero

70. TROPHIMUS
Who accompanied Paul upon his return to Jerusalem. He was later beheaded in Rome under Nero

Basic Sources

A selected list of specific editions of works on the New Testament, the Apocryphal Gospels, legendary biographies of Jesus and the Apostles, general collections of New Testament lore, and miscellaneous related works, is given in the *Reading List with Notes*. But there are several generic sources which everyone interested in the New Testament lore will want to know, as well as their relative importance. For although in a broad sense practically all the lore pertaining to this subject might be designated as apocryphal, there exist great differences between some of them — as to age, authorship, motivation, and general acceptance; and, from the folklore standpoint, value is not determined by either age or authorship alone.

The following are the basic sources of this lore:

(a) *The New Testament:* The canonical books of the New Testament are not only the subject matter and have inspired the vast accumulation of apocryphal legends, but they contain a treasury of parables, precepts and proverbs which are an essential and significant part of this lore.

The New Testament consists of twenty-seven Books. But these are not the works as dictated or written down by their original authors in the first century of our era. The canonical Gospels we now know are based on earlier works, to which their synoptic nature testifies. The Fourfold Gospels were not available before 120 A.D. — nearly ninety years after the Crucifixion. Less than a century later, Origen wrote: "The Church has four gospels; the sects very many." Presumably forty "lost" gospels have been accounted for, upon which the synoptic Gospels of Matthew, Luke, and Mark are believed to be based. To a lesser extent, this is also true of the rest of the New Testament Books. For what we have in the Canon are transcriptions of transcriptions.

It should be remembered that whereas today one transcribing Holy Scriptures would strain for accuracy, in the early days the transcriber, usually, transcribed primarily to interpret. The transcriber's foremost purpose was to underscore his particular concepts within the material transcribed. Also, the earliest gospels were originally written in several languages. Some might have been in Hebrew; some were in almost col-loquial Aramaic; some were in Greek of varying degrees of literary quality. These early gospels were translated back and forth into diverse languages, the original often completely disappearing. We have the in-stance of The Gospel According to the Hebrews mentioned by Origen. A century later, Jerome mentions having seen this Gospel in Aramaic, which was a translation from the Greek, and the Greek version no longer existed in his day. The Greek version in turn was a translation from the Hebrew Gospel, which had also disappeared quite early. Even the most punctilious scholar, when he translates, makes the material his own to some degree. And the early translators of the Books of the New Testa-ment, heads of contending sects, were noted more for zeal than objective scholarship.

To understand this lore, it is helpful to have a fairly clear idea of how the Bible grew and what the canonical New Testament represents. For this is the clue to most of the apocryphal works.

(b) *The Psalter:* Next only to the Books of the New Testament, in the Christian religion and its lore, comes the Psalter. There was a time in the early days of the Christian church when the Psalter was the first book to be put into the hands of converts to Christianity; and it was considered an unfailing light on the road to the gospel. In joy and in sorrow, the Nazarenes turned to the Psalms. In them they found "all the sorrows, troubles, fears, doubts, hopes, pains, perplexities, stormy out-breaks by which the hearts of men are tossed" — as Calvin puts it in his *Commentary of the Psalms.* The Psalter has been called the primer of Christian teachings. No other book has so deeply influenced Christianity; and this influence is clearly evident throughout the lore of the New Testa-ment.

(c) *The Ante-Nicene Apocrypha of the New Testament:* These are contained in the gathered works of the early church fathers, down to 325 A.D. The Gospels, Letters, Acts and Revelations in this vast collec-tion are all of a very early date, though, of course, not in the form they have today. The most important of these works, as a rich source of lore, are: *The Protevangelium of James, The Gospel of Thomas, The Gospel of Pseudo-Matthew,* and *The History of Joseph the Carpenter,* for the In-fancy legends; the various forms of *The Gospels of Nicodemus, The Book of John,* and *The Assumption of Mary,* for the Passion legends; the *Acts of Peter and Paul,* the *Acts of John,* the *Acts of Philip,* the *Acts of An-drew and Matthias,* and the *Acts of Thomas,* for the adventures and martyrdom of the apostles.

(d) *The Apocryphal New Testaments:* These are collections of works, dealing with New Testament figures or events, either now completely lost and known only through references to them by early Church Fathers, or available in fragments, or existing in full in many and, often, diverse versions. The number of these works is very great; and there is no agreement among scholars as to which should be included in a collection of New Testament Apocrypha, and which should be excluded. Many Gnostic, or heretical, or "hostile," or mystical works of a very early period are frequently excluded; though, as lore, some of them are as worthy as the more acceptable records.

In English there are two collections under the same title that deserve special mention: One, collected and translated by William Hone in 1820, claims to have included all the Gospels, Epistles, and other documents "attributed in the first four centuries to Jesus Christ, His Apostles and and their companions," but excluded from the Canon, according to Hone, by the Council of Nice. This volume starts with the *Gospel of the Birth of Mary* and ends with the Visions, Commands, and Similitudes of the *Shepherd of Hermas.* The second volume, also entitled *The Apocryphal New Testament,* was prepared over a century later by the distinguished scholar Montague Rhodes James, and is the most complete one-volume collection of fragments of early Gospels, Agrapha, the Infancy and Passion Gospels, the Acts, Epistles and Apocalypses to be found in English.

(e) *The New Testament Legends of the Middle Ages:* As a group, these legends pertaining to the Holy Family and, more particularly, the Lives of the Apostles and the Saints, reflect the superstitions of the period.

(f) *Recent Apocryphal Works:* These represent a group of comparatively modern works; some claiming to be of ancient origin but recently discovered, and others frankly presented as present-day "revelations." Several of these are of particular interest primarily because they deal with the so-called "hidden years" in the life of Jesus. Though all the recent and strange works, particularly those dealing with the youth of Jesus in foreign lands, are frowned upon by most theologians, they are nevertheless telling records of the unending preoccupation of people the world over with the hopes that the teachings of Jesus inspired in them.

Beyond these sources, a vast literature of *Anecdota,* beliefs, superstitions, poems and romances are available, touching on every conceivable aspect of the New Testament story. A number of poets and writers have taken episodes or personalities in the New Testament and, with the older lore as their base, created new and often inspiring works, whose strength and beauty resided not so much in the original creative talent as in the apocryphal material.

Notes on Sources

The extensive sources of the New Testament lore are divided very broadly into three main divisions:

1. The New Testament Apocrypha, which include a vast number of so-called secondary Gospels, Acts, Epistles, Letters, Apocalypses, Agrapha, and diverse fragments of unequal worth in their claim to a place among the supplements of the New Testament, and of unequal value in the lore.

2. The romantic and miraculous adventures, which include the various Lives of the Saints; the trials and tribulations of the apostles and the disciples (generally known as the Clementine literature); and the body of lore pertaining to the New Testament characters and events in Jewish and Mohammedan sources.

3. The perplexing documents, which consist of works that have caused the scholars to raise their eyebrows. These range from *The Life of Saint Issa,* as recorded by Notovich, and Dr. Dowling's twentieth-century *Aquarian Gospel,* to the claims of the Ahmadiya movement in Kashmir and the *Letter of Benan.*

However eccentric some of the works may be in certain categories, those which assumed importance in the folk imagination properly belong in the lore.

In this book the sources used represent a given translation or edition. Some of the sources are available in many differing versions. At times a source was used which is not generally held in high favor by modern biblical scholars, but which seemed more interesting in the lore elements. Hone's *Apocryphal New Testament,* for instance, was given preference to the superior and more reliable work (by the same name) by Montague Rhodes James, for it preceded the James book by over a century and has a flavor in its prefaces that adds color to the legendary material; and *The Golden Legend,* to cite another instance, "as Englished by William Caxton," was given preference to later and better editions, for similar reasons.

To avoid confusion, the number of titles in these sources has been limited. The symbols represent the specific editions used, which may differ in wording and numeration from other translations. The reader who wishes to trace some of the material but cannot obtain the edition cited here, should consult the index of the work available to him, or consult, topically, *The Dictionary of the Bible* by James Hastings.

(For a brief estimate of most of the sources given here, see *Reading List with Notes*.)

SYMBOLS USED:

AAM   *The Acts of Andrew and Matthias in the City of the Man-Eaters* (see ANL)

AG   *The Aquarian Gospel of Jesus the Christ*, "Transcribed from the Book of God's Remembrances," by Levi (Dr. Levi H. Dowling)

ALC   *The Apocryphal and Legendary Life of Christ*, compiled by James deQuincey Donehoo

ANL   *Ante-Nicene Christian Library*, edited by Alexander Roberts and James Donaldson; the Apocryphal Gospels, Acts and Revelations translated by Alexander Walker, in 24 volumes

ANT   *The Apocryphal New Testament*, translated by William Hone. (The individual apocryphal works from this volume are marked [H] as in AP[H] below.)

APA   *The Acts of Peter and Andrew* (see ANL; NTA)

AP[H]   *The Acts of Philip* (see ANL)

APP   *The Acts of the Holy Apostles Peter and Paul* (see ANL)

APT   *The Acts of Paul and Thecla*, a work of great antiquity written by an ancient presbyter as a glorification of Saint Paul (see ANL; ANT; NTA — there are many versions of this story)

AR   *The Arabic Gospel of the Infancy of the Savior*, a compilation showing many influences, mostly Arabic, with parts of the legends reading as if taken from *The Arabian Nights* (see ANL; NTA)

BB   *The Book of the Bee*, edited and translated from the Syriac text into English by Ernest A. Wallis Budge

BG   *Old Testament Characters; The Lives of the Saints; Curious Myths of the Middle Ages* by S. Baring-Gould

BLM   *Biblical Legends of the Mussulmans*, by G. Weil

BVM   *The History of the Blessed Virgin Mary*, Syriac text edited and translated into English by Ernest A. Wallis Budge

DA   *Devotional and Ascetic Practices in the Middle Ages*, by Dom Louis Gougard

DP   *Daily Prayer Book*, Hebrew text, with English translation by Joseph H. Hertz

ECL   *The Extra-Canonical Life of Christ*, by Bernhard Pick

EJA[H]   *The Epistles of Jesus Christ and Abgarus of Edessa* (see ANT)

GBM   *The Gospel of the Birth of Mary* (see ANT)

GL   *The Golden Legend* or *The Lives of the Saints*, by Jacobus de Voraigne, Archbishop of Genoa in 1275, in 7 volumes

GI[H]   *The First Gospel of the Infancy of Jesus Christ* (see ANT). According to Hone, "It has been supposed that Mahomet and his coadjutors used it in compiling the Koran."

GN[H]   *The Gospel of Nicodemus, formerly called the Acts of Pontius Pilate* (see ANT). There are several versions of this Gospel (see ANL; NTA), and the one given by Hone corresponds to the First Latin Version

GT   *The Gospel of Thomas,* a work of great antiquity, known for its portrayal of young Jesus as arrogant and vengeful (see ANL)

HAT   *The Acts of the Holy Apostle Thomas* (see ANL; NTA)

JA   *The Narrative of Joseph of Arimathea,* a work popular during the Middle Ages, and probably written not later than the twelfth century. The version in ANL differs considerably from the one given in NTA and other sources.

JC   *The History of Joseph the Carpenter,* a work dating back to the fourth century according to some scholars and rich in lore (see ANL). James (NTA) states that this work is an Egyptian document of the fourth century or later; fragments of this work exist in Sahidic, the dialect of Upper Egypt of that time; and the book exists complete in Arabic.

JN   *Jesus of Nazareth,* by Joseph Klausner; translated from the Hebrew by Herbert Danby

JT   *The Acts of the Holy Apostle and Evangelist John the Theologian* (see ANL)

LC   *Legends of the Child,* by Mildred Ockert Waugh; in *The American Scholar,* Vol. 18, No. 1; New York, 1948–49

LCC *Legends of the Christ Child,* by Frances Margaret Fox; Sheed & Ward, New York, 1941

LJ   *The Legends of the Jews,* by Louis Ginzberg; translated from the German manuscript by Henrietta Szold, in 7 volumes

LOT *The Lore of the Old Testament,* by Joseph Gaer; Little, Brown & Company, Boston, 1951

MAA *The Mythological Acts of the Apostles,* translated from the Arabic manuscript by Agnes Smith Lewis

NIC *The Gospel of Nicodemus,* in ANL, contains "The Acts of Pilate" in the first and second Greek forms; the Greek form of "The Descent of Christ into Hell"; the Latin form of "The Acts of Pilate" and the first and second Latin version of "The Descent of Christ into Hell" (see GN[H])

NM   *The Gospel of the Nativity of Mary* is a derivative work, based on *The Gospel of Pseudo-Matthew,* which enjoyed great popularity toward the end of the Middle Ages and inspired much of the poetry and art of that time (see ANL)

NTA *The Apocryphal New Testament,* translated by Montague Rhodes James

PJ   *The Protevangelium of James,* one of the oldest of the Apocryphal Gospels, attributed to James the Lesser. This work was named "protevangelium" (the first evangel or gospel) by one of the sixteenth-century translators. There are many versions of this work which is a basic source of the Infancy Legends (see ANL; ANT; NTA)

PM   *The Gospel of Pseudo-Matthew,* also known as *The Book of
              the Infancy* (see ANL; NTA)

REV   *Revelation of John* (see ANL)

SK   *The Short Koran,* edited by George M. Lamsa; Ziff-Davis,
              Chicago, 1949

SNG   *Strange New Gospels,* by Edgar J. Goodspeed

TGI   *Thomas' Gospel of the Infancy,* sometimes called *The Second
              Gospel of the Infancy of Jesus Christ* (see ANT)

PART I: *The Lineage*

CHAPTER ONE: JOACHIM AND ANNA

1. *The Good Joachim Takes a Bride* (BVM: 3–4 gives Joachim's name
as Yonakhir, and Anna's name as Dinah. BB: 76–77 also calls Joachim
"Zadok." ALC: 1–2. ANT: The Gospel of the Birth of Mary, 17–18.
ANL, XVI: The Gospel of the Nativity of Mary, 53. SK: 145 calls Mary's
mother "the wife of Imram" as given in the Koran: Sura 3:35.)

2. *Issachar's Rebuke* (BB: 76. BVM: 5–6 gives the priest's name as
Rubhil. ECL: 43–44. ALC: 2–4. ANT: The Gospel of the Birth of Mary,
18; The Protevangelium of James, 24–25. ANL, XVI: The Protevangelium,
1–2 gives the rebuker's name as Rubim and does not mention that he
belonged to the priesthood; The Gospel of Pseudo-Matthew, 18–19; The
Gospel of the Nativity of Mary, 53–54 corrects the spelling of Issachar
to Isaschar. Scriptures quoted: Ex. 23:26.)

3. *Visions in the Night* (BB: 76. ALC: 4–5. ANT: The Gospel of the
Birth of Mary, 18–19. BLM: 249.)

4. *Joachim and the Angel* (ANL, XVI: The Gospel of Pseudo-
Matthew, 20–22; The Gospel of the Nativity of Mary, 54–55 refers to
the Golden Gate of Jerusalem as the meeting place. ALC: 7–10. BVM:
11. ANT: The Gospel of the Birth of Mary, 18–19. BB: 74–75 gives
Mary's genealogy all the way back to Adam and also shows that Mary's
father and Joseph's father were cousins; 77 claims that Mary's name
meant "exalted" and not Sea-Bitter or *Mar-yam.*)

5. *Tidings Under the Laurel Tree* (BVM: 7–9. ECL: 44–45. ALC: 4,
5, 11. ANT: The Gospel of the Birth of Mary, 19–20; The Protevan-

gelium of James, 25–26. ANL, XVI: The Protevangelium, 2–4; The Gospel of the Nativity of Mary, 54–55.)

6. *Reunion at the Gate* (BVM: 12–14. ANT: The Gospel of the Birth of Mary, 20. ANL, XVI: The Protevangelium, 3; The Gospel of the Nativity of Mary, 56. Scriptures quoted: Ps. 24: 1–2.)

7. *The Great Celebration* (BVM: 14. BB: 76 claims that Dinah changed her name to Anna or Hannah the day Mary was born, "for the Lord had compassion on her." GL: V, 76ff. ALC: 12–15. ANT: The Protevangelium of James, 27. ANL, XVI: The Protevangelium, 4.)

In religious lore there are many instances of the devout being relieved of barrenness in their old age, often miraculously, and rewarded with a child destined from birth to become the joy of his parents and the pride of his nation. In the Old Testament there is the story of Abraham's son born to aged parents; later there is the story of Samson born to the aged and barren Manoah; and still later, comes the story of Samuel's parents, who seem the nearest model for the story of Joachim and Anna. Centuries before any of these stories were told and written down, there already existed numerous legends of this nature, the most remarkable of which is the story of the ancient hermit and his barren wife who were promised a son by an angel, and told by the angel to name him Alpha. The wife dreamt that a star from the sky fell into her mouth and she thereby conceived. The moment the child left her womb, he was surrounded by a great light; and though it was in the middle of winter, all the trees produced fruit. Alpha walked and talked on the day he was born, and his knowledge and wisdom was without parallel. And during all the days of his life, Alpha, who became the Buddha, did many miraculous things.)

CHAPTER TWO: MARY IN THE TEMPLE

1. *The Late Weaning* (BB: 76–77 gives Mary's age, when taken to the temple, as "two years after she was weaned." BVM: 14–16 claims Mary was ten years old when taken to the temple. ECL: 45. ANL, XVI: The Protevangelium, 4–5; The Gospel of Pseudo-Matthew, 22–23, 25. ANT: Protevangelium of James, 27.)

2. *Anna's Three Marys* (ALC: 19. GL: V, 97. BVM: 16 gives an entirely different version, claiming that after Mary went to dwell in the temple, her parents were consoled by her younger sister, named Paroghitra, meaning "The Pullet.")

3. *Mary's Guardian* (BVM: 17–18. ALC: 19–20. SK: 145–146. BLM: 250.)

4. *Mary and the Sabbath* (DA: 66. GL: V, 96–112 gives many legends about the rewards of those devoted to Mary.)

5. *What Was Mary Like?* (ALC: 20–23. ANL, XVI: The Gospel of Pseudo-Matthew, 23–24.)

CHAPTER THREE: JOSEPH'S ROD

1. *Abiathar and the High Priest* (ALC: 23–24. ANL, XVI: The Gospel of Pseudo-Matthew, 24–25.)

2. *The Complaint of the Pharisees* (ANT: The Gospel of the Birth of Mary, 21. ANL, XVI: The Protevangelium, 6–7; The Gospel of Pseudo-Matthew, 25. ALC: 25–26. Scriptures cited: Num. 30:2; Gen. 1:28.)

3. *The Advice of the Oracle* (ECL: 46. ANT: The Gospel of the Birth of Mary, 21–22; The Protevangelium of James, 28. ANL, XVI; The Protevangelium, 6; The Gospel of Pseudo-Matthew, 25–26; The Gospel of the Nativity of Mary, 57–58. BVM: 18–19 gives quite a different version from those found in most of the other apocryphal sources. Scriptures cited: Ex. 28:33–35.)

4. *The Old Carpenter* (BVM: 19. BB: 77. ECL: 46. ALC: 27. ANL, XVI: The History of Joseph the Carpenter, 63–64 gives another version of how Joseph was chosen as Mary's guardian until her marriage.)

5. *One of the Ten Wonders* (ALC: 29–30. BB: 50–65 claims that the rod was originally a branch from the tree of good and evil, brought forth from Eden by Adam; it also gives a different account of the rod's progression to Moses. GL: V, 115ff.)

6. *The Dove Whiter Than Snow* (BVM: 20. ANT: The Gospel of the Birth of Mary, 22 tells that, because of his age, Joseph did not turn in his rod the first time; but when no sign was given, the high priest was told to ask Joseph to bring his rod to the temple; The Protevangelium of James, 29. ANL, XVI: The Protevangelium, 6; The Gospel of Pseudo-Matthew, 26–27. LJ: V, 23.)

7. *Mary in Joseph's House* (ALC: 33–34. ANL, XVI: The Gospel of Pseudo-Matthew, 27 gives the names of Mary's companions as: Rebecca, Sephora, Susanna, Abigea and Cael. LJ: V, 23.)

CHAPTER FOUR: TRIAL BY WATER

1. *The Veil for the Temple* (BVM: 21. BB: 77–78. ECL: 48. ANT: The Protevangelium of James, 29. ANL, XVI: The Protevangelium, 6–7. LJ: VI, 228.)

2. *Mary and the Angel* (BVM: 22–24. BB: 78 gives the exact hour, day and date when the archangel Gabriel appeared to Mary and states that Mary was told to name her son Emmanuel, who "shall be called the Son of the Highest." ALC: 35–36 states that the view that Mary conceived "by the hearing of the ear" is generally accepted by the church fathers. ANT: The Gospel of the Birth of Mary, 22–23; The Protevangelium, 29–30 gives the scene of the Annunciation at the well. ANL, XVI: The Gospel of Pseudo-Matthew, 28 gives the Annunciation "at the fountain"; The Gospel of the Nativity of Mary, 58–60. SK: 146, 149. BLM: 252–254. GL: III, 97–102.)

(A startlingly curious version of the Annunciation and the birth of Jesus is given in a Muslim legend (BLM) which relates that Mary conceived when the angel Gabriel breathed upon her after announcing that she would have a son miraculously conceived and that she should call him Issa. Thereupon Mary ran out of the house, and had scarcely reached the trunk of a withered date palm, when she was delivered of a son. Mary cried out: "Oh that I were dead and forgotten, rather than the suspicion of having sinned should fall upon me!" And the angel Gabriel said: "Fear nothing, Mary! Behold a fresh fountain flowing at your feet and the dead tree upon which you lean blossoming and covered with fruit. Eat and drink and refresh yourself. Then return home with your child. If any one shall inquire of you about him, be silent and leave your answer to Him." Mary plucked a few dates, which tasted like the fruit of paradise; and she drank from the water of the fountain, which tasted like milk; then she returned home.)

3. *Joseph Returns* (BVM: 26–29. BB: 78–79. ECL: 49. ANT: The Gospel of the Birth of Mary, 23–24; The Protevangelium of James, 31. ANL, XVI: The Protevangelium, 8–9; The Gospel of Pseudo-Matthew, 28–29; The Gospel of the Nativity of Mary, 60–61. Is. 7:14.)

4. *Annas Accuses Joseph* (ECL: 49–50. ANT: The Protevangelium of James, 31. ANL, XVI: The Protevangelium, 9–10.)

5. *Trial Before the Altar* (BVM: 30–31. BB: 79. ECL: 50. ANT: The Protevangelium of James, 31–32. ANL, XVI: The Protevangelium, 10

gives a different version of the procedure at the trial; The Gospel of
Pseudo-Matthew, 29–31. Num. 5:11–31. Ps. 91:1–2; 131:2; 27:1.)

PART II: *The Infancy*

CHAPTER FIVE: THE BIRTH IN A CAVE

1. *The Census* (BVM: 31–32. BB: 79–80. GL: I, 25. ANT: The
Protevangelium of James, 32–33. ANL, XVI: The Gospel of Pseudo-
Matthew, 31; The History of Joseph the Carpenter, 65; The Arabic Gos-
pel of the Infancy, 100. II Sam. 24:1–15.)

2. *When the World Stood Still* (BVM: footnote on 32–33. ECL: 50.
ANT: The Protevangelium of James, 33; The First Gospel of the Infancy, 38–39. ANL, XVI: The Protevangelium, 11. SK: 149–151 gives
another version of the birth of Jesus and the miracles that took place at
his birth "near the trunk of a palm-tree" as given in the Koran: Sura
19:16.)

3. *The Doubting Zebel* (ECL: 50–51. BB: 80 gives the midwife's
name as Salome and adds that the "heretics say that she was called
Hadyok, but they err from the truth." ANT: The Protevangelium of
James, 33–34; The First Gospel of the Infancy, 39. ANL, XVI: The Gos-
pel of Pseudo-Matthew, 31–33 gives the names of the two midwives as
Salome and Zelomi.)

4. *The Night of Miracles* (ALC: 52–54.) . . . *How the Nightingale
Learned to Sing* (LCC: 1–6.) . . . *How the Firefly Acquired Its Light*
(LCC: 12–15.) . . . *Why the Robin Is Called Robin* (LCC: 16–19. In
Selma Lagerlof's *Christ-Legends* the robin's red breast is accounted for
not at the Nativity but at the Crucifixion. According to this version, one
day a gray little mother robin saw three men led to a hill by soldiers
with spears, and followed by a multitude of people. On the crest of
the hill the three men were crucified; and on the head of the one in
the center was placed a crown of thorns. The robin, stirred by pity,
swooped down to pull out a thorn that had become embedded in the
bleeding brow. And when the bird returned to its nest, all the young
robins exclaimed: "Look at your breast feathers, mother! They are redder
than the rose!" The mother bird explained: "It is only a drop of blood
from the poor man's brow. I shall wash it off in the pool." But no matter
how much and how often the robin bathed, the blood-red color remained

on the feathers of her breast. And when the young birds grew up, their breast feathers showed the same blood-red.)

5. *The Shepherds in the Hills* (BVM: 33–34. BB: 81 gives seven shepherds, and names them: Asher, Zublon, Justus, Nicodemus, Joseph, Barshabba and Jose. ANA, XVI: The Arabic Gospel of the Infancy, 101.)

6. *The Adoration of the Animals* (LCC: 23–29. ALC: 59. ANL, XVI: The Gospel of Pseudo-Matthew, 33 states that Mary and her child moved from the cave to the stable on the third day after the birth of Jesus.)

CHAPTER SIX: SETH'S PROPHECY

1. *Zoroaster's Prediction* (BB: 81–82 refers to Zoroaster as "This Zaradosht is Baruch the scribe." ALC: 63–65. ANL, XVI: Arabic Gospel of the Infancy, 102.)

2. *In the Temple of Juno* (ALC: 65–69. BVM: 34–35. BB: 82–84 advances the novel idea that the star of Bethlehem appeared long before the birth of Jesus so that the Magi might be guided by it on their long journey and arrive on the day of his birth. ECL: footnote to p. 53 gives the number of the Magi as three, and their names as: King Melchior, the old man; King Caspar, the beardless youth; and King Balthasar, the swarthy man in the prime of life. Practically all fifteenth-century paintings portray the Magi as three in number, with the youngest invariably black. This is based upon the assumption that the Magi represented all ages and all races of mankind who shall ultimately come to accept Jesus. GL: I, 43 gives the names of the Magi in Hebrew as: Magalath, Galgalath and Tharath; in Greek: Appelius, Amerius and Damascus; and in Latin: Jaspar, Melchior and Balthasar.)

3. *The Gold of the Magi* (BB: 85. ECL: 55. ALC: 70.)

4. *The Magi in Herod's Court* (ELC: 54. BVM: 37. ANT: The Protevangelium of James, 35. ANL, XVI: The Gospel of Pseudo-Matthew, 34–35. BB: 84–85 gives the number of the Magi as "twelve Persian kings," names each of them, and states who carried the gold, who carried the frankincense, and who brought the myrrh. Micah 5:2–4.)

5. *The Exchange of Gifts* (BB: 85. BVM: 35–36, 37–38. ECL: 55. ANL, XVI: Arabic Gospel of the Infancy, 103. ANT: The First Gospel of the Infancy, 40.)

6. *The Magi Return Home* (ALC: 75–76. ANT: The Protevangelium of James, 35; The First Gospel of the Infancy, 41. BVM: 39.)

7. *The Circumcision* (DP: 1024–1028. GL: I, 28–29. BVM: 30. ECL: 52. ANL, XVI: The Arabic Gospel of the Infancy, 101–102. ANT: The First Gospel of the Infancy, 39 claims that Jesus was circumcised in the cave. GL: I, 28–41.)

8. *Jesus in the Temple* (ECL: 52–53 gives Simeon's age as 113 years. ANT: The First Gospel of the Infancy, 40, ANL, XVI: The Arabic Gospel of the Infancy, 102. BVM: 40–41. DP: 1034.)

CHAPTER SEVEN: THE FLIGHT TO EGYPT

1. *The Massacre of the Innocents* (ALC: 77–78. BVM: 41. ANT: The Protevangelium of James, 35. LJ: I, 187 on Nimrod story.)

2. *Joseph's Escape* (ALC: footnote to p. 78 states that, since the Church commemorates the Massacre of the Innocents on December 28, the flight to Egypt must have taken place when Jesus was one or two years and three days old. ANL, XVI: The Gospel of Pseudo-Matthew, 35–36 records that Joseph, in his flight to Egypt, was accompanied by three boys, and that Mary was accompanied by a girl to assist her on the journey. BVM: 44. Ps. 18:3.)

3. *The Palm for Victory* (ECL: 60–62. BVM: footnote on 44–45. ANL, XVI: The Gospel of Pseudo-Matthew, 20–21, 37–38.)

4. *Adventures in Sotrina* (BVM: 54–58 gives the age of the priest's son as thirty instead of three. ANT: The First Gospel of the Infancy, 41–42. ANL, XVI: The Gospel of Pseudo-Matthew gives the name of the city as Sotien; The Arabic Gospel of the Infancy, 103–104.)

5. *The Possessed and the Leprous* (ECL: 68–69. BVM: 49–50. ANT: The First Gospel of the Infancy, 42–43; The Arabic Gospel of the Infancy, 105.)

6. *The Shame of the Father* (ECL: 72–74. BVM: 52–54. ANT: The First Gospel of the Infancy, 44. ANL, XVI: The Arabic Gospel of the Infancy, 106–108.)

7. *The Bewitched Bridegroom* (BVM: 55–59. ECL: 75–78. ANL, XVI: The Arabic Gospel of the Infancy, 108–110. ET: 247, 260–262 on demons and evil spirits and the formulas to banish them as given in the Talmud.)

8. *The Good Robber* (BVM: 59–60 gives the names of the two thieves as Titus and Damachus. BB: 87. ECL: 79–80. The footnote on p. 80 gives the names of the robbers as Matha and Joca. ANL, XVI: The Arabic Gospel of the Infancy, 110. ALC: footnote on p. 94 gives the various names of the two robbers; The Narrative of Joseph, 241.)

9. *Sea-Bitter and Bethaven* (ECL: 85–87. BVM: 62–64 gives the names of the two mothers as Mary and Arzami. ANT: The First Gospel of the Infancy, 48–49 gives the name of Sea-Bitter's son as Caleb, and the gift brought to Mary as "a very handsome carpet." ANL, XVI: The Arabic Gospel of the Infancy, 112–113.)

10. *A Boy Named Bartholomew* (ECL: 87–88. ANL, XVI: The Arabic Gospel of the Infancy, 113. BVM: 64–65 gives the boy's name as Thomas called Didymus.)

11. *Jesus Before Pharaoh* (LC.)

12. *The Pledge of Lazarus* (BB: 87.)

13. *Miracles Without Number* (ALC: 104–107.) . . . *The Blooming Staff* (ALC: 107.) . . . *Three Staves of a Tub* (ALC: 107.) . . . *The Dried Fish that Swam Away* (NTA: The Gospel of Thomas, 58; Acts of Peter, 316 for the Note.) . . . *The Fountain of Heliopolis* (ALC: 105–106. AG: Chapter 24. ANL, XVI: The Arabic Gospel of the Infancy, footnote to p. 111 relates that at the Paris Exhibition of 1867, Ismail Pasha presented the Empress of France with the tree, called Matarea, and the ground surrounding it, located on the site of the ancient city of On, not far from Cairo.) . . . *The Choicest Balm* (BB: 87–88. *Persian Life of Christ,* by Xaverius, 102.) . . . *The Guilt of the Blind and the Lame* (ALC: 103–104.)

14. *A Double Holiday* (BB: 88. ANL, XVI: The History of Joseph the Carpenter, 65–66.)

PART III: *Boyhood in Nazareth*

CHAPTER EIGHT: THE LITTLE BOY JESUS

1. *The Clay Sparrows* (BVM: 76. ECL: 108. ANT: The First Gospel of the Infancy, 53.)

2. *The Kids and the Goats* (BVM: 77–78. ECL: 110–111. ANL, XVI: The Arabic Gospel of the Infancy, 118–119.)

3. *If You Could Make a Wish* (LC.)

4. *The Boy on the Roof* (ECL: 105–106. BVM: 81–82. ANT: The First Gospel of the Infancy, 56–57. ANL, XVI: The Gospel of Pseudo-Matthew, 46; The Gospel of Thomas, 81–82; The Arabic Gospel of the Infancy, 121.)

5. *Satan the Mad Dog* (ECL: 94–95. ANT: The First Gospel of the Infancy, 52–53. ANL, XVI: The Arabic Gospel of the Infancy, 116–117.)

6. *The Boy with a Crown* (BVM: 78–79. ECL: 114–115. ANT: The First Gospel of the Infancy, 55–56. ANL, XVI: The Arabic Gospel of the Infancy, 119–120 presents a good example of occult powers the AR attributes to Jesus, counter to Old Testament prohibitions.)

7. *The Miraculous Cloak* (BVM: 75. ANT: The First Gospel of the Infancy, 57. ANL, XVI: The Gospel of Pseudo-Matthew, 46; The Gospel of Thomas, 82.)

8. *The Lily at the Doorstep* (LC).

9. *The Seventh Birthday* (AG: V: 16, 42.)

10. *Jesus in the Lions' Den* (ALC: 120–121. ECL: 111–113. ANL, XVI: The Gospel of Pseudo-Matthew, 46–48.)

11. *Jesus and the Old Woman* (ALC: 145–146 states that this story, attributed to the medieval period, was influenced by GT.)

12. *Jesus in the Tile Factory* (ALC: 146–149. In his footnote on p. 146 the editor complains about the original author of this legend who "either does not know, or does not care to observe the geographical properties that apply to the situation of Nazareth.")

13. *The Avenger and the Healer* (ALC: 122–149.) . . . *Son of Iniquity* (ECL: 96–97. ANT: The First Gospel of the Infancy, 57. ANL, XVI: The Gospel of Pseudo-Matthew, 41; The Arabic Gospel of the Infancy, 121.) . . . *The Plague of Blindness* (ANT: The First Gospel of the Infancy, 57; Thomas' Gospel of the Infancy, 61. ANL, XVI: The Gospel of Thomas, 79.) . . . *The Foolish Sodomite* (ECL: 96–97. ANT: Thomas' Gospel of the Infancy, 61. ANL, XVI: The Gospel of Pseudo-Matthew, 41–42; The Gospel of Thomas, 78–79.) . . . *The Healing Breath* (BVM: 73. ANT: The First Gospel of the Infancy, 56. ANL, XVI: The Gospel of Pseudo-Matthew, 50–51; The Gospel of Thomas, 84; The Arabic Gospel of the Infancy, 120.) . . . *The Healing Touch* (ECL: 106. ANL, XVI: The Gospel of Thomas, 82 gives his age as six years when this occurred.) . . . *The Healing Word* (ECL: 107. ANL, XVI: The Gospel of Thomas, 84.)

CHAPTER NINE: STUDENT AND APPRENTICE

1. *Jesus Before the Teacher* (BVM: 71–73. ECL: 98–104 gives another version. ALC: 157–160. ANT: The First Gospel of the Infancy, 57–58; Thomas' Gospel of the Infancy, 61–62. ANL, XVI: The Gospel of Pseudo-Matthew, 42–45; The Gospel of Thomas, 80–81 presents Jesus as denouncing his teacher, laughing at and frightening his elders and, as might be expected of the GT, no one dares to make the child Jesus angry "lest He should curse him, and he should be maimed.")

2. *The Meaning of the Alpha* (BVM: 71–75. ALC: 152–156. ET: 178. SK: 154 states that God, himself, taught Jesus all he knew of "the Scripture and Wisdom and the Law and the Gospel" as given in the Koran: Sura 5:112.)

3. *Hillel's Pupil* (AG: V: 18, 44–45.)

4. *Jesus and Joseph* (ECL: 117. BVM: 75–76. ANT: The First Gospel of the Infancy, 45. ANL, XVI: The Gospel of Pseudo-Matthew, 48; The Arabic Gospel of the Infancy, 118.)

5. *The Tools of the Mind* (AG: V: 20, 47.)

6. *The Rich Man's Couch* (BVM: 75–76 gives another version. ALC: 111–112.)

CHAPTER TEN: JESUS IN THE TEMPLE

1. *The Visit to Jerusalem* (ALC: 162–163. See also footnote 1 on p. 163. ANL, XVI: The Arabic Gospel of the Infancy, 123. DP: 760–768. AG: V: 20, 47.)

2. *Who Is that Boy?* (ECL: 121–124. ANT: The First Gospel of the Infancy, 58–59. ANL, XVI: The Arabic Gospel of the Infancy, 123–124.)

3. *Jesus and the Astronomer* (ECL: 121–124. ANT: The First Gospel of the Infancy, 58–59. ANL, XVI: The Arabic Gospel of the Infancy, 123–124.)

4. *Jesus and the Physician* (ECL: 121–124. ANT: The First Gospel of the Infancy, 58–59. ANL, XVI: The Arabic Gospel of the Infancy, 123–124.)

5. *Are You the Mother?* (ECL: 121–124. ANT: The First Gospel of the Infancy, 58–59. ANL, XVI: The Arabic Gospel of the Infancy, 123–124.)

6. *Life in Nazareth* (ANL, XVI: The History of Joseph the Carpenter, p. 66 records the discourse of Jesus to his disciples on the accord with which he lived with his family, never arousing their anger. "On the contrary, I cherished them with great love, like the pupil of my eye." ALC: 166–168. Footnote 5 on p. 168 gives interesting data on the custom of grace in those days. DP: 964–978.)

CHAPTER ELEVEN: THE DEATH OF JOSEPH THE CARPENTER

1. *Joseph's Illness* (ANL, XVI: The History of Joseph the Carpenter, 66–68.)

2. *The Last Visit* (ANL, XVI: The History of Joseph the Carpenter, 69–71.)

3. *Jesus and the Angel of Death* (ALC: 179–183. ANL, XVI: The History of Joseph the Carpenter, 71–73.)

4. *Lamentation for Joseph* (ECL: 125–128.)

5. *Joseph's Burial* (ALC: 183–187. DP: 1085.)

PART IV: *The Unknown Life of Jesus*

CHAPTER TWELVE: THE LIFE OF SAINT ISSA

Entire chapter devoted to the document on the unknown years by Nicolas Notovich, called *The Unknown Life of Jesus Christ*. See also comments on this work by SNG: 10–24. NTA: 90.

CHAPTER THIRTEEN: THE AQUARIAN GOSPEL

1. *The Golden Cord* (AG: V: 17, 43–44.)

2. *Jesus in India* (AG: VI: 21–22, 47–49.)

3. *Udraka the Healer* (AG: VI: 23–28, 49–57.)

4. *Parable of the Nobleman and the Unjust Sons* (AG: VI: 25, 52–53.)

5. *Jesus and the Buddhist Sage* (AG: VI: 32, 60–62.)

6. *Parable of the Rocky Field* (AG: VI: 33, 62–68.)

7. *Miracle in Leh* (AG: VII: 36–37, 65–68.)

8. *Jesus in the City of Ur* (AG: X: 42–43, 72–74.)

9. *The Seven Degrees* (AG: XI: 47–55, 78–87.)

CHAPTER FOURTEEN: THE LETTER OF BENAN

Another document on the unknown years. SNG: 73–74. NTA: 90. *Der Benanbrief: Eine Moderne Leben-Jesu-Fälschung*, by Dr. Carl Schmidt. (Josephus: *Antiquities of the Jews*, XVIII: I: 5.)

PART V: *The Great Teacher*

CHAPTER FIFTEEN: THEY WHO SAW JESUS

1. *The Death of a Priest* (ALC: 189–194.)

2. *Rumors from Along the Jordan* (GL: I, 14–15. ECL: 294–295. ALC: 262–263. Josephus, *Wars of the Jews*, II: VIII, 2ff. LJ: I, 221, 236, 293–294. Tobit 13:10–13, 16–18.)

3. *The Story of John the Baptist* (ALC: 32–33, 38–40. SK: 145–146 as given in the Koran: Sura 3:35. GL: III, 253–261.)

4. *The Murder of John's Father* (BVM: 42–44. BB: 86, 89. ALC: 80–82. GL: III, 254ff. ANL, XVI: The Protevangelium, 13–14. SK: 143–144 as given in the Koran: Sura 19:1. LOT: 293.)

5. *John and His Teacher Matheno* (AG: IV, 38–41. BB: 89. ET: 104.)

6. *When Jesus Was Baptized* (BVM: 83–86. BB: 89–91. JN: 251–253. ECL: 213 gives the Baptism of Jesus as described in the Gospel of the Ebionites. ALC: 195–197 records that "Jesus was by his mother Mary almost unwillingly brought to the receiving of the baptism of John." This is derived from the Gospel of the Twelve Apostles. See: Footnote 3 on p. 195. JN: 251–252.)

7. *Behold, the Man!* (ECL: 210–211 gives a description of Jesus as found in the *Letter of Lentulus;* 211–212 gives quite a different description according to *Epiphanius the Monk.* SK: 148 states that "the likeness of Jesus in the sight of God is as the likeness of Adam" as given in the Koran: Sura 3:35. Is. 52:14.)

8. *Two Heads on a Silver Charger* (BB: 90–91. ALC: 197.)

CHAPTER SIXTEEN: THE WONDERFUL HEALER

1. *Where There Is Faith* (BVM: 86–88. ALC: 208–210.)

2. *Jesus and the Sphinx* (ANL, XVI: The Acts of Andrew and Matthias, 354–356. ALC: 210–213 has valuable footnotes on the AAM legend. NTA: 454–455 has a slightly different version of the AAM story.)

3. *The Three Merchants* (ALC: 278.)

4. *Veronica the Wise* (ALC: 214–218. ANL, XVI: The Death of Pilate Who Condemned Jesus, 234–235 relates how Veronica obtained a picture of Jesus and how the Emperor Tiberius was healed by the sight of it; The Avenging of the Savior, 251–254.)

5. *The Rich Young Man* (Matt. 19:16–24. Luke 18:18–25. Mark 10:17–25. ANL, XXII: Part II, 157–217.)

6. *King Abgar of Edessa* (NTA: Epistles, 476–477. ECL: 221–223. ANT: The Epistles of Jesus Christ, 62–63 presents both the letter to Jesus from King Abgarus and the answer. Up to about a century ago, in many English homes the Epistle of Jesus to Abgarus could be seen framed with a picture of Jesus and hung prominently as a bulwark against evil. ANL, XVI: Acts of the Holy Apostle Thaddaeus, 440–443. ALC: 219–224 has many interesting footnotes on Abgar Ucomo, or Abgar the Black, fifteenth king of Edessa. GL: VI, 73–75.)

7. *Loaves and Fishes* (ALC: 224–226. There are many variations of this story in the lore, some versions stating that Jesus turned stones into bread.)

8. *The Table from Heaven* (ALC: 226–229. SK: 154–155 as given in the Koran: Sura 5:112. BLM: 259–262.)

9. *The Report of the Skull* (ALC: 236–239. BVM: 254–259.)

10. *Poor Man, Rich Man* (ALC: 282, 285.)

11. *Doubting Thomas* (ALC: 230–236.)

CHAPTER SEVENTEEN: THE MASTER STORYTELLER

(Author's essay on the parables)

CHAPTER EIGHTEEN: LETTERS, DISCOURSES AND SAYINGS

1. *The Letters* (ANT: The Epistles of Jesus Christ and Abgarus, King of Edessa, 62–63. ALC: 220–223, 253, 405. NTA: 476–477. SNG: 96–107. ECL: 221–222.)

2. *Discourses* (ANL, XVI: The History of Joseph the Carpenter, 62–77. NTA: 84–86 gives a synopsis of the entire Death of Joseph and states that it is of Egyptian origin.)

3. *The Sayings of Jesus* (ALC: 242–285 gives many sayings, with notes on sources, where most of the sayings given here will be accounted for; the others will be found in ECL: 218–245; and in the *Sayings of Jesus*, from the *Oxyrhyncus Papyri* discovered by Grenfell, B. P. and Hunt, A. S. These eight *Sayings* are found in many essays and books on the *Oxyrhyncus Papyri*.)

PART VI: *From Mount Olivet to Calvary*

CHAPTER NINETEEN: THE CONSPIRACY

1. *Carius' Report to Herod* (ALC: 298–300.)

2. *Herod's Plot* (ALC: 300.)

3. *The Secret Meeting* (ECL: 223–225. ALC: 304–305.)

4. *Judas Ish Sekharyut* (GL: III, 35.)

5. *Pontius Pilate* (ECL: footnotes to p. 144. Josephus, *Antiquities of the Jews*, XVIII: III: 1. GL: I, 80–82.)

6. *Judas Repents* (ALC: footnote to pp. 135–136. GL: VII, 61–62.)

7. *Gestas and Demas* (ANL, XVI: The Narrative of Joseph of Arimathea, 237–238.)

8. *Thirty Pieces of Gold* (ANL, XVI: The Narrative of Joseph of Arimathea, 238–240.)

9. *The Cock that Entered Paradise* (ALC: 307. NTA: 150, citing from the Coptic *Book of the Cock*. Here Paul of Tarsus is associated with instigating Judas to betray Jesus. His name is given as Paul of Tarsus, son of Josue Almason, son of Cadafana.)

10. *The Hymn of Preparation* (BB: 92–94. NTA: Acts of John, 253).

CHAPTER TWENTY: THE SENTENCE

1. *Jesus Accused* (ANT: Gospel of Nicodemus, 64. ANL, XVI: Gospel of Nicodemus, 126.)

2. *The Adoration of the Runner* (ECL: 140–144. ANT: The Gospel of Nicodemus, 64–65. ANL, XVI: The Gospel of Nicodemus, 127.)

3. *The Standards Bow Down* (ANT: The Gospel of Nicodemus, 65. ANL, XVI: The Gospel of Nicodemus, 127–128. ECL: 142–144.)

4. *Procla's Dream* (ECL: 145–148. ANT: The Gospel of Nicodemus, 66. ANL, XVI: The Gospel of Nicodemus, 128–129.)

5. *The Inquiry* (ECL: 149–156. ANT: The Gospel of Nicodemus, 66–72. ANL, XVI: The Gospel of Nicodemus, 129–135.)

6. *Pilate's Verdict* (ECL: 226–229. ANT: The Gospel of Nicodemus, 72.)

CHAPTER TWENTY-ONE: THE SORROWFUL JOURNEY

1. *The Roman Scourging* (ALC: 337 footnote 2.)

2. *The Wood of the Cross* (ALC: 338–342. BG: *Curious Myths of the Middle Ages,* 341–385 contains many legends pertaining to the cross.)

3. *From the Judgment Hall to Golgotha* (ALC: footnote 5 to p. 338. ANL, XVI: The Gospel of Nicodemus, 135–136.)

4. *My Son!* (ALC: 345–346. ANL, XVI: The Gospel of Nicodemus, 158–159.)

5. *Veronica's Veil* (BG: *Lives of the Saints,* II, 73–75. ANL, XVI: The Avenging of the Savior, 251–255. There are many versions of a legend about the Roman Emperor Tiberius who suffered from an incurable disease, and sent his officer Volusianus to find a certain Jew named Thomas who was said to have performed miraculous cures. During his long search for Thomas, Volusianus learned of a woman named Veronica, who had a true image of Jesus on a veil which cured the hopelessly afflicted. Veronica and the true image were brought to the Emperor. And as soon as Tiberius looked at the image on the veil and touched it, he was healed. Baring-Gould, in his *Lives of the Saints,* Vol. II: 74–80 suggests that Veronica's name and the legends about her arose after the belief

was established that a true image [*vera icon*] of Jesus could affect miraculous cures; that *vera icon* became *Veraicon*, and then, by a transposition of letters, *Veronica*.)

6. *The Wandering Cartaphilus* (ALC: 347. BG: *Curious Myths of the Middle Ages*, 7.)

7. *Ahasuerus the Shoemaker* (ALC: 346–347.)

CHAPTER TWENTY-TWO: CRUCIFIXION AND BURIAL

1. *Where the Cross Was Planted* (ANT: The Gospel of Nicodemus, 72–73. ALC: 348–349. The claim that the cross was placed exactly over the cranium of Adam's skull is of Arabic origin. SK: 162 states that Jesus was never crucified, "but was represented by one in his likeness," and taken up by God "into Himself," as given in the Koran: Sura 4:156.)

2. *"They Know Not What They Do"* (ANT: The Gospel of Nicodemus, 72.)

3. *Demas the Repentant* (ECL: 160–162. ANT: The Gospel of Nicodemus, 72–73. ANL: The Gospel of Nicodemus, 136; The Narrative of Joseph of Arimathea, 240–241. NTA: 161–165.)

4. *The Letter to Heaven* (ANL, XVI: The Narrative of Joseph of Arimathea, 241.)

5. *Darkness at Noon* (ANL, XVI: The Gospel of Nicodemus, 187; The Report of Pilate, 229.)

6. *The Baptism of Demas* (BB: 95. Most sources name the centurion "Longinus," though BB calls him "Legorrius.")

7. *The Fate of Judas* (ALC: 343–344. ECL: 137–139. BLM: 263.)

8. *The Burial* (ANT: The Gospel of Nicodemus, 73–74.)

9. *The Tomb in Srinagar* (*Mirza Ghulam Ahmad*, by H. D. Griswold; *The Ahmadiya Movement*, by H. A. Walter; *The "Greatest Discovery" Exploded*, by G. L. Dhakur Dass. The concept that Jesus was never crucified but that "God took him up into Himself" is found in the Koran, Sura 4:156. See also: Hasting's Encyclopedia, Vol. X, 830–831, under Quadiani.)

10. *The Names of Jesus* (ALC: 271–272. ET: 23. The significance of the Names of Jesus becomes clearer when one realizes that in those

days the soul of a man resided in his name; just as the Holy Spirit resided in the name of God. According to the Talmud, God has not one but many names, each representing one of his attributes, such as: the Compassionate; the Just; the Patient; the Omniscient; the Forgiving; the Eternal Light, and so on. In the mystic names of Jesus we find a parallel to the names of God, based on the same doctrine of divinity residing in the Ineffable Name, and which the lore expresses in its own inimitable way.)

CHAPTER TWENTY-THREE: THE ASCENSION

1. *The Descent to Hades* (ECL: 175–197. ANT: The Gospel of Nicodemus, 83–88. ANL, XVI: The Gospel of Nicodemus, 169–176. NTA: 139. ALC: 375–395 gives a number of legends on the Descent and the delivery of the patriarchs from hell, based, principally, on GN.)

2. *Joseph's Release* (ANT: The Gospel of Nicodemus, 74–78. ANL, XVI: The Gospel of Nicodemus, 141–144.)

3. *Phinees, Adas, and Haggai* (ANL, XVI: The Gospel of Nicodemus, 139–141. In the Latin version of GN the names of these three are given as: Finees, Addas, and Egias; and there is great diversity in the spelling of the names in different versions of the same Gospel.)

4. *What Happened to the Cross* (ALC: 458–459.) . . . *The Cross in the Tomb* (ALC: 458.) . . . *The Healing Cross* (ALC: footnote 1 to p. 359.)

5. *The Stranger on the Road* (AG: XXI: 173, 246–247.)

6. *At Ravanna's Feast* (AG: XXI: 176, 250–251.)

7. *The News in Capernaum* (AG: XXI: 179, 255–256.)

8. *Christ Is Risen!* (ECL: 198–204. ALC: 439. GL: I, 108–122.)

PART VII: *The Acts of the Apostles*

CHAPTER TWENTY-FOUR: THE ADVENTURES OF JOHN THE FISHERMAN

1. *The Storm at Sea* (MAA: 37–40.)

2. *Domna Acquires Two Slaves* (MAA: 40–43.)

3. *John's Revelation* (ANT: Revelation of John, 493–503.)

4. *Miracle in the Bathhouse* (MAA: 43–46.)

5. *John Before Domitian* (ANL, XVI: The Acts of John the Theologian, 445–449. NTA: Acts of John, 228.)

6. *John and the Robber* (ANL, XXII: Part II, 214–216. GL: II, 170–172.)

7. *Epistle from Ignatius* (ANL, I: Second Epistle of Ignatius, 492.)

8. *The Sandals at the Fountain* (MAA: 54–59 gives another version of the death of Saint John. NTA: Acts of John, 270. GL: II, 161–176 accounts for many miraculous deeds of John the Evangelist.)

CHAPTER TWENTY-FIVE: THE ADVENTURES OF THOMAS DIDYMUS

1. *Thomas Sold As a Slave* (MAA: 80–82. NTA: Acts of Thomas, 365. ANL, XVI: The Acts of the Holy Apostle Thomas, 389–390.)

2. *Thomas and the Flute-girl* (ANL, XVI: The Acts of the Holy Apostle Thomas, 390–397. NTA: Acts of Thomas, 365–371; Acts of John, 266 presents an even more virulent attack on the institution of marriage than given in this legend.)

3. *Plan for a Palace* (MAA: 233. NTA: Acts of Thomas, 371–372. ANL, XVI: The Acts of the Holy Apostle Thomas, 397–399.)

4. *Thomas Makes a Convert* (MAA: 82–89.)

5. *The Palace of King Gundaphoros* (NTA: Acts of Thomas, 372–375. ANL, XVI: The Acts of the Holy Apostle Thomas, 399–406.)

6. *The Man Who Killed His Bride* (NTA: Acts of Thomas, 388–393. ANL, XVI: The Acts of the Holy Apostle Thomas, 416–422.)

7. *The Girdle from Heaven* (NTA: The Assumption of the Virgin, 194–227. AN, XVI: The Passing of Mary, 515–530. There are many versions of this legend, varying greatly in the incidents attending Mary's Assumption; the length of time that elapsed between the Crucifixion and her passing; and between her death and corporal assumption. James, NTA: 218, observes that the Narrative by Joseph of Arimathea, the only version in which the girdle episode is related, is an Italian composition certainly not earlier than the thirteenth century. In the Syriac Narratives

NTA: 220 the names of the virgins ministering to Mary are given as: Gallathea, daughter of Nicodemus; Neshra, daughter of Gamaliel; and Tabitha, daughter of Archelaus. GL: IV, 234–271.)

8. *The Martyrdom of Judas Thomas* (MAA: 94–99. NTA: Acts of Thomas, 434–438. ANL, XVI: Consummation of Thomas the Apostle, 423–428 gives different versions of Thomas's martyrdom.)

CHAPTER TWENTY-SIX: THE ADVENTURES OF ANDREW AND MATTHIAS

1. *Matthias in the Land of the Cannibals* (ANL, XVI: The Acts of Andrew and Matthias, 348–349. NTA: The Acts of Andrew and Matthias, 453 calls the land to which Matthias went "the land of the antropophagi," and it identifies Matthias with Matthew.)

2. *Andrew and the Pilot* (ANL, XVI: The Acts of Andrew and Matthias, 349–357. NTA: 453–455.)

3. *The Empty Prison* (ANL, XVI: The Acts of Andrew and Matthias, 358–360. NTA: 455–456.)

4. *The Conversion of the Men-Eaters* (ANL, XVI: The Acts of Andrew and Matthias, 360–368. NTA: 456–458. GL: II, 94ff.)

CHAPTER TWENTY-SEVEN: THE ADVENTURES OF PHILIP

1. *Worshipers of the Golden Idol* (MAA: 60–65. LOT: 219.)

2. *Philip in the City of the Serpents* (ANL, XVI: The Acts of Philip, 301–316 presents "from the Fifteenth Act until the End, and among them the Martyrdom," which indicates that this is part of an incomplete work, the rest having been lost. MAA: 66–68 gives a quite different version. NTA: The Acts of Philip, 448–450.)

CHAPTER TWENTY-EIGHT: THE ADVENTURES OF PETER AND PAUL

1. *It Is Easier for a Camel* (ANL, XVI: The Acts of Peter and Andrew, 368–372. NTA: The Acts of Peter and Andrew, 458–460.)

2. *The Cure for Luhith* (MAA: 175–182.)

3. *Satan and the Apostles* (MAA: 182–192.)

4. *Thecla of Iconium* (ANT: The Acts of Paul and Thecla, 99–111. NTA: Acts of Paul, 272–281. ANL, XVI: The Acts of Paul and Thecla, 279–292 gives many adventures in the life of "the first Martyr and Apostle Thecla.")

5. *Paul Goes to Rome* (ANL, XVI: The Acts of Peter and Paul, 256–262.)

6. *The Encounter with Simon the Magian* (ANL, XVI: The Acts of Peter and Paul, 262–275. NTA: Acts of Peter, 313 also gives the story of the talking dog.)

7. *Perpetua's Reward* (ANL, XVI: The Acts of Peter and Paul, 276–278.)

CHAPTER TWENTY-NINE: THE SERMON ON THE MOUNT

Presented as it appears in *The Life and Morals of Jesus of Nazareth,* arranged by Thomas Jefferson from the Four Gospels.

Reading List with Notes

TEXT AND CANON OF THE NEW TESTAMENT, by Alexander Souter; Scribner's, New York, 1913.

This book gives a good scholarly account of the stages in the development of the New Testament; the stages the manuscripts have gone through from the earliest documents on papyrus, which have long since disappeared, through the vellum copies; and down to our times and the printed works. It shows the changes that have taken place in the twenty-seven Books during the numerous transcriptions and editorial interpretations.

HOW THE BIBLE GREW, by Frank Grant Lewis; University of Chicago Press, Chicago, 1919.

A good, popular account of the origins, growth, and final establishment of the Bible as we know it today and as humanity has known it for centuries. Anyone interested in the times of the various Books of the Bible, both Old and New Testaments, will find this volume rewarding. It is particularly explicit on the relationship between the Palestinian and the Egyptian Jews, in the days of Jesus and Paul, and the basic theological differences between these two Jewish communities during the three centuries before the Christian Era.

CANON AND TEXT OF THE NEW TESTAMENT, by Casper René Gregory; Scribner's, New York, 1907.

An informative description of early Christian writings and how the Canon of the New Testament came to be.

NEW SOLUTIONS TO NEW TESTAMENT PROBLEMS, by Edgar J. Goodspeed; University of Chicago Press, Chicago, 1927.

A small book that attempts to clarify the chronology of the twenty-seven Books of the New Testament and the synoptic nature of some of them.

THE GROWTH OF THE GOSPELS, by Frederick C. Grant; The Abingdon Press, New York, 1933.

Though intended for the student, this book is so lucidly written and well organized that the layman can read it with profit and enjoyment. Gives an enlightening differentiation between the Four Gospels as we have them today and "the Gospel before the Gospels," as Dr. Grant puts it.

THE NEW TESTAMENT IN LIFE AND LITERATURE, by Jane T. Stoddart; Hodder and Stoughton, London and New York, 1915.

A vast compilation of familiar and unfamiliar quotations from literature, mostly English, dealing in one form or another with the New Testament material and arranged to follow the chronology of the twenty-seven Books, with sources of the material given in footnotes.

THE PRAISES OF ISRAEL, by John Paterson; Scribner's, New York, 1950.

A valuable study of the Psalter in terms of its contents and religious value.

PSALMS IN HISTORY AND BIOGRAPHY, by John Ker; Andrew Elliot, Edinburgh, 1888.

This small book arranges the Psalms numerically, then fits each into historical or biographical incidents, showing the place of the particular psalm in the life of a given individual or nation. Quaint and full of lore.

THE POETRY AND THE RELIGION OF THE PSALMS, by James Robertson; Dodd, Mead, New York, 1898.

This is a profound study not only of the Psalms but, by implication, of the entire Bible. The author separates the psalms into groups belonging to different historical periods and serving different spiritual needs, and shows why psalmody, which began at a very early date, continued to be the outlet and expression of Judaism.

THE PARABLES AND SAYINGS

THE PARABLES OF THE SYNOPTIC GOSPELS, by B. T. D. Smith; Cambridge University Press, London, 1937.

Excellent exposition of the literary characteristics of the parable; and its evolution; the parables of the Synoptic Gospels and their historical background; and a rich commentary on the parables in the Gospels.

TEACHING OF JESUS IN PARABLES, George Henry Hubbard; The Pilgrim Press, Boston, 1907.

This book divides the parables into major and minor; then organizes them into topical groups: the Parables of the Kingdom; the Parables of New and Old, and so on. Around each parable the author develops an interpretation which assumes the form of a sermon.

THE POETRY OF OUR LORD, by C. F. Burney; The Clarendon Press, Oxford, 1925.

A scholarly study of the influence of the poetry of the Old Testament, in Hebrew, upon the sayings and discourses of Jesus; with particular stress on the psalmic influences and parallelisms.

APOCRYPHAL GOSPELS, ACTS, EPISTLES

ANTE-NICENE CHRISTIAN LIBRARY, edited by Alexander Roberts and James Donaldson; 24 volumes; T. and T. Clark, Edinburgh, 1867–1872. (The American edition of this work, edited and rearranged by A. Cleveland Coxe, was published in 1899 by Scribner's, New York.)

This immense work contains practically everything from Polycarp and Ignatius to Origen and the early Liturgies. It is primarily a theological work; but Volume XVI, containing the Apocryphal Gospels, Acts and Revelations, is devoted to the lore. There are many other collections and studies of the works of the ante-Nicene, the Nicene and the post-Nicene fathers of the Christian church.

CODEX APOCRYPHUS NOVI TESTAMENTI, by Johann Albert Fabricius; 2 volumes; Hamburg, 1719.

Johann Albert Fabricius (1668–1736) was perhaps the greatest theological bibliographer and compiler of apocryphal materials, and his work published in its final and revised form in 1719 has remained the indispensable source for study on this subject.

THE MYTHOLOGICAL ACTS OF THE APOSTLES, translated by Agnes Smith Lewis; Cambridge University Press, London, 1904.

These manuscripts are rich in lore. They are translations from the Arabic manuscript in the Convent of Deyr-Es-Suriani, Egypt, and from manuscripts in the Convent of St. Catherine on Mount Sinai and in the Vatican Library.

THE APOCRYPHAL NEW TESTAMENT, collected and translated by William Hone; Ludgate Hill, London, 1820.

The title page claims that this book contains "all the Gospels, Epistles, and other pieces now extant, attributed in the first four centuries to Jesus Christ, His Apostles, and their companions, and not included in the New Testament by its compilers." This work presents twenty-four "books," beginning with "The Gospel of the Virgin Mary" and ending with the Visions, Commands and Similitudes of "The Shepherd Hermas." Each book is preceded by a note on its antiquity, how it was regarded by the church fathers, and how it was regarded by the common people. A curious and, as lore, interesting volume.

THE APOCRYPHAL NEW TESTAMENT, translated by Montague Rhodes James; The Clarendon Press, Oxford, 1924.

An excellent one-volume collection of Gospels, Acts, Apocalypses, Epistles and diverse fragments, with invaluable notes and appraisals. A scholarly work for the layman and newcomer into this field.

THE LOST AND HOSTILE GOSPELS, by S. Baring-Gould; William and Norgate, London, 1874.

This book contains the Jewish "anti-gospels" (including the first and second *Toledoth Jeschu*); the Lost Petrine Gospels; and the Lost Pauline Gospels. The reader is introduced to a number of rare documents that are part of the New Testament Apocrypha, among them the Gospel of the Hebrews; the Gospel of the Egyptians; the Gospel of Eve; and the strange, now lost, Gospel of Judas.

THE APOCRYPHAL LITERATURE, by Charles Cutler Tomey; Yale University Press, New Haven, 1945.

A brief but good introduction to the meaning and origin of the Old Testament "Outside Books"; with short and penetrating studies of twenty-seven apocryphal books.

JEWISH AND CHRISTIAN APOCALYPSES, by F. Crawford Burkitt; Oxford University Press, London, 1914.

This book contains the essence of three lectures which illuminate in a scholarly way the origin and development of the apocalyptic idea among the Jews and the early Christians during the three centuries preceding and the three centuries following the advent of Christianity — the period known as the age of the Mystery religions. The analysis of the Book of Enoch is particularly perceptive.

THE KORAN, translated from the Arabic by J. M. Rodwell; J. M. Dent & Sons, London, and E. P. Dutton, New York, 1909. (There are other good translations, in many editions.)

Although the New Testament material in the Koran is scant and strictly uncanonical, it is the basis for the extensive Arabic folklore on this subject.

THE "HIDDEN YEARS"

THE UNKNOWN LIFE OF JESUS CHRIST, by Nicolas Notovich, G. W. Dillinger, New York, 1894.

The romantic author of this book claimed to have discovered a rare document dealing with the "hidden years" of Jesus, in the mountains of Tibet. When the book, containing a translation of this Buddhist document, was first published it stirred up a lively controversy. Theologians regard it with distrust, but as lore it is of undisputed interest and value.

THE AQUARIAN GOSPEL OF JESUS THE CHRIST, "Transcribed from the Book of God's Remembrances" by Levi [Dr. Levi H. Dowling]; E. S. Dowling, Los Angeles, 1911.

This work, described on the title page as "The Philosophic and Practical Basis of the Religion of the Aquarian Age of the World and of the Church Universal," begins with the birth and early life of Mary, and ends with the materialization of the Spiritual Body of Jesus, and the establishment of the "Christine Church." Forty chapters of this work are devoted to the "hidden years." First appeared in 1908; but the 1911 and subsequent editions have, in addition, an introduction by Eva S. Dowling, wife of Dr. Levi H. Dowling, which undertakes to explain the origin of this Gospel and the meaning of its symbols. An interesting work both as religious lore and as an attempt to merge in the teachings of Jesus the ethics of the world's great religions.

DER BENANBRIEF (Eine Moderne Leben-Jesu-Fälschung des Hern Ernest Adler von der Planitz) by Dr. Carl Schmidt; J. C. Hinrichs'-sche Buchhandlung, Leipzig, 1921.

This monograph, synopsizing and analyzing The Letter of Benan, is to be found in Texte und Untersuchungen zur Geschichte der Altchristlichen Literatur, Volume 44. It is the only detailed criticism of this strange document.

STRANGE NEW GOSPELS, by Edgar J. Goodspeed; University of Chicago Press, Chicago, 1931.

A brief and unsympathetic account of a number of modern apocryphal works dealing with given periods in the "hidden years" of Jesus.

MIRZA GHULAM AHMAD, by H. D. Griswold; American Tract Society, Lodiana, India, 1902.

A good though biased pamphlet on the Mahdi Messiah of Qadian, founder of the Ahmadiya movement.

LIFE AND TIMES OF JESUS

JESUS OF NAZARETH, by Joseph Klausner, translated from the Hebrew into English by Herbert Danby; Macmillan, New York, 1925.

A great scholarly work, beautifully written, which gives the reader a clear insight into the life of Jesus in terms of the world conditions, in general, in that time, and of the political and economic conditions, in particular, in Palestine. Analyzes the teachings of Jesus and gives the clearest account of the trial and Crucifixion to be found anywhere. As rich in understanding as in scholarship.

LIFE OF JESUS, by Ernest Renan, translated from the French by Charles Edwin Wilbour; Carleton Publisher, New York, 1874. (There are a number of more recent editions, but none better in text.)

One of the earliest of the "modern" books dealing with the life of Jesus, and still a stirring account; which explains why it has survived and become a classic.

RELIGIOUS DEVELOPMENT BETWEEN THE OLD AND THE NEW TESTAMENTS, by R. H. Charles; Henry Holt, New York and London, 1914.

This book, Number 88 in the Home University Library of Modern Knowledge, gives lucidly and convincingly the unbroken continuity between the Old and the New Testaments, as found in the writings of the Apocrypha and Pseudepigrapha during the centuries between Malachi and Matthew. Contains excellent descriptions of the Old Testament Apocrypha and Pseudepigrapha, written between 200 B.C. and 100 A.D. or later.

THE ANCIENT LOWLY, by C. Osborne Ward; 2 volumes; Charles H. Kerr, Chicago, 1907.

An excellent portrayal of the unrest of workers and slaves during the times of Jesus, and why Christianity found such an eager following among the lowly outside of Palestine.

BOOKS WHICH INFLUENCED OUR LORD AND HIS APOSTLES, by John E. H. Thomson; T. & T. Clark, Edinburgh, 1891.

A good analysis of the Old Testament Apocrypha and the evolution of the apocalyptic works that multiplied immediately before the birth of Jesus. These are given against the background of the political-religious sects of those times and the general literature of the period. A reading of this book would be helpful toward a better understanding of most of the New Testament lore as it clarifies the apocalyptic element of the New Testament, particularly the Gospel According to St. John and Revelation.

THE TRIAL OF JESUS OF NAZARETH, by Max Radin; University of Chicago Press, Chicago, 1931.

A juridical and historical re-evaluation of the trial of Jesus by a brilliant professor of law.

ENCYCLOPEDIAS AND CONCORDANCES

THE NEW SCHAFF–HERZOG ENCYCLOPEDIA OF RELIGIOUS KNOWLEDGE, edited by Samuel Macauley Jackson; 12 volumes; Funk and Wagnalls, New York and London, 1911. (Earlier and later editions available.)

An encyclopedia of Protestant learning, based on the work of Albert Hauck, the German theologian, and adapted for the American public by Philip Schaff and J. J. Herzog. It is comprehensive and thorough, though sometimes dry.

THE CATHOLIC ENCYCLOPEDIA, 15 volumes; Robert Appleton Company, New York, 1907.

A presentation of every phase of the Catholic church from the devout point of view. It covers a vast field, from art and archaeology to philosophy and theology; and is a rich source of Christian lore.

ENCYCLOPEDIA OF RELIGION AND ETHICS, edited by James Hastings; 12 volumes; Scribner's, New York, 1908. (Later editions available.)

This great work embraces all religions and great systems of ethics, and presents them with admirable impartiality. Many of the beliefs, superstitions and legends pertaining to the New Testament are treated topically and often extensively.

COLLECTIONS OF NEW TESTAMENT LORE

THE GOLDEN LEGEND, or THE LIVES OF THE SAINTS, by Jacobus de Voraigne, "as Englished by William Caxton"; 7 volumes; J. M. Dent & Sons, London, 1800.

For anyone wishing to gain insight into the religious thought, beliefs and superstitions of the Middle Ages, these strange books of *The Golden Legend* will lead him into an incredible wonderland — incredible even within the realm of myth and legend.

THE LIVES OF THE SAINTS, by S. Baring-Gould; 12 volumes; John Hodges, London, 1877.

This work is a colossal task accomplished by a master storyteller and follows the Christian saints of eighteen centuries, and of practically every nation under the sun, around the calendar, day by day. These books contain more, and more rewarding, New Testament lore than any other single collection. The comments are brief and clear; the sources impeccable. An invaluable collection for anyone interested in any kind of folklore.

THE BOOK OF THE BEE, by Bishop Shelomon of Khilat, Armenia; edited and translated from the Syriac Text by Ernest A. Wallis Budge of the Department of Egyptian and Assyrian Antiquities, British Museum; Volume I, Part II of the Semitic Series of *Anecdota Axoniensia;* The Clarendon Press, Oxford, 1889.

This strange book by the Nestorian bishop of the thirteenth century deals, as the author explains in his introduction, with matters relating to "the beginning of the creation of this world, and concluding with the consummation of the world to come." The author explains the title of the book: "As the common bee with gauzy wings flies about, and flutters over and lights upon flowers of various colors, and upon blossoms of divers odors, selecting and gathering from all of them materials which are useful for the construction of her handiwork; and having first of all collected the materials from the flowers, carries them upon her thighs, and bringing them to her dwelling, lays a foundation for her building with a base of wax; then gathering in her mouth some of the heavenly dew which is upon the blossoms of spring, brings it and blows into these cells; and weaves the comb and honey for the use of men and her own nourishment: in like manner have we, the infirm, hewn the stones of corporeal words from the rocks of the Scriptures which are in the Old Testament, and have laid them down as a foundation for the edifice of the spiritual law." In this manner the rich collection of lore is presented.

THE EXTRA–CANONICAL LIFE OF CHRIST, by Bernhard Pick; Funk & Wagnalls, New York and London, 1903.

A miscellany of easy-to-read acanonical narratives, arranged in continuity from the birth of Jesus to the Resurrection and Ascension; appended by a few records and sayings from diverse sources.

DAS LEBEN JESU IM ZEITALTER DER NEUTESTAMENT–LICHEN APOKRYPHEN, by Walter Bauer; Verlag J. C. B. Mohr, Tübingen, 1909.

A comprehensive and scholarly study of the legends pertaining to the life of Jesus, with a great number of sources for those wishing to make a more thorough search of this field.

THE APOCHRYPHAL AND LEGENDARY LIFE OF CHRIST, compiled by James deQuincey Donehoo; Macmillan Company, 1903.

The most complete one-volume collection of New Testament Apocryphal lore; arranged to present the biography of Jesus; thoroughly annotated; with valuable lists of sources and their authors. A book of great value to those interested in New Testament folklore.

CHRIST–LEGENDS, by Selma Lagerlöf, translated from the Swedish by Velma Swanston Howard; Henry Holt, New York, 1908.

A group of enduring folk legends gathered orally from diverse Oriental sources and retold for young readers with impressive simplicity by a great Swedish novelist.

CURIOUS MYTHS OF THE MIDDLE AGES, by S. Baring-Gould; J. B. Lippincott, Philadelphia, 1869.

Inimitable storyteller Baring-Gould gives us in this, one of his many books, a rich collection of lore, some bearing directly on the lore of the New Testament.

MISCELLANEOUS WORKS

CHRISTIAN ICONOGRAPHY, by Adolphe-Napoléon Didron, translated from the French by E. J. Millington; H. G. Bohn, London, 1851.

A valuable discussion of the symbolism in the Christian religion and its lore.

THE AHMADIYA MOVEMENT, by H. A. Walter; Association Press, Calcutta, 1918, Oxford University Press, London and New York.

A monograph in the series, *The Religious Life of India*, edited by J. N. Farquhar. A good and fair-minded statement on a religious movement little known in the West. Of particular interest because of its association with the life of Jesus; and the claim put forward by Mirza Ghulam Ahmad that he represented the Second Coming of the Messiah.

BIBLICAL LEGENDS OF THE MUSSULMANS, by G. Weil; translated from the German; Harper & Brothers, New York, 1846.

A charming collection of Muslim legends concerning many Biblical characters, from Adam to Solomon, and ending with some curious stories about John, Mary, and Jesus. These stories are taken from the Koran as well as later Arabic sources.

MUHAMMAD AND CHRIST, by Moulvi Muhammad Ali; Ahmadiah Anjuman-i-Ishaat-i-Islam; Lahore, India, 1921.

A valuable discussion for anyone interested in knowing how the devout Muslims regard the New Testament, in general, and Jesus as he appears in the Gospel. Simply if devoutly presented.

THE LEGENDS OF THE JEWS, by Louis Ginzberg, translated from the German manuscript by Henrietta Szold; 7 volumes; Jewish Publication Society of America, Philadelphia, 1909–1938.

A treasury for the student of the lore of the New Testament who wishes to understand the sources of many concepts, beliefs, and folk attitudes in the times of Jesus.

DEVOTIONAL AND ASCETIC PRACTICES IN THE MIDDLE AGES, by Dom Louis Gougard; Burns Oates & Washbourne, London, 1927.

A strange collection of unusual legends from many sources, presenting beliefs and practices pertaining to New Testament characters and events, rarely found in the more popular collections.

THE BIBLE AND THE COMMON READER, by Mary Ellen Chase;
Macmillan, New York, 1949.

Although this is the last book on the Reading List it is decidedly
the first that should be read by anyone interested in biblical folklore and in the Bible as literature.

Acknowledgments

I am deeply indebted to all those who labored to gather and record the lore, created in so many lands and over so many centuries; and to those who read this book before publication and helped so generously with their valuable suggestions and criticism: Professor Frederick C. Grant of the Union Theological Seminary; Professor Malcolm Pitt, Hartford Seminary Foundation; Professor George Johnston, Hartford Theological Seminary; Dr. A. William Loos of the Church Peace Union; Dr. Dwight J. Bradley; Mr. Stewart Meacham, now with the Methodist Mission Board in India; Dr. Paul Schubert of the Yale Divinity School; Dr. Guy Emery Shipler, Editor of *The Churchman;* Dr. R. Duncan Luce; and especially to Stanley Salmen whose perceptive suggestions gave me perspective on the book as a whole. But, of course, for all the shortcomings and weaknesses of this book the author alone is responsible.

It is a pleasure to express my thanks to the librarians of the Union Theological Seminary for their helpfulness to me while this book was in preparation.

J. G.

Index

ABBANES, 250, 251, 252, 254, 255
Abel, the Righteous, 27
Abgar, King of Edessa, 169, 183
Abgarus. *See* Abgar
Abiathar, 27
Abigea, companion of Mary, 32, 260
Aboth d'Rabbi Nathan, 179
Abracadabra, magic of, 64
Abraham, the Patriarch, 13, 19; inherits Adam's rod, 30, 45; and the star, 62; awakened by the sphinx, 165
Abraxas, an idol, 64
Abyater, a mystic name of Jesus, 224
Achias, 193
Acts of Andrew and Matthias, 165, 313
Acts of Andrew and Paul, 309, 318
Acts of the Apostles, 5
Acts of Peter, 76
Acts of Peter and Andrew, 313
Acts of Thomas, 311
Adam, 5; rod of, 30; names Seth, 52, 54; gold buried with, 55; grave of, 210; cross at grave of, 214–215, 293
Adanael, a mystic name of Jesus, 224
Adas, 228–230
Adronicus, a disciple, 316
Afera, a mystic name of Jesus, 224
Affrodosius, governor of Sotrina, 64
Afrael, a mystic name of Jesus, 224
Africa, 272, 291
Afrona, a mystic name of Jesus, 224
Agabus, a disciple, 317
Agrapha, 186
Ahasuerus, 213
Ahikar, story of, 180
Ahmad, Mirza Ghulam, 222
Ahmadiya, Muslim sect, 222–223

Ahura-Mazda, 53
Akasha, 130
Akashic Records, 130
Akonou, a mystic name of Jesus, 224
Akrosina, wife of Simon the Leper, 197
Alexander, a disciple, 278
Alexander, the Syrian, 289
Alpha, the meaning of, 98–99; legend of the Buddha, 328
Amanouel, a mystic name of Jesus, 224
Ampilus. *See* Amplias
Amplias, a disciple, 316
Ampliatus. *See* Amplias
Ananias, a disciple, 314
Ananias, the painter sent by Abgar, 169
Andrew, the apostle, 65, 171, 234, 260; does not recognize Jesus, 264–267; rescues Matthias from prison, 267–268; tortured by cannibals, 270–271, 278, 309
Angar, Apostle of the North, 307
Angel Gabriel. *See* Gabriel, Angel
Angel of Death, 112, 173
Angel of the Sabbath, 24–25
Animals, adoration of the, 51
Anna, Mary's mother, 5, 6; childlessness of, 16; miracle that happened to, 16; vision of, 18; and the angel, 19; gives birth to Mary, 20–21, 87, 88
Annas, the high priest, 93, 192, 195, 227, 228, 229
Annas, the Scribe, 37
Annunciation, the, 34–35; Muslim legend of, 330
Antioch, 240, 289

Origen, gospel mentioned by, 186
Orissa, city of, 132, 232
Orsis, country of, 119
Orthodoxy, Jewish, 10
Ox, in the adoration of the animals, 51
Oxyrhynchite, province, 186
Oxyrhynchus papyri, 5, 186

PAGANS, in Israel, 122
Palestine, 6; Rabbinic literature of, 178
Pali, document in, 117
Palm tree, miracle of the, 63
Paneas, city of, 166, 167, 175
Papyri, discovery of Greek, 186
Parables, canonical, 179
Parables, of the Old Testament, 178
Para-Brahma, 119
Parmenas, a disciple, 315
Passion Gospels, 189
Passover, 99, 104, 139, 143, 197–199
Paterson, Dr. John, 8
Patmos, Island of, 245, 248
Patriarch Abraham. *See* Abraham
Patriarchs, awakened by the sphinx, 165
Patrick, Apostle of Ireland, 307
Patrobulus, a disciple, 317
Patrobus. *See* Patrobulus
Paul, of Tarsus, 11; Benan visits, 142, 260, 281; brought from Philippi, 285; imprisoned in Iconium, 288, 290; reaches Peter in Rome, 292; appears before Nero, 293–296; death of, 297, 307, 313–314
Perpetua, 296–297
Persia, 61, 121, 137
Persia, King of, 54, 58
Peter, the apostle, 234, 250, 260; accompanies Philip on his mission, 272; performs miracle with camel, 279–280; speaks with a bird, 282–283; brought in chains from Philippi, 285; learns Paul is alive, 292; meets Simon Magian, 293–296; causes death of Simon Magian, 296
Pharaoh, and the Magi's gold, 55; and Jesus, 72–75; accepts pledge of Lazarus, 75, 191
Pharisee, testifies for Jesus, 205

Pharisees, complaint of the, 27–28; Mary and the, 108; gathered in the temple, 143
Philemon, a disciple, 318
Philip, the apostle, 234, 260, 310; and the idolaters, 272–277; martyrdom of, 276–277
Philip, a disciple (sometimes confused with the apostle), 314
Philip, Herod's brother, 161; countries of, 191
Philippi, Peter and Paul in, 284, 285
Philo and Jesus, 144
Philologus, a disciple, 308, 317
Phinees, testimony of, 228–230
Phlegon, a disciple, 317
Phutiphares, 193
Phygellus, a disciple, 316
Physician, Jesus and the, 107
Physician of Anu, Jesus as the, 144, 145
Pilam, daughter of Atus, 194
Pilam-Atus (Pilate), 194
Pilate, Pontius, 123, 125, 127, 128, 194–195, 200–207, 219
Pinehas, Rabbi, 143, 144
Pirke Aboth, 180
Plague, of blindness, 92
Planitz, Ernest Adler von der, 141
Polia, wife of Herod, 161
Pontiole, 291, 292
Pontius Pilate. *See* Pilate, Pontius
Pontus, Island of, 194
Potters, Jesus and the, 90–91
Prochorus, a disciple, 239, 240; as bathman, 241–242, 314
Procla, dream of, 202–203
Prophets, 8
Propippius, the priest, 53
Protevangelium of James, 5, 41, 312
Proverbs, 8
Psalms, 8
Psalter, 8
Ptolomaeus, 193
Pudens, a disciple, 318
Punjab, 222
Putiphra, the astronomer, 142, 143

QATANAOUK, a mystic name of Jesus, 224